Welcome to the 2009 edition of Condé Nast Johansens Hotels & Spas, Great Britain and Ireland.

Each year we are able to bring you a more diverse and comprehensive portfolio of places to stay thanks to the concerted effort of our experienced inspection team. We pride ourselves on understanding the expectations of our discerning readership and in anticipating those needs, not only for high standards, a welcoming atmosphere, relaxation and a good night's sleep but also for discovering new and special corners of Great Britain and Ireland.

Whether you are looking for a delightful old coaching inn, all the charm of a classic country house, the sophistication of a city hotel, the magic of a castle or a prestigious hotel & spa, we have found plenty to inspire you for the year ahead.

Few guides offer such rich diversity and accommodation experience which makes your search for that extra special stay easier and more rewarding.

You may be in need of inspiration or simply want to search a specific location, either way our guide is designed to help you make the right choice. Now also interactive on www.johansens.com you can 'check availability' and communicate directly with the Recommendation of your choice. Each hotel's entry page invites you to 'Tell us about your stay' so we look forward to your comments when you return.

Our portfolio comprises 6 published Guides, featuring more than 1,100 annually inspected and recommended hotels, resorts, inns, spas and venues across more than 60 countries. See them all at www.johansens.com.

Wishing you safe and rewarding travels in 2009.

Andrew Warren
Managing Director

L'INSTANT
TAITTINGER

Vitalie Taittinger, who works for the family Champagne house

About this Guide

Introduction 1
County Maps 4, 5
Key to Symbols 6
Awards for Excellence 11

Recommendations and regional maps:
Channel Islands 14
England 22
Ireland 206
Scotland...232
Wales 250

Mini Listings:
Small Hotels, Inns & Restaurants –
Great Britain & Ireland 2009 268
Historic Houses, Castles & Gardens 2009 270
Hotels & Spas – Europe & The Mediterranean 2009 275
Hotels, Inns, Resorts & Spas –
The Americas, Atlantic, Caribbean & Pacific 2009 281

Indexes..304
Guest Survey Report...311

To find a hotel by location:
- Use the **county maps** at the front of the Guide to obtain a page number for the area of the country you wish to search.
- Turn to the **indexes** at the back of the book, which start on page 304.
- Alternatively, use the **maps** at the front of each colour coded country section where each hotel is marked.

If you cannot find a suitable hotel you may decide to choose one of the properties within the *Condé Nast Johansens Recommended Small Hotels, Inns & Restaurants Guide.* These more intimate establishments are listed on pages 268–269.

Once you have made your choice please contact the hotel directly. Rates are per room, including VAT and breakfast (unless stated otherwise) and are correct at the time of going to press but you should always check with the hotel before you make your reservation. **When making a booking please mention that Condé Nast Johansens is your source of reference.**

Readers should be aware that by making a reservation with a hotel, either by telephone, e-mail or in writing, they are entering into a legal contract. A hotelier under certain circumstances is entitled to make a charge for accommodation when guests fail to arrive, even if notice of the cancellation is given.

Lake Vyrnwy Hotel, Powys, Wales, p264

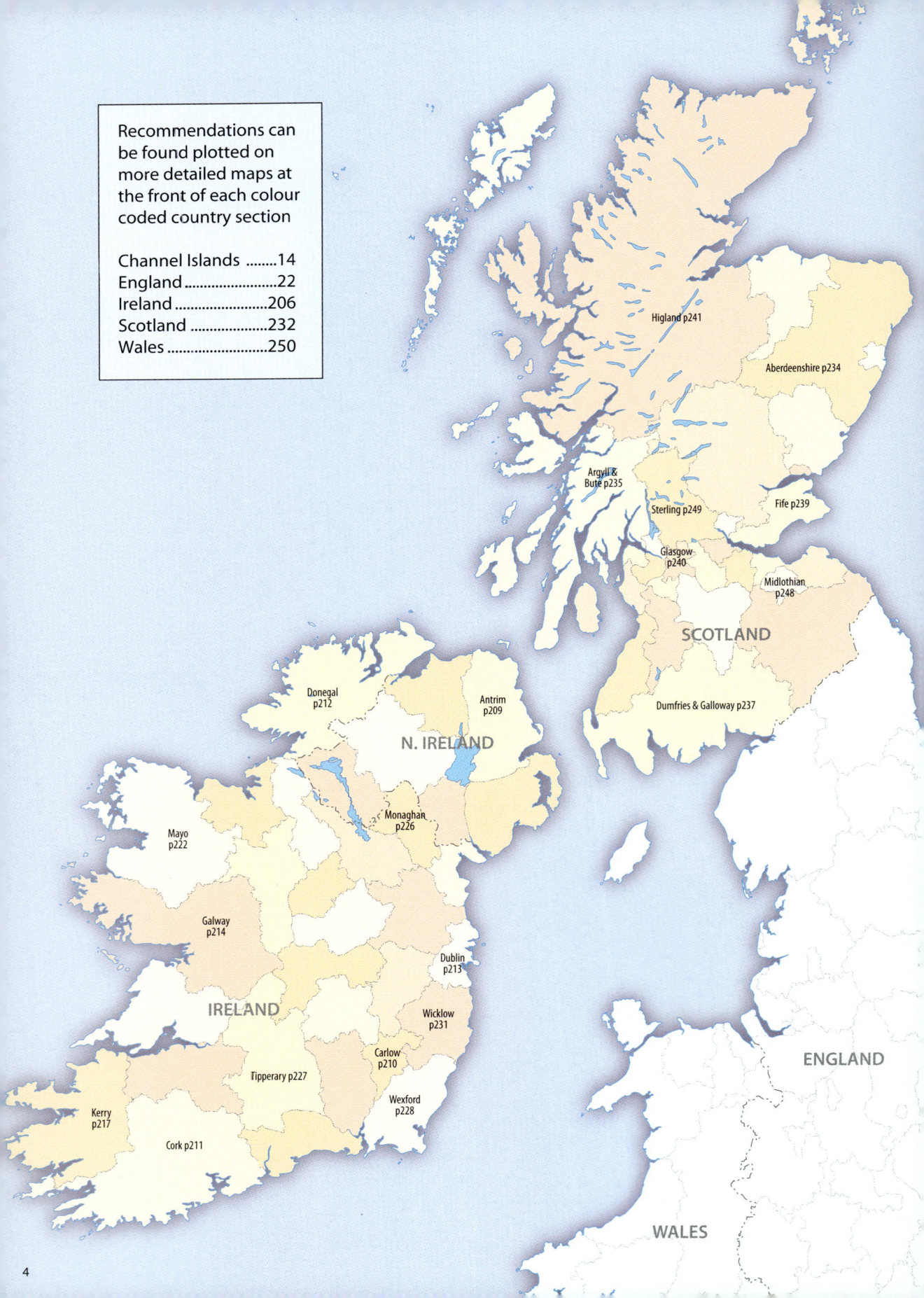

Recommendations can be found plotted on more detailed maps at the front of each colour coded country section

Channel Islands 14
England 22
Ireland 206
Scotland 232
Wales 250

Higland p241
Aberdeenshire p234
Argyll & Bute p235
Sterling p249
Fife p239
Glasgow p240
Midlothian p248
SCOTLAND
Dumfries & Galloway p237

Donegal p212
Antrim p209
N. IRELAND
Monaghan p226
Mayo p222
Galway p214
Dublin p213
IRELAND
Wicklow p231
Carlow p210
Tipperary p227
Wexford p228
Kerry p217
Cork p211

ENGLAND

WALES

Map of the United Kingdom and Ireland

- N. IRELAND
- SCOTLAND
- IRELAND
- WALES
- ENGLAND

England counties
- Cumbria p61
- Tyne & Wear p182
- Durham p97
- North Yorkshire p198
- Lancashire p120
- Cheshire p49
- Derbyshire p74
- Nottinghamshire p145
- Lincolnshire p122
- Staffordshire p157
- Leicestershire p121
- Rutland p152
- Norfolk p141
- Worcestershire p193
- Warwickshire p183
- Northamptonshire p143
- Herefordshire p115
- Suffolk p158
- Gloucestershire p99
- Bedfordshire p38
- Buckinghamshire p45
- Hertfordshire p116
- Essex p98
- South Gloucestershire p107
- Oxfordshire p148
- Bath & NE Somerset p32
- Berkshire p39
- London p123
- Wiltshire p187
- Somerset p153
- Hampshire p108
- Surrey p164
- Kent p119
- Devon p79
- Dorset p93
- West Sussex p177
- East Sussex p167
- Cornwall p51

Wales counties
- Conwy p255
- Gwynedd p257
- Ceredigion p253
- Powys p263
- Pembrokeshire p260
- Vale of Glamorgan p266
- Cardiff p252
- Newport p259

Channel Islands
- Guernsey p16
- Jersey p18

Key to Symbols

- 23 Total number of bedrooms
- Owner managed
- CC Credit cards not accepted
- Quiet location
- Wheelchair Access. We recommend that you contact the hotel to determine the level of accessibility for wheelchair users.
- Chef-patron
- M 23 Meeting/conference facilities with maximum number of delegates
- 8 Children welcome, with minimum age where applicable
- Dogs welcome in rooms or kennels
- At least 1 bedroom has a four-poster bed
- Cable/satellite TV in all bedrooms
- CD player in bedrooms
- DVD player in bedrooms
- ISDN/modem point in all bedrooms
- WiFi Wireless Internet connection available in part or all rooms
- Non-smoking bedrooms available
- Lift available for guests' use
- Air conditioning in all bedrooms
- Gym/fitness facilities on-site
- SPA A dedicated spa offering extensive health, beauty and fitness treatments together with water treatments
- Indoor swimming pool
- Outdoor swimming pool
- Tennis court on-site
- Walking – details of local walking routes and packed lunches can be provided and an overnight drying room for clothes is available.
- Fishing on-site
- Fishing can be arranged
- Golf course on-site
- Golf course nearby, which has an arrangement with the property allowing guests to play
- Shooting on-site
- Shooting can be arranged
- Horse riding can be arranged
- Property has a helicopter landing pad
- Licensed for wedding ceremonies

Dale Hill, Eeast Sussex, England, p176

In partnership with Condé Nast Johansens

Café DU MONDE®
LUXURY COFFEE SYSTEMS

Sans Pareil - Without Equal

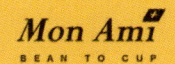

Photography by tandi.co.uk

www.cafedumonde.co.uk tel: 01322 284804

Cafetiere SYSTEM | Mon Ami BEAN TO CUP | GAGGIA® ESPRESSO | Bulk BREW | SERVICE EN CHAMBRE

photo: M. Marcato – Verona, Italy

Beautiful Furniture for Hotels and Homes.

SELVA

40 Years of Timeless Beauty

photo: © Moreno Maggi
Hotel St. George, Roma

Selva SpA   Via Luigi Negrelli 4   39100 Bolzano (Italia)   Tel. +39 0471 240 111   Fax +39 0471 240 112   selva@selva.com   www.selva.com

Condé Nast Johansens

Condé Nast Johansens Ltd, 6-8 Old Bond Street, London W1S 4PH
Tel: +44 (0)20 7499 9080 Fax: +44 (0)20 7152 3565
E-mail: info@johansens.com
www.johansens.com

Publishing Director:	Patricia Greenwood
PA to Publishing Director:	Clare Freeman
Hotel Inspectors:	Jean Branham
	Peter Bridgham
	Geraldine Bromley
	Robert Bromley
	Charlie Bronks
	Tim Fay
	Audrey Fenton
	Maureen Flynn
	Edward Gallier
	David Innes-Edwards
	Marie Iversen
	Pauline Mason
	John Morison
	Mary O'Neill
	Fiona Patrick
	Liza Reeves
	Leonora Sandwell
	Nevill Swanson
	Kevin Smyth
Production Manager:	Kevin Bradbrook
Production Editor:	Laura Kerry
Senior Designer:	Michael Tompsett
Copywriters:	Norman Flack
	Debra O'Sullivan
	Rozanne Paragon
	Leonora Sandwell
Client Services Director:	Fiona Patrick
Venue Advisory Service:	Lesley Ulrick
Managing Director:	Andrew Warren

Whilst every care has been taken in the compilation of this Guide, the publishers cannot accept responsibility for any inaccuracies or for changes since going to press, or for consequential loss arising from such changes or other inaccuracies, or for any other loss direct or consequential arising in connection with information describing establishments in this publication.

Recommended establishments, if accepted for inclusion, pay an annual subscription to cover the costs of inspection, the distribution and production of copies placed in hotel bedrooms and other services.

No part of this publication may be copied or reproduced, stored in a retrieval system or transmitted, in any form or by any means, electronic, mechanical, photocopy, recording or otherwise, without the prior permission of the publishers.

The publishers request readers not to cut, tear or otherwise mark this Guide except Guest Survey Reports and Order Forms. No other cuttings may be taken without the written permission of the publishers.

Copyright © 2008 Condé Nast Johansens Ltd.
Condé Nast Johansens Ltd. is part of The Condé Nast Publications Ltd.
ISBN 978-1-903665-39-8
Printed in England by St Ives plc
Distributed in the UK and Europe by Portfolio, Brentford (bookstores).
In North America by Casemate Publishing, Pennsylvania (bookstores).
Front cover picture: Sharrow Bay, Cumbria, p70

The Priory Hotel, Dorset, England, p95

Divine Bathing Products — Stunning Boutique Design

Introducing a Bold and Distinctive New Line of Luxury Guest Toiletries from Internationally Renowned Interior Designer Nina Campbell

Exclusively from Pacific Direct, Condé Nast Johansens Preferred Partner for 10 Years

www.pacificdirect.co.uk

Pacific Direct
Email: sales@pacificdirect.co.uk
Tel: +44 (0)1234 347 140

PENHALIGON'S LONDON · Elemis · FLORIS LONDON · NP NATURAL PRODUCTS · Nina Campbell · BRONNLEY · Salvatore Ferragamo · THE WHITE COMPANY LONDON

Awards for Excellence

The Condé Nast Johansens 2008 Awards for Excellence were presented at our Awards Dinner held at Jumeirah Carlton Tower, London, on 12th November, 2007. Awards were received by properties from all over Europe that represented the finest standards and best value for money in luxury independent travel.

An important source of information for these awards was the feedback provided by guests who completed Condé Nast Johansens Guest Survey Reports. Forms can be found on page 312.

You can also nominate a hotel via its entry page on the website www.johansens.com, under 'Tell Us About Your Stay'.

2008 Winners appearing in this Guide:

Most Excellent Hotel
- INVERLOCHY CASTLE – Fort William, Highland, p242

Most Excellent London Hotel
- SOFITEL ST JAMES – Piccadilly, London, p139

Most Excellent Service
- HARVEY'S POINT – Donegal Town, Donegal, Ireland, p212

Most Excellent City Hotel Award
- ROCPOOL RESERVE – Inverness, Highland, p244

Most Excellent Hotel Restaurant
- THE CAPITAL HOTEL & RESTAURANT – Knightsbridge, London, p131

Most Excellent Country House Hotel Award
- LLANGOED HALL – Brecon, Powys, p263

Condé Nast Johansens Readers' Award
- NEWICK PARK – Lewes, East Sussex, p175

Champagne Taittinger Most Excellent Wine List Award
- THE GEORGE OF STAMFORD – Stamford, Lincolnshire, p122

To us, no two hotels are the same

Insurance cover exclusive to Condé Nast Johansens recommended hotels

Tel: 0044 7768093718
Email: Johansens@jltgroup.com

Insurance | Experience | Excellence
Preferred insurance partner of Condé Nast Johansens

JARDINE LLOYD THOMPSON
Leisure

The Perfect Combination...

Condé Nast Johansens Gift Vouchers

Condé Nast Johansens Gift Vouchers make a unique and much valued present for birthdays, weddings, anniversaries, special occasions and as a corporate incentive.

Vouchers are available in denominations of £100, £50, €140, €70, $150, $75 and may be used as payment or part payment for your stay or a meal at any Condé Nast Johansens 2009 recommended property.

To order Gift Vouchers call +44 (0)207 152 3558 or purchase direct at www.johansens.com

Condé Nast Johansens Guides

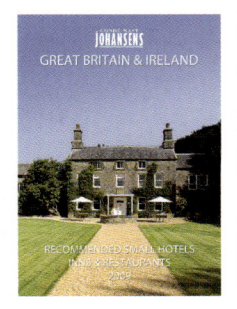

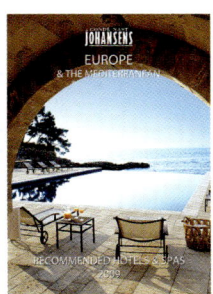

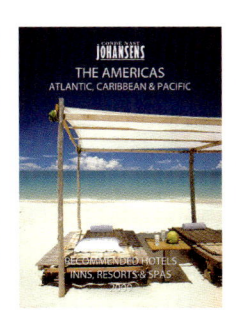

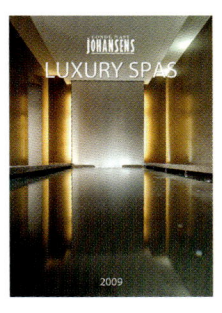

As well as this Guide, Condé Nast Johansens also publish the following titles:

- Recommended Small Hotels, Inns & Restaurants, Great Britain & Ireland 2009
- Recommended Hotels & Spas, Europe & The Mediterranean 2009
- Recommended Hotels, Inns, Resorts & Spas, The Americas, Atlantic, Caribbean & Pacific 2009
- Luxury Spas Worldwide 2009
- Recommended International Venues for Meetings & Special Events 2009

To purchase Guides please call FREEPHONE 0800 269 397 or visit our Bookshop at www.johansens.com

Channel Islands

GUERNSEY

- La Fontenelle
- St Sampson
- Saint Peter Port — 17
- 16
- Richmond
- La Planque

HERM ISLAND

SARK

JERSEY

- Saint John
- Saint Peter
- Saint Mary
- Trinity
- Quennevais — 18
- Saint Helier — 20, 19
- 21
- Gorey

Channel Islands

For further information on the Channel Islands, please contact:

Visit Guernsey
North Esplanade, St Peter Port, Guernsey GY1 2LQ
Tel: +44 (0)1481 723552
Internet: www.visitguernsey.com

Jersey Tourism
Liberation Place, St Helier, Jersey JE1 1BB
Tel: +44 (0)1534 448800
E-mail: info@jersey.com
Internet: www.jersey.com

Sark Tourism
The Visitors Centre, The Avenue, Sark, GY9 0SA
Tel: +44 (0)1481 832345
E-mail: office@sark.info
Internet: www.sark.info

Herm Tourist Office
Administration Office, Herm Island, Guernsey GY1 3HR
Tel: +44 (0)1481 722377
E-mail: admin@herm-island.com
Internet: www.herm-island.com

or see **pages 270-273** for details of local historic houses, castles and gardens to visit during your stay.

For additional places to stay in the Channel Islands, turn to **pages 268-269** where a listing of our Recommended Small Hotels, Inns & Restaurant Guide can be found.

CHANNEL ISLANDS - GUERNSEY (ST PETER PORT)

Fermain Valley Hotel

FERMAIN LANE, ST PETER PORT, GUERNSEY GY1 1ZZ
Tel: 0845 365 3950 **International:** +44 (0)1481 235 666 **Fax:** 01481 235 413
Web: www.johansens.com/fermainvalley **E-mail:** info@fermainvalley.com

Our inspector loved: Lunching on the delightful terrace with its spectacular view down the valley to the sea.

Price Guide:
single £100-£200
silver/gold £120-£190
platinum £180-£220

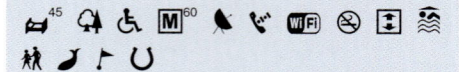

Discover this stunning 4 star hotel nestling in a pretty valley high above Fermain Bay where most of the rooms offer breathtaking views out to sea. Down a sleepy lane, surrounded by greenery and superb cliff walks, this is a peaceful world of comfort and excellent service. The property was originally 2 adjoining hotels, which were the subject of a complete redesign and renovation resulting in a combination of stylish originality with the best of traditional hospitality. There is a choice of excellent restaurants to enjoy, including the most celebrated, Christophe's, with its impressive décor and cuisine. It stands apart in the grounds and holds the island's only Michelin star. Take a dip in the indoor pool and, for something a little different, feel like a VIP and attend a special showing at the private cinema.

Awards/Recognition: 1 Star Michelin 2008

Location: Fermain Bay, 0.25 miles; Guernsey Airport, 2.5 miles; St Peter Port, 1.75 miles

Attractions: Sausmarez Manor; Underground Military Museum; Boats to Sark and Herm; Tax Free Shopping

CHANNEL ISLANDS - GUERNSEY (ST PETER PORT)

THE OLD GOVERNMENT HOUSE HOTEL

ST. ANN'S PLACE, ST PETER PORT, GUERNSEY, CHANNEL ISLANDS GY1 2NU
Tel: 0845 365 3927 **International:** +44 (0)1481 724 921 **Fax:** 01481 724 429
Web: www.johansens.com/oldgovernmenthouse **E-mail:** ogh@theoghhotel.com

Our inspector loved: The Governor's fine dining room serving wonderful cuisine.

Price Guide:
single £135-£295
double £160-£320
feature rooms £320

Awards/Recognition: 2 AA Rosettes 2008-2009

Location: Harbour and Ferry Port, 1 mile; Guernsey Airport, 4 miles

Attractions: Tax free shopping; Boat trips to neighbouring islands of Herm and Sark; Castle Cornet; Sausmarez Manor

Dignified and traditional, you will find this historic hotel in the heart of St Peter Port with fabulous sea views over Guernsey's harbour. The OGH, as it is affectionately known, dates from 1858 and was formerly the residence of the Lieutenant Governor. Restored to reach modern day expectations, it retains a great many original features and the timeless charm and elegance of that era. You will definitely be impressed by the rich décor, glamorous pool area and the Moroccan style spa created for total relaxation. Bedrooms and suites are styled and furnished to a standard you will love, and the Governor's restaurant has gained an enviable reputation for it's cuisine and for serving fresh seafood ripe from the local waters. Its easy to see why state banquets, society weddings and company events can all work so brilliantly here.

CHANNEL ISLANDS - JERSEY (ST BRELADE)

The Atlantic Hotel and Ocean Restaurant

LE MONT DE LA PULENTE, ST BRELADE, JERSEY, JE3 8HE
Tel: 0845 365 2395 **International:** +44 (0)1534 744101 **Fax:** 01534 744102
Web: www.johansens.com/atlantic **E-mail:** info@theatlantichotel.com

Our inspector loved: *the outstanding levels of comfort, food and service achieved at this superbly located hotel. Staff are committed to anticipate your every need.*

Price Guide:
single £150–£200
double/twin £200–£300
suite/deluxe £300–£550

Awards/Recognition: Condé Nast Johansens Most Excellent Service 2007; 1 Star Michelin 2008

Location: A13, 0.5 miles; St Helier, 5 miles; Jersey Airport, 3 miles

Attractions: Jersey War Tunnels; Jersey Zoo; Orchid Farm; La Mare Vineyards

This stunning hotel is the object of continuous and thoughtful investment by its owner who places the needs of his guests first. Be spoiled by superb service and contemporary interiors that are decorated with vibrant island art. The Atlantic stands in 6 acres of private grounds alongside La Moye Golf Course with sympathetic cliff-top landscaping that has opened a vista, allowing an uninterrupted view of the ocean across a 5-mile sweep of St Ouen's Bay. Enjoy a special treat and stay in the prestigious Atlantic Suite with its own entrance hall, living room, guest cloakroom and service pantry. Gaining a much deserved Michelin Star, the restaurant showcases modern British cuisine, with an emphasis on seafood and fresh local produce. Be sure to book in advance.

CHANNEL ISLANDS - JERSEY (ST HELIER)

The Club Hotel & Spa, Bohemia Restaurant

GREEN STREET, ST HELIER, JERSEY JE2 4UH
Tel: 0845 365 2419 **International:** +44 (0)1534 876500 **Fax:** 01534 720371
Web: www.johansens.com/theclubjersey **E-mail:** reservations@theclubjersey.com

Our inspector loved: *The chef's table - 4 to 6 guests can eat in the heart of chef's empire, enjoying wonderful food and the drama of a busy kitchen - just like on TV!*

Price Guide:
double/twin from £195
suite from £350

Awards/Recognition: 1 Star Michelin 2008; 4 AA Rosettes 2007-2008

Location: A15, 0.25 miles; Jersey Airport, 5 miles

Attractions: Shopping in St Helier; Maritime Museum; Jersey Pottery; Elizabeth Castle and Harbour

The Club Hotel and Spa reflects the real buzz that exudes from St Helier itself. Designed with contemporary elegance and understated luxury in mind, bedrooms and suites are furnished to a standard you'll love - LCD TVs and CD players feature - while sleek bathrooms have granite surfaces, power showers and all-enveloping sumptuous bathrobes. The sophisticated Bohemia Restaurant has rapidly gained an enviable reputation and the place to be seen in is the hotel's chic, popular bar. At the Club Spa, you're encouraged to savour a slower pace of life to maximise the treatments and benefits on offer and once refreshed take a walk along the sandy beaches, surf, sail, or explore the secret places of this beautiful island.

CHANNEL ISLANDS - JERSEY (ST HELIER)

The Royal Yacht Hotel

WEIGHBRIDGE, ST HELIER, JERSEY JE2 3NF
Tel: 0845 365 3873 **International:** +44 (0)1534 720 511 **Fax:** 01534 767 729
Web: www.johansens.com/theroyalyacht **E-mail:** reception@theroyalyacht.com

Our inspector loved: The creature comforts, and St Helier's vibrant evening culture.

Price Guide:
silver/gold double £115-£175
penthouse suite £650-£750

Location: Opposite the Harbour at Liberation Square; St Helier; Jersey Airport, 5 miles

Attractions: Sailing Packages; Durrell Conservation Center; Beaches; Shopping

The Royal Yacht Hotel is a newly extended and renovated hotel which keeps its distinct style that alludes to its esteemed history. Contemporary chic design at its finest, the modern bedrooms are spacious and beautifully decorated with soothing colour schemes that enhance the harmonious and peaceful ambience. Try and stay in a penthouse suite or one of the guest rooms with its own balcony and from where you can watch the boats and yachts in St Aubins Bay and St Helier Marina sail in and out. The numerous bustling bars and restaurants located within the hotel are all of the highest quality and offer a wide variety of choice from informal al fresco dining to delicious gourmet cuisine. Spa Sirène is a superb experience that can be used by guests over the age of 16, and offers an extensive array of massages and treatments for both men and women.

CHANNEL ISLANDS - JERSEY (ST SAVIOUR)

LONGUEVILLE MANOR

ST SAVIOUR, JERSEY, CHANNEL ISLANDS JE2 7WF
Tel: 0845 365 2038 **International:** +44 (0)1534 725501 **Fax:** 01534 731613
Web: www.johansens.com/longuevillemanor **E-mail:** info@longuevillemanor.com

Our inspector loved: *The cottage in the garden - an ideal hideaway.*

Price Guide:
single from £175
double/twin £230–£480
suite £500–£800

Awards/Recognition: 3 AA Rosettes 2007-2008; Relais & Châteaux

Location: Just off A3; St Helier, 1.25 miles; Jersey Airport, 7 miles

Attractions: Jersey Pottery; Durrell Wildlife Conservation Trust; Jersey War Tunnels; La Mare Vineyards

Upon arrival at this restored 14th-century Norman manor house you are greeted by staff that know exactly how to blend professionalism with warmth, which is no doubt part of the reason behind this years AA inspectors Choice five star award. The guest rooms with their welcome of champagne and homemade shortbread are all decorated in warm tones with carefully chosen antiques, beautiful fabrics, digital widescreen TVs and DVD/CD players. Honeymooners are in for a real treat in their secluded suite complete with four-poster bed and hand-painted bath for two. Credited with numerous awards the Oak Room restaurant offers a wonderful atmosphere in which you could spend hours enjoying the fine food and engaging in recommendations from the Master Sommelier. It is also licensed to hold civil wedding ceremonies and with doors opening onto a pretty rose garden this would make a dreamy venue.

North West England

SCOTLAND

Berwick-Upon-Tweed

Northumberland National Park

Carlisle

61

67
68
69 71 70
Lake District National Park
63
64
Windermere
62
Kendal
72
73
66

199
Yorkshire Dales National Park

Isle of Man

Douglas

Barrow-in-Furness

Fleetwood

Skipton
198

120

Blackpool
Preston

Southport

Bolton
Wigan
Manchester

Liverpool

WALES

22

© Lovell Johns Limited, Oxford

North East England

Central England

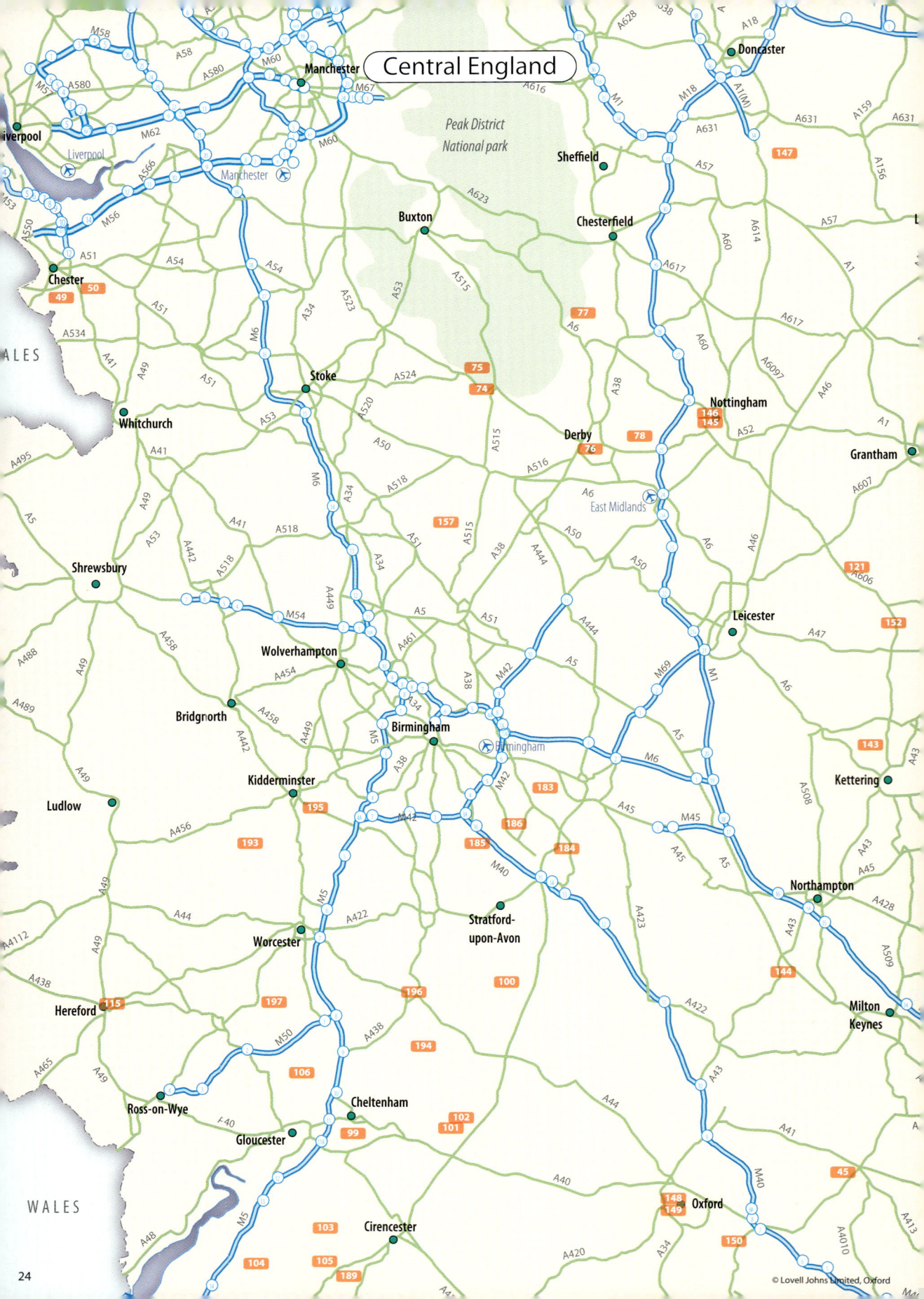

Eastern England

South West England

WALES

Exmoor National Park

Barnstaple
Bideford
Okehampton
Launceston
Newquay
St Austell
Truro
Plymouth
Falmouth
Helston
Penzance
St Ives

Dartmoor National Park

ISLES OF SCILLY

26 © Lovell Johns Limited, Oxford

South West England

Southern England

South East England

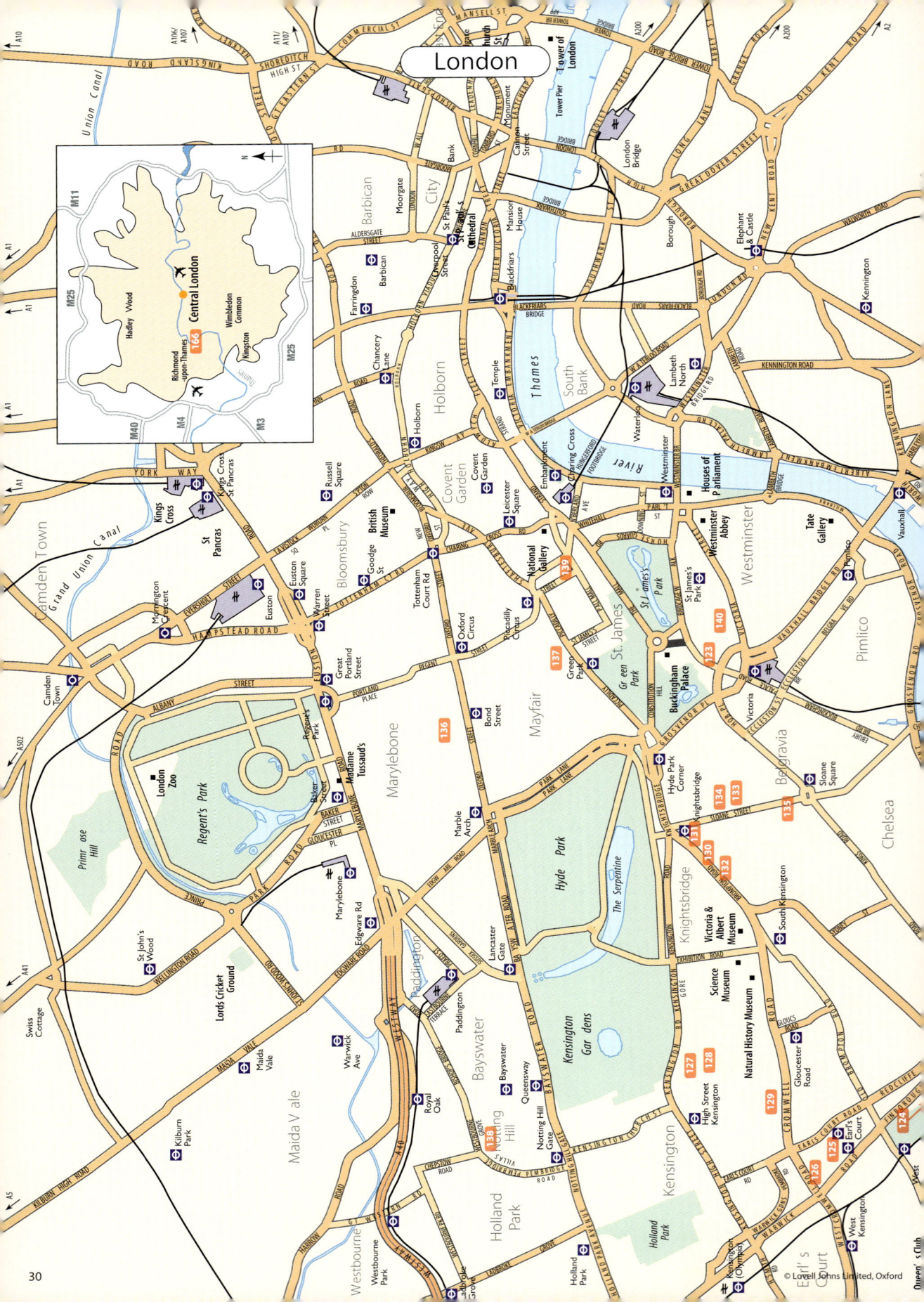

London

England

For further information on England, please contact:

Cumbria Tourist Board
Tel: +44 (0)1539 822222
E-mail: info@cumbriatourism.org
Web: www.golakes.co.uk

East of England Tourist Board
Tel: +44 (0)1284 727470
E-mail: info@eet.org.uk
Web: www.visiteastofengland.com

Heart of England Tourism
Web: www.visitheartofengland.com

Visit London
Tel: 0870 156 6366
Web: www.visitlondon.com

North East England Tourism Team
Web: www.visitnortheastengland.com

North West Tourist Board
Web: www.visitnorthwest.com

Tourism South East
Tel: +44 (0)23 8062 5400
Web: www.visistsoutheastengland.com

South West Tourism
Tel: 0870 442 0880
E-mail: info@westcountryholidays.com
Web: www.visitsouthwest.co.uk

Yorkshire Tourism Network
Tel: +44 (0)1904 707961
Web: www.ytb.org.uk

English Heritage
Tel: +44 (0) 870 333 1181
Web: www.english-heritage.org.uk

Historic Houses Association
Tel: +44 (0)20 7259 5688
E-mail: info@hha.org.uk
Web: www.hha.org.uk

The National Trust
Tel: 0844 800 1895
Web: www.nationaltrust.org.uk

or see **pages 270-273** for details of local historic houses, castles and gardens to visit during your stay.

For additional places to stay in England, turn to **pages 268-269** where a listing of our Recommended Small Hotels, Inns & Restaurant Guide can be found.

BATH & NORTH EAST SOMERSET - BATH

The Bath Priory Hotel, Restaurant & Spa

WESTON ROAD, BATH, SOMERSET BA1 2XT
Tel: 0845 365 2397 **International:** +44 (0)1225 331922 **Fax:** 01225 448276
Web: www.johansens.com/bathpriory **E-mail:** mail@thebathpriory.co.uk

Our inspector loved: *The beautifully decorated bedrooms overlooking the terrace and gardens.*

Price Guide: (incl. full English breakfast, use of the Garden Spa facilities)
double/twin from £250

Awards/Recognition: 1 Star Michelin 2008; 3 AA Rosettes 2007-2008

Location: Bath, 1 mile; M4 jct 18, 7.5 miles; Bristol Airport, 14 miles

Attractions: Roman Baths; Theatre Royal; The Cotswolds; Thermae Bath Spa

Standing close to some of England's most famous and finest architecture, The Bath Priory Hotel is very easy on the eye, this Georgian mellow stone building dating from 1835 formed part of a row of fashionable residences on the west side of the city. You will sense this history as you enter the hotel - antique furniture, oil paintings and objets d'art greet you - and well-defined colour schemes uplift throughout. Experience Michelin-Starred, modern British cuisine in the charming restaurant, where wines are well chosen to complement the food. You can arrange private parties in the Terrace, Pavilion and Orangery. Bath, of course, has so much to offer - The Pump Rooms, Museum of Costume and wonderful bijou shops.

BATH & NORTH EAST SOMERSET - BATH

Dukes Hotel

GREAT PULTENEY STREET, BATH, SOMERSET BA2 4DN
Tel: 0845 365 3274 **International:** +44 (0)1225 787960 **Fax:** 01225 787961
Web: www.johansens.com/dukesbath **E-mail:** info@dukesbath.co.uk

Our inspector loved: Lunch on the outside terrace, lovely al fresco dining in the centre of Bath.

Price Guide:
single £100
double/twin £135–£155
suite £195–£215

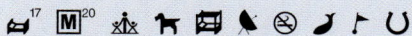

Awards/Recognition: 3 AA Rosettes 2008-2009

Location: A36, 0.5 miles; M4 jct 18, 8 miles; Bristol Airport, 15.5 miles; London, 90-min train

Attractions: Roman Baths & Pump Room; Thermae Bath Spa; Theatre Royal; Bath Abbey

Dukes Hotel introduces itself as charming, full of character and style as soon as you walk through the elegant entrance below half-moon shaped decorative glass and edged by slim, black, wrought-iron railings. Grade I listed and built from Bath stone, the hotel is a former Palladian mansion, and today basks in a sense of understated luxury. Most guest rooms and suites have original intricate plasterwork and large sash windows, and from front rooms you can see more Palladio-inspired façades, while those at the back look out to rolling hills. Recently refurbished, the Cavendish Restaurant is light, airy and relaxing, and you can enjoy the best organic and free-range British ingredients, including Cornish lamb, local Somerset beef and seafood delivered daily from Devon.

BATH & NORTH EAST SOMERSET - BATH

The Royal Crescent Hotel & The Bath House Spa

16 ROYAL CRESCENT, BATH, SOMERSET BA1 2LS
Tel: 0845 365 2679 **International:** +44 (0)1225 823333 **Fax:** 01225 339401
Web: www.johansens.com/royalcrescent **E-mail:** info@royalcrescent.co.uk

Our inspector loved: *The Bath House spa, a wonderful place to relax and unwind.*

Price Guide:
single from £215
double/twin £295–£400
suite £450–£850

Awards/Recognition: Relais & Châteaux; 2 AA Rosettes 2008-2009

Location: City Centre; A4, 1.5 miles; M4 jct 18, 10 miles; Bath Spa Station, 1 mile

Attractions: The Roman Baths; Stourhead; Longleat; Cotswolds

Hidden in the middle of one of the great architectural masterpieces of Europe, The Royal Crescent Hotel, part of the prestigious Relais & Chateaux collection, is far more than a remarkable collection of buildings. Staying here offers an opportunity, all too rare in today's frantic world, to experience gracious living from the age when Bath was the centre of the civilized world. Restored to their original splendour, the individual bedrooms are rich in period features with 21st century creature comforts hidden amongst them. Beyond the main mansion stretches an acre of hidden garden and four original coach houses where The Dower House restaurant is found. A further coach house houses the tranquil oasis of The Bath House, a spa specialising in an holistic approach. If all that is not enough, why not enjoy a champagne cruise along the Kennet and Avon waterway in the hotel's private river launch. A von Essen hotel.

BATH & NORTH EAST SOMERSET - BATH (HINTON CHARTERHOUSE)

Homewood Park

HINTON CHARTERHOUSE, BATH, BA2 7TB
Tel: 0845 365 1875 **International:** +44 (0)1225 723731 **Fax:** 01225 723820
Web: www.johansens.com/homewoodpark **E-mail:** info@homewoodpark.co.uk

Our inspector loved: *The fabulous new decoration and Room 3!*

Price Guide:
single from £145
double/twin £245-£355
suite £395–£485

Awards/Recognition: 2 AA Rosettes 2008-2009

Location: On the A36; Bath 6 miles; M4 jct 18, 15 miles; Bristol Airport, 20 miles

Attractions: Longleat; Stonehenge; Stourhead; Roman Baths; Thermae Bath Spa

A gloriously quintessential English country house hotel in an area of outstanding natural beauty amid acres of award winning gardens and woodland just 6 miles from the centre of Bath. A recent refurbishment has been sympathetic to the relaxed elegance found in the best of English homes. Rich fabrics, warm neutrals and traditional floral prints have been used in the bedrooms. Each individually styled and enhanced by extraordinary antique furniture, personal details and many with superb views over the garden. The restaurant is a destination in its own right; stylish, innovative and great English cuisine. The hotel's drawing room, study and bar ensure guests always have a cosy corner in which to relax and in winter enjoy the roaring log fires. The warmth of service and atmosphere along with outstanding food make this an ideal retreat. A von Essen hotel.

BATH & NORTH EAST SOMERSET - BATH (HUNSTRETE)

Hunstrete House

HUNSTRETE, NR BATH, SOMERSET BS39 4NS
Tel: 0845 365 1906 **International:** +44 (0)1761 490490 **Fax:** 01761 490732
Web: www.johansens.com/hunstretehouse **E-mail:** reception@hunstretehouse.co.uk

On the edge of the Mendip Hills stands Hunstrete House, largely built in the 18th century and surrounded by lovely gardens. Bedrooms are individually decorated and furnished, many offer uninterrupted views over fields and woodlands. The reception areas feature beautiful antiques and log fires burn in the hall and drawing room through the winter. Popham's Restaurant overlooks an Italianate, flower-filled courtyard. A highly skilled head chef prepares light, elegant dishes using produce from the extensive garden, including organic meat and vegetables. The hotel would make a great venue for exclusive use, a wedding or company event. A von Essen hotel.

Our inspector loved: *The beautiful setting surrounded by fields and woodland.*

Price Guide:
single from £135
double/twin from £190
suite from £290

Awards/Recognition: 2 AA Rosettes 2008-2009;

Location: A368, 0.1 miles; A37, 1.8 miles; Bath, 8 miles; Brsitol Airport, 15.5 miles

Attractions: Roman Baths; Bristol; Wells Cathedral; Cheddar Caves & Gorge

BATH & NORTH EAST SOMERSET - BATH (WICK)

THE PARK

WICK, NEAR BATH BS30 5RN
Tel: 0845 365 2619 **International:** +44 (0)117 937 1800 **Fax:** 0117 937 1813
Web: www.johansens.com/thepark E-mail: info@tpresort.com

Our inspector loved: *The Park Room, a fabulous room for a wedding or banquet.*

Price Guide:
single from £135
double/twin from £185
luxury from £280

Awards/Recognition: 2 AA Rosettes 2007-2008

Location: Off the A420; A46, 2.3 miles; M4 jct 18, 7 miles; Bath, 4 miles

Attractions: Stonehenge; Bristol; Thermae Bath Spa; Cotswolds

If you're a golfer you'll be in 18th heaven at this hotel with its 2 championship golf courses filled with mature trees, lakes and modern specification greens, if you're not, you'll love it anyway for its beauty, stylish bedrooms and glorious natural parkland. The Park's restaurant, Oakwood, was originally an old stone Masonic lodge, and has an open-plan kitchen under the instruction of Chef Mark Treasure. Menus specialise in the simple treatment of roasted meats and fish cooked in a wood burning oven. There are 7 conference and syndicate rooms accommodating up to 150 delegates, and the attractive Park Room, with views over the golf course, seats up to 130 for a private banquet or wedding reception. You're conveniently located between Bristol and Bath. Take the park & ride, just 2 miles from the hotel and enjoy a fabulous day out in the beautiful, Georgian city of Bath

BEDFORDSHIRE - LUTON

Luton Hoo Hotel, Golf & Spa

THE MANSION HOUSE, LUTON HOO, LUTON, BEDFORDSHIRE LU1 3TQ
Tel: 0845 365 3458 **International:** +44 (0)1582 734437 **Fax:** +44 (0)1582 485438
Web: www.johansens.com/lutonhoo **E-mail:** reservations@lutonhoo.co.uk

Our inspector loved: *The Romanov Suite - formerly a Russian Orthodox chapel.*

Price Guide:
single £235-£810
double £275-£850
suite £360-£850

The sweeping drive builds a sense of excitement and you are not disappointed as you arrive at the front of this impressive grade 1 listed historic mansion. Recently restored to its original splendour it sits overlooking 1000 acres of Bedfordshire parkland and formal gardens once designed by Capability Brown. Remarkable care as been taken with the restoration of the stonework and with the soft furnishing of silks, panelling and marquetry. The master bedrooms in the mansion house give a luxurious glimpse of the past. More contemporary bedrooms are to be found in the outbuildings close by; the Parklands and Flower Garden Wood. Take tea in the Italianate drawing room or experience the elegance of the former state dining room, now the Wernher Restaurant. There is plenty to occupy you including the spa, a challenging 18-hole golf course and tennis courts.

Location: A1081, 1 mile; M1 jct 10, 3 miles; Luton Airport, 10-min drive; London, 30-min train

Attractions: London; St.Albans; Hatfield House; Woburn Abbey

BERKSHIRE - MAIDENHEAD

Fredrick's – Hotel Restaurant Spa

SHOPPENHANGERS ROAD, MAIDENHEAD, BERKSHIRE SL6 2PZ
Tel: 0845 365 1758 **International:** +44 (0)1628 581000 **Fax:** 01628 771054
Web: www.johansens.com/fredricks **E-mail:** reservations@fredricks-hotel.co.uk

Our inspector loved: *This excellent hotel with its lovely grounds, elegant spa and personal welcome*

Price Guide:
single from £245
double/twin from £325
suite from £450

Awards/Recognition: 3 AA Rosettes 2007-2008

Location: A4, 1 mile; M4 jct 8/9, 1 mile; Windsor, 6 miles; Heathrow, 17 miles

Attractions: Windsor Castle; Henley; Royal Ascot; Legoland

"Putting people first" is the guiding philosophy behind this superb hotel, whose extensive landscaped gardens are filled with contemporary artwork and overlook a broad swathe of Maidenhead Golf Club. Fredrick's is now under new management who intend to uphold the friendly attention to detail the hotel has become renowned for. Its exclusive spa, the first in the UK equipped with its own private flotation suite, is ideal for spa day experiences where you can indulge in restorative treatments such as Rasul or LaStone therapies. And the large bedrooms all benefit from free WiFi access and have comfortable, spacious bathrooms; some even have their own patio or balcony. Dine in the elegant restaurant where a new, more contemporary and relaxed menu is available or savour a more informal meal alfresco. As well as being suitable for relaxation, spa breaks, romantic escapes and fine dining, this is the perfect place for conferences and corporate hospitality.

BERKSHIRE - MAIDENHEAD (TAPLOW)

Cliveden & The Pavilion Spa

TAPLOW, BERKSHIRE SL6 0JF
Tel: 0845 365 3236 **International:** +44 (0)1628 668561 **Fax:** 01628 661837
Web: www.johansens.com/cliveden **E-mail:** Reservations@clivedenhouse.co.uk

Our inspector loved: *It does not matter how many times you visit Cliveden, the experience is as rewarding on each occasion.*

Price Guide: (room only, excluding VAT)
double/twin from £370
suites from £650

One of the world's finest luxury hotels, this grand stately home is set in the heart of the Berkshire countryside, surrounded by magnificent formal gardens. From the moment you enter the beautiful Great Hall with its grand fireplace, oak panelling and priceless artworks, you will feel like a treasured, personal guest, treated to the very highest standards of quality conveyed in the excellence of every detail. Where else can you be surrounded by such extraordinary extravagance and remarkable refinement, but at the same time feel so welcomed and at ease. Set amidst 376 acres of parkland, yet conveniently near to London and Heathrow Airport, Cliveden overlooks an idyllic bend in the River Thames, which affords the house with panoramic views over the beautiful grounds and beyond. Enjoy award-winning cuisine, a luxury spa, idyllic river cruises and state-of-the-art meeting room facilities. A von Essen hotel.

Awards/Recognition: 3 AA Rosettes 2008-2009 (Waldo's Restaurant) 2 AA Rosettes 2008-2009 (The Terrace Dining Room); Best Hotel for Food Condé Nast Traveller Gold List 2007

Location: A4, 3 miles; M4 jct 7, 4 miles; Heathrow Airport, 12 miles

Attractions: Windsor Castle / Windsor Great Park; Ascot Racecourse; Henley; Legoland

BERKSHIRE - NEWBURY

Donnington Valley Hotel and Spa

OLD OXFORD ROAD, DONNINGTON, NEWBURY, BERKSHIRE RG14 3AG
Tel: 0845 365 3267 **International:** +44 (0)1635 551199 **Fax:** 01635 551123
Web: www.johansens.com/donningtonvalley **E-mail:** general@donningtonvalley.co.uk

Our inspector loved: *The fabulous Spa, spacious bedrooms and all round excellence of this friendly hotel.*

Price Guide:
classic from £190
executive £230
suite from £260

Awards/Recognition: 2 AA Rosettes 2007-2008

Location: A34, 3 miles; M4 jct 13, 3 miles; Newbury, 2 miles; Heathrow Airport, 45 miles

Attractions: Donnington Castle; Newbury Racecourse; Highclere Castle; Lambourn Downs

Experience England's most exciting spa at this highly-acclaimed 4-star hotel with its 111 elegantly designed bedrooms and suites, an award-winning WinePress restaurant and challenging 18-hole, par 71 golf course. Classic features such as an open log fire, wood-beamed bar and lounge area create a friendly, warm and intimate ambience. Donnington Valley Health Club and Spa has everything you could wish for, from an 18m pool, Signature Lifefitness Gym, Jacuzzi, sauna, steam room, aromatherapy room and monsoon shower to 7 treatment suites. The hotel offers a variety of Spa and Leisure Breaks for families and friends seeking a peaceful, rural setting as well as mid-week and weekend Golf Breaks suitable for leisurely getaways and corporate breaks alike. The closing 4 holes are considered one of the toughest finishes in the country, so after a challenging day at the course head to the clubhouse, a Grade II listed Victorian building where 2 bars welcome you in.

41

BERKSHIRE - NEWBURY

The Vineyard At Stockcross

NEWBURY, BERKSHIRE RG20 8JU
Tel: 0845 365 2716 **International:** +44 (0)1635 528770 **Fax:** 01635 528398
Web: www.johansens.com/vineyardstockcross **E-mail:** general@the-vineyard.co.uk

Sir Peter Michael's "restaurant-with-suites" showcases 600 top Californian wines, including those from the Peter Michael Winery. The Head Sommelier has a wide and innovative list with 2000 wines to complement the modern British cuisine created by Executive Chef, John Campbell. Dishes combine a unique blend of flavours and textures creating an unforgettable multi-sensory feast! Awards include 5 Red Stars and 4 AA Rosettes and 2 Michelin Stars. An arresting collection of paintings and sculptures including the keynote piece "Fire and Water" by William Pye FRBS will inspire you further. The 49 bedrooms include 32 suites which provide stylish comfort. The refurbished Vineyard Spa features a new indoor pool as well as steam room, jacuzzi and poolside relaxation area. The treatment rooms offer a range of ESPA and Choco, Vino and TruffleTherapy treatments. There are a number of tempting spa packages and other special offers which include celebration breaks.

Our inspector loved: As soon as you walk into this hotel, you experience a very special atmosphere which remains throughout your stay.

Price Guide: (room only)
classic £210
luxury £295
suite from £345

Awards/Recognition: Condé Nast Johansens Taittinger Wine List Awards, Range of Wine by the Glass and Connoisseur List 2008; 2 Star Michelin 2007; Relais & Châteaux; 4 AA Rosettes 2007–2008

Location: A4, 500 metres; M4 jct 13, 2.5 miles; Newbury, 2.5 miles; Heathrow, 45 miles

Attractions: Highclere Castle; Newbury Racecourse; Bath; The Cotswolds

BERKSHIRE - READING (SONNING-ON-THAMES)

The French Horn

SONNING-ON-THAMES, BERKSHIRE RG4 6TN
Tel: 0845 365 2496 **International:** +44 (0)1189 692204 **Fax:** 01189 442210
Web: www.johansens.com/frenchhorn **E-mail:** info@thefrenchhorn.co.uk

Our inspector loved: *The relaxed atmosphere and traditional values of this family-run hotel.*

Price Guide:
single £125–£170
double/twin £160–£215

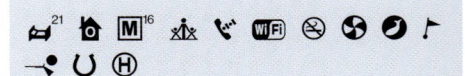

Awards/Recognition: 2 AA Rosettes 2007-2008

Location: A4, 1 mile; M4 jct 10, 3 miles; Reading, 3 miles; Heathrow Airport, 20 miles

Attractions: Henley; Windsor Castle; Stratfield Saye; The Mill Theatre

For over 150 years The French Horn has provided a charming riverside retreat. Today, it continues that fine tradition of comfortable accommodation, notably excellent service and outstanding cuisine. Choose to stay in bedrooms or suites located in the hotel or within riverside cottages that are ideally suited for longer stays, and make sure to request a riverside view. The old panelled bar provides an intimate scene for pre-dinner drinks in the award-winning restaurant with its speciality of locally reared duck, spit roasted on-site over an open fire. The restaurant is a lovely setting for lunch, while at night, diners can enjoy the floodlit view of the graceful weeping willows which fringe the river. Dinner is served by candlelight and the cuisine is a mixture of French and English cooking that uses the freshest ingredients alongside a fine and extensive wine list. This is the perfect location for a romantic getaway, special celebration or corporate event.

43

BERKSHIRE - WINDSOR

Harte & Garter Hotel & Spa

HIGH STREET, WINDSOR, BERKSHIRE SL4 1PH
Tel: 0845 365 3813 **International:** +44 (0)1753 863426 **Fax:** 01753 830527
Web: www.johansens.com/harteandgarter **E-mail:** res@harteandgarter.com

Our inspector loved: *The complete transformation of this hotel into a modern, character filled, elegant venue - suitable for all sorts of occasions.*

Price Guide: (room only)
single £175-£350
double £225-£350
junior suites from £350

Location: A332, 0.5 miles; M4 jct 6, 1 mile; Heathrow Airport, 7 miles

Attractions: Royal Ascot Racecourse; Windsor Castle; Windsor Great Park (for the polo); Sunningdale Golf Course; Legoland

This beautiful hotel is ideal for a romantic weekend getaway or hosting a special occasion. Standing directly opposite Windsor Castle, it enjoys a spectacular position right in the heart of the charming town of Windsor. Originally two inns dating back to the 14th century, they were lovingly joined together in the late 19th century in a popular Jacobethan style. Now, after a total refurbishment, the result is this stylish hotel that is a remarkable, contemporary space retaining its historic beauty. You will love the light, airy rooms with their high ceilings, and the exquisite ballroom is dazzling. There are 5 treatment rooms and a thermal experience including steam room, sauna, Jacuzzi, experience showers, rasul oven and 4 senses beds. If you are in the mood for a glorious walk along the river, the Thames is only a short stroll away, while a quick trip to London is very easy.

BUCKINGHAMSHIRE - AYLESBURY

HARTWELL HOUSE HOTEL, RESTAURANT & SPA

OXFORD ROAD, NEAR AYLESBURY, BUCKINGHAMSHIRE HP17 8NR
Tel: 0845 365 1824 **International:** +44 (0)1296 747444 **Fax:** 01296 747450
Web: www.johansens.com/hartwellhouse **E-mail:** info@hartwell-house.com

Our inspector loved: *The sweeping drive, glorious surrounding parkland and above all, the very special attention to detail from the attentive staff.*

Price Guide: (including continental breakfast)
single from £145
double/twin from £240
suites from £340

Awards/Recognition: 3 AA Rosettes 2008-2009

Location: A418, 0.2 miles; M40, 10 miles; Luton Airport, 29 miles; Heathrow, 40 miles

Attractions: Waddesdon Manor (NT); Stowe Landscaped Gardens; Oxford; Bicester Village

Standing in 90 acres, landscaped by a contemporary of Capability Brown, Hartwell House is a beautiful Grade 1 listed building with Jacobean and Georgian facades - the residence in exile of King Louis XVIII of France from 1809 to 1814. The large ground floor reception rooms, with oak panelling and decorated ceilings, have antique furniture and fine paintings. There are 46 individually designed bedrooms and suites, 30 in the main house and 16 in the Hartwell Court, where dogs are permitted. The dining room at Hartwell is the setting for award winning cuisine, there are also 2 private dining rooms. The Old Rectory, provides superb private accommodation and swimming pool. The Hartwell Spa is the perfect place to be pampered. Owned and restored by Historic House Hotels Limited.

BUCKINGHAMSHIRE - MARLOW-ON-THAMES

Danesfield House Hotel and Spa

HENLEY ROAD, MARLOW-ON-THAMES, BUCKINGHAMSHIRE SL7 2EY
Tel: 0845 365 3261 **International:** +44 (0)1628 891010 **Fax:** 01628 890408
Web: www.johansens.com/danesfieldhouse **E-mail:** sales@danesfieldhouse.co.uk

Our inspector loved: *The grandeur yet comfort of this splendid Country House with its exceptional staff and excellent facilities.*

Price Guide:
single from £240
double/twin from £275
suites from £300

Danesfield House Hotel and Spa is set within 65 acres overlooking the River Thames, with panoramic views across the Chiltern Hills. It is the third house on this site since 1664 and was built in sumptuous Victorian style at the end of the 19th century. The executive bedrooms are richly decorated and furnished. Guests may relax in the magnificent Grand Hall, with its minstrels' gallery, in the sun-lit atrium or comfortable bar before taking dinner in one of the 2 restaurants. The Oak Room features the delicious cuisine of award-winning chef Adam Simmonds and the Orangery Brasserie which offers a more traditional menu. Leisure facilities include the award-winning spa with 20-metre ozone-cleansed pool, sauna, steam room, gymnasium and superb treatment rooms. There are also 10 private banqueting and conference rooms.

Awards/Recognition: 4 AA Rosettes 2008-2009; Buckinghamshire Restaurant of the Year - Good Food Guide 2007

Location: A4155, 0.2 miles; M40 jct 4, 7 miles; Marlow, 3 miles; Heathrow airport, 23 miles

Attractions: Henley; Windsor; Ascot; River Walks

BUCKINGHAMSHIRE - SLOUGH

Stoke Place

STOKE GREEN, STOKE POGES, BUCKINGHAMSHIRE SL2 4HT
Tel: 0845 365 2843 **International:** +44 (0)1753 534 790 **Fax:** 01753 560 209
Web: www.johansens.com/stokeplace **E-mail:** enquiries@stokeplace.co.uk

Our inspector loved: *The mix of contemporary with traditional style - sumptuous, quirky, fun and flexible - all rolled into one.*

Price Guide:
double from £225
suite £275-£350

Location: A4, 2.5 miles; M4, 4 miles; Heathrow Airport, 10 miles; Central London, 20-min train

Attractions: Windsor and Windsor Castle; Legoland; Henley

This beautiful 17th-century Queen Anne mansion is sure to impress you with its wonderfully refurbished, contemporary interior that is both elegant and incredibly comfortable. Quirky touches and individuality has been encouraged here which helps create the warm atmosphere that is enhanced by the friendly staff. All the bedrooms have views over the hotel's extensives grounds and some of the spacious suites benefit from giant bay windows and fireplaces. The Vyse Room Restaurant produces a modern seasonal English menu. For total indulgence there is an in-room spa service. Stoke Place is an excellent location for business, midweek breaks, exclusive use, weddings, and family Sundays

47

BUCKINGHAMSHIRE - STOKE POGES (HEATHROW)

STOKE PARK

PARK ROAD, STOKE POGES, BUCKINGHAMSHIRE SL2 4PG
Tel: 0845 365 2374 **International:** +44 (0)1753 717171 **Fax:** 01753 717181
Web: www.johansens.com/stokepark **E-mail:** info@stokeparkclub.com

Our inspector loved: *The traditional, elegant yet relaxed atmosphere of the mansion contrasted with the contemporary spa and new bedrooms.*

Price Guide:
single from £285
executive from £345
suite from £400

Location: Off the B416; M4 jct 6, 4.5 miles; Windsor, 5 miles; Heathrow Airport, 7 miles

Attractions: Windsor Castle; Ascot; Henley; Legoland

Stoke Park offers 5 star hotel accommodation set amidst 350 acres of parkland and has for more than 900 years been at the heart of English heritage, playing host to royalty and the aristocracy. The magnificence of the Palladian mansion is echoed by the beautifully decorated interior, enhanced by antiques, exquisite fabrics and original paintings. All 21 individually furnished bedrooms and suites have marble bathrooms some with terraces. A further 28 luxury contemporary rooms have been added above the £20 million health and racquet pavillion. Private bars, cosy lounges, 8 function rooms and the finest restaurants outside London are perfect for entertaining. Since 1908 the hotel has been home to one of the finest 27-hole championship parkland golf courses in the world. The all indulging spa, health and racquet pavilion re-affirms the hotel's position as one of the country's leading sporting venues. A selection of indulgence breaks are often available.

CHESHIRE - CHESTER

GREEN BOUGH HOTEL

60 HOOLE ROAD, CHESTER, CHESHIRE CH2 3NL
Tel: 0845 365 1796 **International:** +44 (0)1244 326241 **Fax:** 01244 326265
Web: www.johansens.com/greenbough **E-mail:** luxury@greenbough.co.uk

Our inspector loved: The Roman theme prevalent throughout this small luxurious hotel.

Price Guide:
single from £105
double/twin from £175
suites from £245

Location: on the A56, M53 jct 12, 1 miles; Chester, 1 miles; Manchester Airport, 32 miles

Attractions: Chester Super Zoo; Chester Racecourse; Erdigg (NT); Cheshire Plains;

Proprietors Janice and Philip Martin have worked ceaselessly to make this place what it is, a friendly and relaxing haven, whilst collecting a fistful of awards in the process, including the Condé Nast Johansens Most Excellent City Hotel in 2004. Arguably Chester's premier small luxury hotel, the 15 bedrooms and suites have been refurbished using Italian wall coverings and fabrics in keeping with the Roman theme throughout the hotel. Original oil paintings depict scenes from a bygone era in Pompeii and antique cast-iron beds, four-posters and Jacuzzi baths add extra drama. You will certainly be tempted into The Olive Tree restaurant by an eclectic mix of aromas and flavours, complemented by a wine list from an extensive cellar. The hotel is within walking distance of historic Chester, and centrally placed for Snowdonia, Cumbria and Manchester.

49

CHESHIRE - CHESTER (ROWTON)

Rowton Hall Hotel, Health Club & Spa

WHITCHURCH ROAD, ROWTON, CHESTER, CHESHIRE CH3 6AD
Tel: 0845 365 2308 **International:** +44 (0)1244 335262 **Fax:** 01244 335464
Web: www.johansens.com/rowtonhall **E-mail:** reception@rowtonhallhotelandspa.co.uk

There is so much to say about this hotel that it's difficult to know where start - its original oak panelling, self-supporting hand-carved staircase, inglenook and elegant Robert Adam fireplaces, or the comfortable bedrooms with every contemporary amenity from satellite TV to broadband and voicemail, and even a goodies tray! Just enjoy it all, especially eating great food in Langdale Restaurant - created from local market and hotel garden ingredients - knowing you can exercise to make up for it in the Health Club. Work out in the gym, on 2 floodlit all-weather tennis courts, or the dance studio, then relax in the fabulous spa with pool Jacuzzi, steam room and sauna. Rowton Hall is perfect for corporate events as 4 main conference and banqueting suites hold up to 150 people.

Our inspector loved: *The double treatment room in the spa above the swimming pool, health club and gym.*

Price Guide:
single from £145
double/twin £170–£205
suites £380–£525

Awards/Recognition: 2 AA Rosette 2007-2008

Location: A41, 0.5 miles; M53 jct 12, 2 miles; Chester, 2 miles; John Lennon International Airport, 35 miles

Attractions: Chester Zoo; Chester Racecourse; Cheshire Oaks Outlet Village; Blue Planet Aquarium

CORNWALL - CARNE BEACH (NEAR ST MAWES)

The Nare Hotel

CARNE BEACH, VERYAN-IN-ROSELAND, TRURO, CORNWALL TR2 5PF
Tel: 0845 365 2603 **International:** +44 (0)1872 501111 **Fax:** 01872 501856
Web: www.johansens.com/nare **E-mail:** office@narehotel.co.uk

Our inspector loved: *The panoramic sea views and country house comfort.*

Price Guide:
single £109-£223
double/twin £206-£410
suite £376-£630

Awards/Recognition: Condé Nast Johansens Most Excellent Coastal Hotel 2006; 2 AA Rosettes 2007-2008

Location: St Mawes, 8 miles, Truro, 12 miles; St Austell, 12 miles ; A30, 15 miles

Attractions: Eden Project; Lost Gardens of Heligan; Private Cornish Gardens; National Maritime Museum Falmouth

This absolute gem is superbly positioned overlooking the fine sandy beach of Gerrans Bay. Thanks to Toby Ashworth's proprietorial presence, the hotel has carefully evolved over the years and is considered the most comfortable in Cornwall. Bedrooms overlook the countryside or sea and have patios and balconies that are the best vantage point for spectacular views. There are 2 restaurants at The Nare Hotel for you to choose from. The main dining room overlooks the sea, and offers a fine dining experience off the table d'hôte menus. The traditional English cuisine includes local seafood dishes such as Portloe lobster and crab and delicious home-made puddings with generous helpings of Cornish cream. Dinner is also always available at the more informal Quarterdeck Restaurant where al fresco lunches may be taken on the terrace. Explore the glorious Roseland Peninsula's coastline and villages, not forgetting Cornwall's beautiful houses and gardens.

CORNWALL - FALMOUTH (GYLLYNGVASE BEACH)
St Michael's Hotel & Spa

GYLLYNGVASE BEACH, FALMOUTH, CORNWALL TR11 4NB
Tel: 0845 365 2358 **International:** +44 (0)1326 312707 **Fax:** 01326 211772
Web: www.johansens.com/stmichaelsfalmouth **E-mail:** info@stmichaelshotel.co.uk

Our inspector loved: *The feeling of relaxation and escape from everyday stress.*

Price Guide:
single £50–£165
double/twin £104–£220
suite £170–£244

Awards/Recognition: 1 AA Rosette 2007-2008

Location: Just off A39; Truro, 11.7 miles; Newquay Airport, 25 miles

Attractions: National Maritime Museum; Land's End; Eden Project; Coastal walks

St Michael's Hotel & Spa has been carefully and extensively refurbished, resulting in a state-of-the-art health club, spa, award-winning restaurant, and contemporary bedrooms, bars and conference suites. The Flying Fish Restaurant, overlooking the sea and gardens, changes menus regularly so you can sample Cornwall's best fresh fish, seafood and seasonal produce. The sun terrace is the perfect spot for alfresco dining. Surrounded by sub-tropical gardens, the Spa offers an impressive range of health and relaxation treatments, and you can also take a dip in the indoor pool and work out in the large fitness suite. Feel the sand between your toes on the blue flag beach, directly opposite the hotel, or visit the Eden Project within an hour's drive.

CORNWALL - FALMOUTH (MAWNAN SMITH)

BUDOCK VEAN - THE HOTEL ON THE RIVER

NEAR HELFORD PASSAGE, MAWNAN SMITH, FALMOUTH, CORNWALL TR11 5LG
Tel: 0845 365 3212 **International:** +44 (0)1326 252100 **Fax:** 01326 250892
Web: www.johansens.com/budockvean **E-mail:** relax@budockvean.co.uk

Our inspector loved: *The generously filled crab sandwich at lunch followed by the fillet of beef for dinner that melted in my mouth.*

Price Guide: (including dinner)
single £66–£125
double/twin £132–£250
suite £228–£320

Awards/Recognition: 1 AA Rosette 2007–2008

Location: M5 jct 30, 100 miles; A39, 12 miles; Falmouth, 6 miles; Newquay Airport, 30 miles

Attractions: Trebah Gardens; Glendurgan Gardens; National Maritime Museum Falmouth; Eden Project

A destination in itself, recommended by Condé Nast Johansens since 1983 and current recipient of the Green Tourism Business Scheme Gold Award, this family-run hotel is set in 65 acres of outstanding natural beauty. With award-winning gardens and a private foreshore on the Helford River, Budock Vean is all about relaxation and pampering. Amenities include a large indoor pool, outdoor hot tub, sauna, tennis courts, a billiard room, boating, fishing, and the Natural Health Spa. A local ferry will take you from the hotel's jetty to waterside pubs and Frenchman's Creek and you can even enjoy a trip on the hotel's own river boat. Imaginative 5-course dinners specialise in fresh seafood, which can be walked off on a magnificent myriad of local country and coastal walks.

CORNWALL - FALMOUTH (MAWNAN SMITH)

Meudon Hotel

MAWNAN SMITH, NEAR FALMOUTH, CORNWALL TR11 5HT
Tel: 0845 365 2059 **International:** +44 (0)1326 250541 **Fax:** 01326 250543
Web: www.johansens.com/meudon **E-mail:** wecare@meudon.co.uk

Our inspector loved: *This family owned and run hotel offering all that's expected within beautiful grounds.*

Price Guide: (including dinner)
single £125
double/twin £250
suite £340

Awards/Recognition: 1 AA Rosette 2006-2007

Location: A39, 5 miles; Falmouth, 4 miles; A30, 13 miles

Attractions: National Maritime Museum Falmouth; Trebah Gardens; Pendennis Castle; Eden Project

The French name originates from a nearby farmhouse built by Napoleonic prisoners of war and called after their longed-for home village. Comfortable bedrooms enjoy spectacular views over the hotels sub-tropical gardens which tend to be coaxed into early bloom by the Gulf Stream and mild Cornish climate. Local fishermen and farmers supply the kitchen with ingredients to allow a changing seasonal menu. The Pilgrim's are 5th generation hoteliers and it shows in the attention, care and enthusiasm they put into running the place. There are plenty of watersports and outdoor pursuits to indulge in, you can play golf free at nearby Falmouth Golf Club, sail aboard the hotel's skippered 34-foot yacht or just laze on the private beach.

CORNWALL - FOWEY

Fowey Hall & Aquae Sulis Retreat

HANSON DRIVE, FOWEY, CORNWALL PL23 1ET
Tel: 0845 365 1754 **International:** +44 (0)1726 833866 **Fax:** 01726 834100
Web: www.johansens.com/foweyhall **E-mail:** info@foweyhallhotel.co.uk

Our inspector loved: *The feeling of being able to switch off and relax in this wonderful location*

Price Guide:
double/twin £150–£265
suite £175–£340
interconnecting £260–£440

Awards/Recognition: 2 AA Rosettes 2008-2009

Location: A3082, 0.3 miles; A390, 5.7 miles; Newquay Airport, 23.3 miles

Attractions: Eden Project; Newquay Zoo; Lost Gardens of Helegan; Readymoney Cove

Sitting high on the hill over looking the pretty Fowey Estuary, Fowey Hall Hotel is a superb Victorian mansion with fine panelling and superb ceilings. Spacious and atmospheric public rooms and a beautiful terrace provide ample opportunity for relaxation. Well proportioned bedrooms and suites give families plenty of flexibility and accommodation is split between the main house and the courtyard. With young guests eating early adults can enjoy time to themselves in the intimate surroundings of Hansons restaurant renowned for its use of the best regional produce. An Ofsted Registered Nursery is on hand and for older children "The Beach Hut" in the courtyard is well-equipped with table tennis, table football and many other games. An out door play area is available. The New Aquae Sulis Retreat is all about having a good time together, enjoy the pool and hot tub as well as fantastic treatments designed with the 'exhausted parent' in mind. A von Essen Luxury Family Hotel.

CORNWALL - ISLES OF SCILLY (BRYHER)

Hell Bay

BRYHER, ISLES OF SCILLY, CORNWALL TR23 0PR
Tel: 0845 365 1837 **International:** +44 (0)1720 422947 **Fax:** 01720 423004
Web: www.johansens.com/hellbay **E-mail:** contactus@hellbay.co.uk

Our inspector loved: *This contemporary first class Island retreat offering total escapism.*

Price Guide: (including dinner)
suites £260–£580

Awards/Recognition: 2 AA Rosettes 2008-2009;

Location: Lands End, 30 miles; Exeter Airport, 1 hour; Penzance Heliport, 20 mins; Penzance Ferry Terminal, 2.5 hours

Attractions: Tresco Abbey Garden; Water Sports; Boat Excursions; Fishing

You should visit the magical Isles of Scilly at least once in your life. The 3 Red Star awarded Hell Bay stands on the rugged West Coast of Bryher – the smallest of the island communities where the local transport network relies on bicycles and colourful boats. This is a spectacular getaway-from-it-all destination. Warm winds of the gulf stream, empty beaches and crystal clear water. We love it. Most of the suites have dazzling sea views. The restaurant serves up dawn fresh crab, lobster and fish hand picked from the local boats. On hand is an outdoor heated swimming pool, gym, sauna, spa bath, children's playground, games room and par 3 golf course. Though you should venture out & explore; fishing trips, diving expeditions, inter-island hops and evening gig races. Fly by helicopter or sail from Penzance or by plane from Bristol, Southampton, Exeter, Newquay and Land's End.

CORNWALL - LOOE

TALLAND BAY HOTEL

PORTHALLOW, CORNWALL PL13 2JB
Tel: 0845 365 2386 **International:** +44 (0)1503 272667 **Fax:** 01503 272940
Web: www.johansens.com/tallandbay **E-mail:** info@tallandbayhotel.co.uk

Our inspector loved: *The wonderful fresh seafood at dinner followed by a nightcap on the terrace.*

Price Guide:
single £75–£105
double/twin £95–£225

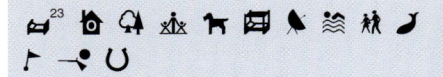

Awards/Recognition: 2 AA Rosettes 2008-2009

Location: A387, 1 mile; A38, 9.5 miles; Looe, 3.2 miles

Attractions: St Ives; National Maritime Museum, Falmouth; Eden Project; Lost Gardens of Heligan

In this wild and romantic location on the Cornish coastline with its cliff tops, estuaries and abundant wildlife you will find all the ingredients you need to unwind. Exuding a relaxed country house atmosphere, this Old Cornish Manor overlooks the dramatic Talland Bay and where, when the tide is out you can walk amongst the rock pools or take a picnic to the beach. Fully deserving of their 2 AA Rosettes the charming wood panelled restaurant serves delectable dishes influenced by the catch of the day at Looe, seasonally grown vegetables and local organically reared beef and lamb. Each bedroom has its own character, and in particular the suites and balcony rooms have an added touch of luxury. Incredibly well positioned to explore both Cornwall and the south coast of Devon. In both winter and summer there's a tremendous amount to do from walking and golf to the Eden Project and Heritage gardens. Well-behaved dogs welcome.

CORNWALL - MULLION (NEAR HELSTON)

The Polurrian Hotel

POLURRIAN COVE, MULLION, HELSTON, CORNWALL TR12 7EN
Tel: 0845 365 2849 **International:** +44 (0)1326 240421 **Fax:** 01326 240083
Web: www.johansens.com/polurrian **E-mail:** relax@polurrianhotel.com

Our inspector loved: Location, welcome and feeling of total relaxation.

Price Guide: (including dinner)
single £56-£88
double £112-£210
suite £196-£270

A stay in this incredibly beautiful Edwardian hotel will certainly be a breathtaking and romantic experience. Perched proudly atop a 300-foot cliff with awe-inspiring views of Mounts Bay and the Atlantic Ocean beyond, you will be hard pressed to ever leave! Top-class service is guaranteed, which together with gorgeous décor that is comfortable and inviting, creates a relaxed and informal environment perfect for adults and children alike. The dining room offers fantastic views across the ocean; a truly memorable experience accompanied by unforgettable fine cuisine. The hotel's magnificent gardens lead to a path that gently meanders down to a quiet cove and a pristine sandy beach.

Location: B3296 Mullion, 1 mile; A394 Helston, 7 miles

Attractions: Flambards Theme Park; Gweek Seal Sanctuary; Marconicentre; Trevarno Gardens

CORNWALL - PORTLOE (ROSELAND PENINSULA)

The Lugger Hotel

PORTLOE, NEAR TRURO, CORNWALL TR2 5RD
Tel: 0845 365 2584 **International:** +44 (0)1872 501322 **Fax:** 01872 501691
Web: www.johansens.com/lugger **E-mail:** reservations@ohiml.com

Our inspector loved: *This enchanting cove surrounded by dramatic Cornish coastline.*

Price Guide: (including dinner)
single from £175
double/twin £220–£310

Awards/Recognition: 1 AA Rosette 2007–2008

Location: A3078, 2.5 miles; A30, 65 miles; M5 jct 31, 87 miles; Newquay Airport, 29 miles

Attractions: Lost Gardens of Heligon; Pendower and Carne Beaches; Truro; Eden Project

With a setting that is almost too good to be true, The Lugger sits tucked away in a cove and tiny harbour where you can watch lobster and crab pots being landed and taken away. It's history is an intriguing mix of a 17th-century inn, boat builder's shed and fishermen's cottages. Now transformed into a warm, welcoming hotel, complete with The Seboni Spa. Rooms are delightful and whilst varying in size have immense character and come stocked with huge bath sheets. You won't be surprised to find out that the menus are heavy on fresh produce such as locally caught seafood, and in the summer you can easily spend hours over lunch and drinks on the sunny terraces admiring the gorgeous, rugged coastline.

CORNWALL - ST IVES

The Garrack Hotel & Restaurant

BURTHALLAN LANE, ST IVES, CORNWALL TR26 3AA
Tel: 0845 365 2497 **International:** +44 (0)1736 796199 **Fax:** 01736 798955
Web: www.johansens.com/garrack **E-mail:** djenquiry@garrack.com

Our inspector loved: *The very tastefully refurbished and well presented restaurant.*

Price Guide:
single £75–£110
double/twin £134–£220

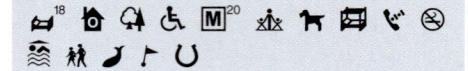

Awards/Recognition: 1 AA Rosette 2007-2008

Location: B3306, 0.65 mile; A3074, 1 mile; A30, 5 miles; Newquay Airport, 27 miles

Attractions: Porthmeor Beach; St Ives Tate Gallery; The Leach Pottery; Coastal Paths

This Kilby family-run hotel is set in 2 acres of gardens with fabulous sea views. You can wander down the hill to Porthmeor beach and its excellent surf, St Ives' old town and the St Ives Tate Gallery, then back up, for a steep, but scenic walk. Bedrooms in the original house maintain the style of the building, while additional rooms are modern in design. A ground floor room has been equipped for guests with disabilities. Lounges have open fires, and a bijou leisure centre contains a small pool, sauna and fitness area. Service is informal yet professional, and the restaurant specialises in seafood, especially fresh lobster. With 70 selected wines. Gateway to wonderful coastal walks, dogs are welcome by prior arrangement.

CUMBRIA - ALSTON

Lovelady Shield Country House Hotel

NENTHEAD ROAD, ALSTON, CUMBRIA CA9 3LF
Tel: 0845 365 2042 **International:** +44 (0)1434 381203 **Fax:** 01434 381515
Web: www.johansens.com/loveladyshield **E-mail:** enquiries@lovelady.co.uk

Our inspector loved: *The delicious dinner at this informal relaxing hotel set in a picturesque valley,*

Price Guide: (Including 4-course dinner)
single £100–£180
double/twin £200–£360

Awards/Recognition: 2 AA Rosette 2008-2009

Location: A689, 0.3 mile; Alston, 2 miles; M6 jct 40, 22 miles

Attractions: High Force - Englands highest waterfall; Hadrians Wall; Penine Way; North Lakes

It's not often we recommend a driving route as well as hotel, but the A686 which leads to Lovelady Shield is officially one of the world's 10 best drives. Bright log fires welcome you on cooler days and owners Peter and Marie Haynes take care to create a relaxed atmosphere in this riverside haven. 4-course dinners prepared by master chef Barrie Garton and rounded off by homemade puddings and a selection of English farmhouse cheeses, have consistently been awarded AA Rosettes for the past 15 years. Many people discover this place en route to Scotland then return to explore the beautiful, unspoilt area properly. For equestrian lovers, pony-trekking and riding can be arranged. The Pennine Way, Hadrian's Wall and the Lake District are within easy reach.

CUMBRIA - AMBLESIDE

Holbeck Ghyll Country House Hotel

HOLBECK LANE, WINDERMERE, CUMBRIA LA23 1LU
Tel: 0845 365 1872 **International:** +44 (0)15394 32375 **Fax:** 015394 34743
Web: www.johansens.com/holbeckghyll **E-mail:** stay@holbeckghyll.com

Our inspector loved: Lowtherwood, the recent addition nearby with 4 bedrooms, a sauna and an outside hotub.

Price Guide: (including 4 course dinner)
single from £175
double/twin £230–£390
suite £300–£595

Holbeck Ghyll was built in the early days of the 19th century and has a prime position overlooking Lake Windermere and the Langdale Fells. Today, its outstanding award winning reputation is due to proprietors, David and Patricia Nicholson. The majority of bedrooms are large and have spectacular lake views. All are refurbished to a very high standard and include decanters of sherry, fresh flowers, fluffy bathrobes and more. There are 6 rooms in the Lodge and houses in the grounds include Lowtherwood, Madison House and the Miss Potter Suite. The oak-panelled restaurant, awarded a coveted Michelin star for 9 consecutive years and 3 AA Rosettes, is a delightful setting for memorable dining and meals are classically prepared, with the focus on flavours and presentation, while an extensive wine list reflects quality and variety. Health Spa on site.

Awards/Recognition: 3 AA Rosettes 2007-2008; 1 Star Michelin 2008; Condé Nast Johansens / Taittinger Wine List Award 2007

Location: A591, 0.5 mile; M6 jct 36, 20 miles; Windermere, 3 miles; Ambleside, 1 mile

Attractions: Lake Windermere; Lake District National Park; Dove Cottage & Rydal Mount; Brockhole Visitors Centre

CUMBRIA - AMBLESIDE

ROTHAY MANOR

ROTHAY BRIDGE, AMBLESIDE, CUMBRIA LA22 0EH
Tel: 0845 365 2307 **International:** +44 (0)15394 33605 **Fax:** 015394 33607
Web: www.johansens.com/rothaymanor **E-mail:** hotel@rothaymanor.co.uk

Our inspector loved: *The friendly and attentive service at this relaxing oasis.*

Price Guide:
single £100–£145
double/twin £160–£190
suite £215

Awards/Recognition: 1 AA Rosette 2008–2009

Location: A593, 100yds; M6 Jct 36, 18 miles; Ambleside, 0.25 miles; Windermere, 4 miles

Attractions: Ambleside; Windermere; Beatrix Potter Museum and Hill Top; Lake District National Park

Take a short walk from the centre of Ambleside to this Regency country house hotel, which, thanks to the Nixon family, has provided a relaxed, comfortable and friendly atmosphere for over 40 years. Choose from a variety of bedrooms, some with balconies, and 3 spacious, private suites, 2 of which are situated in the grounds. Some rooms are suitable for families, while others have been designed for those with disabilities. Varied menus use local produce whenever possible, and it's worth keeping your eye out for special interest holidays which run from October to May - scrabble, gardening, antiques, bridge, painting and Lake District heritage, are just tasters. Otherwise, there's plenty to do in the area, from walking to cycling, sailing, horse-riding, golf and fishing (permits available).

CUMBRIA - AMBLESIDE

The Samling

AMBLESIDE ROAD, WINDERMERE, CUMBRIA LA23 1LR
Tel: 0845 365 4035 **International:** +44 (0)1539 431 922 **Fax:** 01539 430 400
Web: www.johansens.com/samling **E-mail:** info@thesamlinghotel.co.uk

Our inspector loved: *This secluded charming small hotel with stunning views of Lake Windermere.*

Price Guide:
single from £200
double/twin £220–£350
suite £380-£430

Awards/Recognition: 3 AA Rosettes 2008-2009

Location: A 591, 0.5 mile; Ambleside, 1.5 miles; Windermere, 4.5 miles; M6 jct 36, 20 miles

Attractions: Lake Windermere; Lake District National Park; Dove Cottage & Rydal Mount; Brockhole Visitors Centre

Perched above one of the most beautiful lakes in Britain, The Samling is surely everyone's dream of a luxury country get-away. Secluded and private, with stunning views of the lake here you can let the attention to detail and excellent service engulf you. Beautifully decorated bedrooms retain their authentic rustic features which are combined with stylish modern comforts, Turkish rugs and huge baths. Five are in the main house and six have been fashioned out of the original cottages. Food is an important element at The Samling and an innovative kitchen delivers light and seasonal creations. The wine cellar is equally impressive. The inviting ambience of the cosy drawing room is the place to curl up with a good book or towards the end of the day enjoy a drink by the fireside. A von Essen hotel.

CUMBRIA - APPLEBY-IN-WESTMORLAND

Tufton Arms Hotel

MARKET SQUARE, APPLEBY-IN-WESTMORLAND, CUMBRIA CA16 6XA
Tel: 0845 365 2766 **International:** +44 (0)17683 51593 **Fax:** 017683 52761
Web: www.johansens.com/tuftonarms **E-mail:** info@tuftonarmshotel.co.uk

Our inspector loved: *The newly refurbished bedrooms and bathrooms.*

Price Guide:
single £70–£150
double/twin £115–£160
suite £190

Location: A66, 1 miles; M6 Jct 38, 12 mile; Penrith, 13 miles miles

Attractions: Eden Valley; Penine Way; Appleby Golf Course; Lake District National Park

This distinguished Victorian coaching inn, is owned and run by the Milsom family, who also run the The Royal Hotel in Comrie. The bedrooms evoke the style of the 19th century, reflecting the Tufton Arms past Victorian grandeur. The kitchen is run under the auspices of David Milsom and Lee Braithwaite,The restaurant is renowned for its use of locally sourced meat and game as well as its fish dishes.Complementing the cuisine is an extensive wine list. This is an ideal base for touring the Lakes, Yorkshire Dales and Pennines. It is also a convenient stop-over en route to Scotland. Superb fishing for wild brown trout or salmon can be arranged. Shooting parties for grouse, duck and pheasant are a speciality.

65

CUMBRIA - GRANGE-OVER-SANDS

Netherwood Hotel

LINDALE ROAD, GRANGE-OVER-SANDS, CUMBRIA LA11 6ET
Tel: 0845 365 2082 **International:** +44 (0)15395 32552 **Fax:** 015395 34121
Web: www.johansens.com/netherwood **E-mail:** enquiries@netherwood-hotel.co.uk

Our inspector loved: *This majestic hotel overlooking Morecambe Bay.*

Price Guide:
single £80–£115
double £120-£190

Dramatic and stately in appearance, Netherwood was built as a family house in the 19th century, and still exudes a warm, family atmosphere thanks to the care of its longstanding owners, the Fallowfields. Impressive oak panelling is a key feature, and provides a fitting backdrop to roaring log fires in the public areas. Bedrooms come with views of the sea, woodlands and gardens. The light and airy restaurant is housed in the first floor conservatory and maximises dramatic views over Morecambe Bay. If you're a family you'll probably spend the lion's share of your time in the indoor pool and fitness centre - the pool even has toys for our younger friends - while an extensive range of treatments are available at "Equilibrium", the hotel's health spa.

Location: B5277, 500yds; A590, 3 miles; M6 jct 36, 5 miles

Attractions: Morecambe Bay; Holker Hall; Lake District National Park; Leighton Moss RSPB Reserve

CUMBRIA - KESWICK (BASSENTHWAITE LAKE)

Armathwaite Hall Country House, Hotel and Spa

BASSENTHWAITE LAKE, KESWICK, CUMBRIA CA12 4RE
Tel: 0845 365 3617 **International:** +44 (0)17687 76551 **Fax:** 017687 76220
Web: www.johansens.com/armathwaite **E-mail:** reservations@armathwaite-hall.com

Our inspector loved: Dining in the terrace Restaurant with lovely views across Bassenthwaite Lake.

Price Guide:
single £145–£265
double/twin £230–£310
studio suites £350–£370

Awards/Recognition: 1 AA Rosette 2007-2008

Location: A591, 0.25 miles; A66, 1 mile; M6 jct 40, 25 miles; Keswick, 7 miles

Attractions: Trotters World of Animals; Bassenthwaite Lake; Lake District National Park; Wordsworth and Beatrix Potter

If you have a passion for boating, walking and climbing, or to simply relax, this 4-star hotel is a peaceful hideaway. On the shores of Bassenthwaite Lake and with a backdrop of Skiddaw Mountain and Lakeland Fells it provides old-fashioned hospitality, as you would expect of a family-owned hotel. Wood panelling, impressive stonework, art and antiques remain, and you can arrange champagne, chocolates and flowers in your room upon arrival. Master Chef Kevin Dowling creates local, seasonal menus in the Rosette restaurant, and the hotel is family-friendly, with a programme of activities for mini guests. Get in touch with your inner child and visit the estate's Trotters World of Animals, home to traditional favourites and endangered species. Due to open in the winter of 2008 is a luxurious spa, pool and fitness centre.

CUMBRIA - KESWICK (BORROWDALE)

The Lodore Falls Hotel

BORROWDALE, KESWICK, CUMBRIA CA12 5UX
Tel: 0845 365 2581 **International:** +44 (0)17687 77285 **Fax:** 017687 77343
Web: www.johansens.com/lodorefalls **E-mail:** lodorefalls@lakedistricthotels.net

Our inspector loved: *The lovely views of Derwentwater from Lake view bedrooms.*

Price Guide:
single £88–£137
double £150–£220
suite £278–£368

Location: B5289, 10yds; A66, 4 miles; M6 jct 40, 22 miles; Keswick, 3.5 miles

Attractions: Derwentwater Launch; Keswick Golf Club; Trotters world of animals; Honistor Slate Mine with its new Via Ferrata walk/climb

Close your eyes and imagine stunning lake and mountain views, a waterfall in landscaped gardens warm hospitality and good food and service. Open your eyes and see The Lodore Falls Hotel in the picturesque Borrowdale Valley. The 69 en-suite Fell and Lake View Rooms, include family rooms, internet access and luxurious suites, some with balconies. Light meals and coffee can be enjoyed in the comfortable lounges, whilst the cocktail bar is the ideal venue for a pre-dinner drink. The Lake View restaurant serves the best in English and Continental cuisine accompanied by fine wines. The new Beauty Salon with its 4 beautiful treatment rooms use the famous Elemis beauty products in its treatments and offers pamper days, luxury days and a very special Waterfall treatment day. For children an activity programme is also available for 2 hours daily during school holidays.

CUMBRIA - KESWICK (LAKE THIRLMERE)

Dale Head Hall Lakeside Hotel

THIRLMERE, KESWICK, CUMBRIA CA12 4TN
Tel: 0845 365 3258 **International:** +44 (0)17687 72478
Web: www.johansens.com/daleheadhall **E-mail:** onthelakeside@daleheadhall.co.uk

Our inspector loved: *The unrivalled views over Lake Thirlmere - this is the only house on the Lake.*

Price Guide: (including dinner)
single £130–£160
double £210–£330

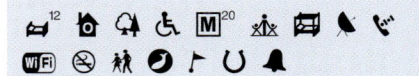

Awards/Recognition: 2 AA Rosettes 2007-2008

Location: A591, 0.25 miles; M6 jct 40, 14 miles; Keswick, 4 miles; Windermere, 14 miles

Attractions: Dove Cottage & The Wordsworth Museum; Honister Slate Mine; Theatre by the Lake; Rookin House Farm Activity Centre.

The key handed to you upon arrival at Dale Head Hall isn't simply the key to a room – it's the key to complete relaxation. This is the boast of the Hill family, caring owners of this fine hotel that stands alone on the shores of Lake Thirlmere. A bird watcher's paradise, the setting is nothing less than idyllic, and inside, the furnishings and atmosphere are warm and welcoming. Some of the rooms are in the Elizabethan house, while others are in the Victorian extension; all have stunning lake and mountain views as do both drawing rooms. You can enjoy superb food from the finest, freshest seasonal local produce, complemented by an extensive international wine list in the award winning restaurant. The hotel also has it's own boat on the Lake.

CUMBRIA - LAKE ULLSWATER

SHARROW BAY COUNTRY HOUSE HOTEL

LAKE ULLSWATER, PENRITH, CUMBRIA CA10 2LZ
Tel: 0845 365 2346 **International:** +44 (0)1768 486 301 **Fax:** 01768 486 349
Web: www.johansens.com/sharrowbaycountryhouse **E-mail:** info@sharrowbay.co.uk

Our inspector loved: *The ever impressive dining experience in the Lakeside Restaurant with lovely views of Ullswater.*

Price Guide:
single from £220
double/twin £250–£400
suite £410–£550

Awards/Recognition: Relais & Châteaux; 1 Star Michelin 2008; 2 AA Rosettes 2008-2009

Location: B592, 2 miles; A66, 6 miles; M6 jct 40, 7 miles; Penrith, 8 miles

Attractions: Overlooking Lake Ullswater; Lake District National Park

With its breathtaking setting on the shore of the Lake Ullswater in the Lake District, Sharrow Bay Hotel with its Michelin star restaurant is built upon innovation, tradition and a history that sets it apart. The internationally renowned kitchen, led by Colin Akrigg and Mark Teesdale, uses the finest local ingredients to produce some exceptional 'British' cuisine. The cellar has a growing international reputation for fine and rare wine. The founding British member of the prestigious Relais & Chateaux, the hotel was where the term 'country house hotel was first coined' and the famous British dish, sticky toffee pudding, was invented. Set up in 1949 the hotel celebrates its diamond anniversary this year and its planned series of events will no doubt be further reason to entice you to this delightful property. A von Essen hotel.

CUMBRIA - LAKE ULLSWATER (GLENRIDDING)

THE INN ON THE LAKE

LAKE ULLSWATER, GLENRIDDING, CUMBRIA CA11 0PE
Tel: 0845 365 2548 **International:** +44 (0)17684 82444 **Fax:** 017684 82303
Web: www.johansens.com/innonthelake **E-mail:** innonthelake@lakedistricthotels.net

Our inspector loved: The four poster bedrooms with lovely views of the lake.

Price Guide:
single from £85
double £144–£232

Awards/Recognition: 1 AA Rosette 2008-2009

Location: A592, 100yds; M6 jct 40, 12 miles; Penrith, 12 miles; Windermere, 14 miles

Attractions: Lake Ullswater; Ullswater Steamers; Rheged Centre; Dalemain Stately Home

This 19th century hotel enjoys one of the most spectacular settings in the Lake District. 15 acres of lawn sweep down to the shore of Lake Ullswater, where you can sail from the private jetty and take trips aboard the Ullswater steamers. Relax with a drink in the comfort of one of the lounges or stroll to The Rambler's Bar in the grounds for a proper Lakeland pub atmosphere. Superb food is served in the Lake View restaurant and most bedrooms have stunning views across the lake, ask for a lake-view four poster room. There is a small leisure suite with sauna, solarium, Jacuzzi and a gym. The hotel makes a particularly romantic wedding venue for civil ceremonies and celebrations. The list of local activities is endless, from rock climbing to pony trekking, canoeing, windsurfing and fishing.

CUMBRIA - WINDERMERE (BOWNESS)

LINTHWAITE HOUSE HOTEL

CROOK ROAD, BOWNESS-ON-WINDERMERE, CUMBRIA LA23 3JA
Tel: 0845 365 2031 **International:** +44 (0)15394 88600 **Fax:** 015394 88601
Web: www.johansens.com/linthwaitehouse **E-mail:** stay@linthwaite.com

Our inspector loved: *The unstuffy and friendly ambiance of this hotel with spectacular views of Lake Windermere.*

Price Guide:
single £120-£160
double £145-£320
suite £265-£400

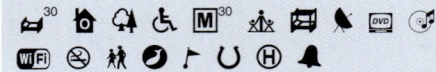

Awards/Recognition: Condé Nast Johansens Most Excellent Country House 2007; 2 AA Rosettes 2008-2009; Condé Nast Traveller Gold List 2006

Location: B5284, 0.25 miles; Windermere, 2 miles; A591, 2 miles; M6 Jct 36, 14 miles

Attractions: Windermere; Beatrix Potter Museums & Dove Cottage; Lake District National Park;

At the heart of the Lake District situated in 14 acres of garden and woodland is Linthwaite House overlooking Lake Windermere and Belle Isle. The hotel combines stylish originality with the best of traditional hospitality. Most bedrooms have lake or garden views whilst the restaurant offers excellent cuisine with the best of fresh, local produce accompanied by a fine selection of wines. There is a 9 hole putting green within the grounds and a par 3 practice hole. You can if you wish, fish for brown trout in the hotel tarn. Fell walks begin at the front door, and you can follow in the footsteps of Wordsworth and Beatrix Potter to explore the spectacular scenery.

CUMBRIA - WINDERMERE (NEWBY BRIDGE)

LAKESIDE HOTEL ON LAKE WINDERMERE

LAKESIDE, NEWBY BRIDGE, CUMBRIA LA12 8AT
Tel: 0845 365 1978 **International:** +44 (0)15395 30001 **Fax:** 015395 31699
Web: www.johansens.com/lakeside **E-mail:** sales@lakesidehotel.co.uk

Our inspector loved: Morning coffee in the Lakeside Conservatory watching the ducks being fed at 11am

Price Guide:
single from £160
double/twin £185–£340
suite from £340

Awards/Recognition: 2 AA Rosettes 2007-2008

Location: A590, 1 mile; M6 jct 36, 15 miles; Newby Bridge, 1 mile

Attractions: Windermere Lake Cruisers; Aquarium of the Lakes; Lakeside and Haverthwaite Steam Railway; Holker Hall and Gardens

Offering a unique location on the edge of Lake Windermere this classic, traditional Lakeland hotel will have cast its spell on you by the time your visit is over. Many bedrooms have breathtaking lake vistas, and menus in both the award-winning Lakeview Restaurant or Ruskin's Brasserie include Cumbrian favourites. To get a real lakes experience there are cruisers berthed adjacent to the hotel ready for further exploration and adventure. For inclement weather the Pool and Spa, exclusively for hotel residents, has a 17m indoor pool, gym, sauna, steam room and health and beauty suites. The hotel's fully equipped conference centre and syndicate suites offer scope and flexibility for business, so whatever your requirements this old coaching inn's facilities and friendly service will deliver!

DERBYSHIRE - ASHBOURNE

CALLOW HALL

MAPPLETON ROAD, ASHBOURNE, DERBYSHIRE DE6 2AA
Tel: 0845 365 3221 **International:** +44 (0)1335 300900 **Fax:** 01335 300512
Web: www.johansens.com/callowhall **E-mail:** Reception@callowhall.co.uk

Our inspector loved: *The feeling of relaxed country estate living in this fine Victorian hall.*

Price Guide:
single from £105
double/twin from £150
suite from £210

Awards/Recognition: 2 AA Rosettes 2007-2008

Location: A515, 2 miles; A52, 3 miles; A50, 10 miles; East Midlands Airport, 24 miles

Attractions: Chatsworth House; Kedleston Hall; Peak District National Park; Uttoxeter Racecourse

Overlooking Bentley Brook and the River Dove, you are treated to a delightful welcome at this fine Victorian hall run by the same family for the last 25 years. Fine antiques and fireplaces combine with ornate ceilings to give a sense of grandeur to this country house, while the bedrooms offer comfortable fabrics and striking vistas across the landscape. The Spencers take great pride in home baking, smoking and curing; skills that have been passed down through the family since 1724. The menu includes local produce and game and Anthony's passion for wines is evident in the extensive list of over 100 labels. Private parties can be accommodated in the formal dining room and groups of 20 in a further function room. Country pursuits including trout fishing can be arranged.

DERBYSHIRE - ASHBOURNE (DOVEDALE)

THE IZAAK WALTON HOTEL

DOVEDALE, NEAR ASHBOURNE, DERBYSHIRE DE6 2AY
Tel: 0845 365 2561 **International:** +44 (0)1335 350555 **Fax:** 01335 350539
Web: www.johansens.com/izaakwalton **E-mail:** reception@izaakwaltonhotel.com

Our inspector loved: *The Dovedale Bar with its stone walls and open fire, a great place to relax with a drink and a light meal after a walk or a day's fishing.*

Price Guide:
single from £110
double/twin from £145

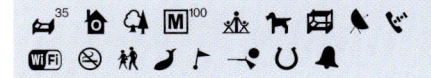

Awards/Recognition: 2 AA Rosettes 2007-2008

Location: A515, 3 miles; A52, 6 miles; Derby, 16 miles; East Midlands Airport, 36 miles

Attractions: Chatsworth House; Stepping Stone and Thorpe Cloud; Kedleston Hall; Alton Towers

The driveway leads you through grazing fields and well kept gardens and lawns to arrive at a handsome whitewashed stone hotel. The Izaak Walton extends a warm welcome, made cosier by the open fires in the reception and bars. Named after the famous author of "The Compleat Angler," this retreat is a great base for fishermen, hikers and lovers of outdoor pursuits. The stunning views out across the rolling hills towards the Stepping Stone and Thorpe Cloud can be admired from many of the bedrooms or from chairs and tables set out on the lawns. After a days activity, the Dovedale Bar, with its beamed roof, bare stoned walls, open fires and quirky fishing memorabilia, is a great place to kick back with a drink before dining in the AA 2 Rosette-awarded Haddon Restaurant.

DERBYSHIRE - DERBY

Cathedral Quarter Hotel

16 ST MARY'S GATE, DERBY, DERBYSHIRE DE1 3JR
Tel: 0845 365 3917 **International:** +44 (0)1332 546080 **Fax:** 01332 546098
Web: www.johansens.com/cathedralquarter **E-mail:** stay@cathedralquarterhotel.com

Our inspector loved: *The well-stocked wine cellar of over 200 bins in the old police station's strong room, all looking for an early release date!*

Price Guide:
single from £85
double from £95
suite from £175

Location: A52, 1/5 mile; M1, 7 miles; Nottingham, 15 miles; East Midlands Airport, 16 miles

Attractions: Royal Crown Derby; Derby Cathedral; Silk Mill Museum of Industry & History; Derbyshire and The Peak District

Following extensive redevelopment, this former police station and local government offices fully lives up to its credentials as a quality boutique hotel. Tucked away in a quiet Victorian street this stylish retreat is an excellent base from which to explore the rejuvenated city of Derby. Behind the red brick exterior you will find a welcoming atmosphere of old and new with many of the original 1890s features restored and blending beautifully with 21st-century luxuries. A city oasis with an attentive, club-like feel, the guest rooms have everything the discerning traveller expects. There's a busy cocktail bar, excellent restaurant, private dining room, a chef's table located in a room adjacent to the kitchen, and for the business visitor, 2 small meeting rooms.

DERBYSHIRE - MATLOCK (RIBER)

RIBER HALL

MATLOCK, DERBYSHIRE DE4 5JU
Tel: 0845 365 2149 **International:** +44 (0)1629 582795 **Fax:** 01629 580475
Web: www.johansens.com/riberhall **E-mail:** info@riber-hall.co.uk

Our inspector loved: *Relaxing on the new terrace in the shade of the grand old weeping copper beach tree enjoying my pre dinner drink.*

Price Guide:
single £95–£105
double/twin £145–£190

Awards/Recognition: 2 AA Rosettes 2007-2008

Location: Matlock, 2 miles; M1 jct 28, 13 miles; Derby, 24 miles; East Midlands Airport, 45 miles

Attractions: Chatsworth House; Heights of Abraham for caves and cable car; Carsington Reservoir for sailing and watersports; Haddon Hall

Perched above the picturesque town of Matlock, you really do feel on top of the world. Bordering the Peak District National Park, with rolling Derbyshire hills and pretty gardens as its backdrop, this welcoming 15th century manor house is a real get away. Graceful antique furniture, open fires and personal details add to the welcoming atmosphere, whilst period bedrooms, most with four poster beds, exude a timeless elegance. The delightful walled garden is definitely worth exploring and where you can enjoy sitting with a good book on a warm summer's day. Mull over the impressive wine list on the terrace before dinner and simply enjoy the stunning views before heading into the contemporary setting of the newly refurbished restaurant for some inspired dishes created from local and seasonal produce.

DERBYSHIRE - RISLEY

Risley Hall Hotel and Spa

DERBY ROAD, RISLEY, DERBYSHIRE DE72 3SS
Tel: 0845 365 3795 **International:** +44 (0)115 939 9000 **Fax:** 0115 939 7766
Web: www.johansens.com/risleyhall **E-mail:** reservations@ohiml.com

Our inspector loved: *The view of the grounds from my armchair in the drawing room while enjoying afternoon tea.*

Price Guide:
single from £110
double from £125
suite from £140

Risley Hall is a delightful country house dating back as far as the 11th century and is set in 17 acres of well-tended gardens. The traditional décor transports you to a bygone era with a charming combination of Victorian features, art-nouveau influenced woodwork details, pretty wallpapers and open fireplaces. You can admire the view across the lawns and hedges from the bay window in the drawing room, or the snug bar that is perfect for pre-dinner drinks. The restaurant is set over 4 rooms which include the atmosheric Oak Room with its panelling, impressive windows and fire place. Bedrooms are very comfortable and vary in style and character with many affording wonderful garden views. If you wish to be pampered during your stay, the hotel's spa and team of therapists will indulge you with soothing treatments, or you simply enjoy a swim or soak in the Jacuzzi.

Awards/Recognition: 1 AA Rosette 2007–2008

Location: A52, 1 mile; M1 jct 25, 1 miles; Nottingham/Derby, 7 miles; East Midlands International Airport, 10 miles

Attractions: Donnington Park; Twycross Zoo; Chatsworth House; Nottingham Castle and Tales of Robin Hood

DEVON - BURRINGTON (NEAR BARNSTAPLE, UMBERLEIGH)

Northcote Manor Country House Hotel

BURRINGTON, UMBERLEIGH, DEVON EX37 9LZ
Tel: 0845 365 2087 **International:** +44 (0)1769 560501 **Fax:** 01769 560770
Web: www.johansens.com/northcotemanor **E-mail:** rest@northcotemanor.co.uk

Our inspector loved: *The newly appointed bedrooms, so striking and tasteful.*

Price Guide:
single from £100
double from £155
suite from £255

Awards/Recognition: 2 AA Rosettes 2006-2007; Condé Nast Johansens Reader Award 2006

Location: Stay on the A377 (not through village); Barnstaple, 14 miles; Exeter, 30 miles

Attractions: RHS Rosemoor; Dartington Crystal; Dartmoor and Exmoor; Various National Trust Properties

It is easy to understand why this luxurious 18th-century manor has won numerous accolades over the years. Following a recent refurbishment including a redesign of the spacious sitting rooms, hall, restaurant and bedrooms, Northcote has retained its charmingly unpretentious atmosphere of timeless tranquillity. Savour seasonal gourmet meals in the elegant restaurant while admiring the view of the pretty gardens, and take afternoon tea on the terrace garden that overlooks the Japanese water garden. Sitting high above the Taw River Valley you might feel like doing nothing more than playing a game of croquet, reading a book under a large shady tree or enjoying a relaxing treatment, such as Indian head massage, manicure or pedicure, in the comfort of your own room. Alternatively, there is a challenging golf course next door, outstanding fishing at the end of the drive, tennis and the area hosts some of the best shoots in the county.

DEVON - CHAGFORD

GIDLEIGH PARK

CHAGFORD, DEVON TQ13 8HH
Tel: 0845 365 1759 **International:** +44 (0)1647 432367 **Fax:** +44 (0)1647 432574
Web: www.johansens.com/gidleighpark **E-mail:** gidleighpark@gidleigh.co.uk

Our inspector loved: *The peace - the ambience and the total experience.*

Price Guide:
Single from £295
Double/twin from £310
Suite from £1,155

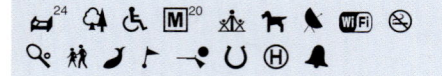

Situated in the heart of Dartmoor National Park you will appreciate Gidleigh Park for its outstanding international reputation for comfort and gastronomy. A clutch of top culinary awards including 2 Michelin stars for its imaginative cuisine and the wine list, make it one of the best in Britain. Service throughout the hotel is faultless. The bedrooms – 2 of them in a converted chapel – are furnished with original antiques. The public rooms are well appointed and during the cooler months, a fire burns in the lounge's impressive fireplace. Privacy is complete, amidst 54 secluded acres in the Teign Valley. A croquet lawn and a splendid water garden can be found in the grounds. A 360 yard long, par 52 putting course designed by Peter Alliss was opened in 1995.

Awards/Recognition: Condé Nast Traveller Gold List Award "Best For Food" 2008; 3 AA Rosettes 2008 - 2009; 2 Star Michelin 2007; Relais & Châteaux

Location: A382, 2.5 miles; A30, 4.79 miles; M5 jct 31, 20 miles; Exeter St. Davids Railway Station, 21 miles

Attractions: Castle Drogo; Exeter Cathedral; Dartington Hall; Dartmouth

DEVON - EXETER (HONITON)

COMBE HOUSE

GITTISHAM, HONITON, NEAR EXETER, DEVON EX14 3AD
Tel: 0845 365 3241 **International:** +44 (0)1404 540400 **Fax:** 01404 46004
Web: www.johansens.com/combehousegittisham **E-mail:** stay@thishotel.com

Our inspector loved: *Everything other than having to leave.*

Price Guide:
single from £150
double/twin £170–£280
suite £320–£375

Awards/Recognition: Michelin Rising Star 2007/2008

Location: M5 jct 28/29, 11 miles; A303/A30, 2 miles; Exeter Airport, 10 miles; Honiton Railway Station, 4 miles

Attractions: South West Coastal Path; Sidmouth to Lyme Regis Jurrasic Coast; Cathedral City of Exeter; Honiton Antique Shops and Galleries

The Small Hotel of the Year, 2007/8 winner – South West Tourism Excellence Awards, this hidden away country estate is set in 3,500 acres and is simply magical. Ken and Ruth Hunt have enjoyed 10 years of resident ownership that has resulted in this very special retreat which continues to tirelessly pursue the desire to find new ways to delight. For instance, many of the bedrooms provide a stunning combination of contemporary furnishings, fine antiques and fresh flowers. A romantic thatched cottage for 2 with private walled garden is tucked away within the estate. There are 2 Master Chefs of Great Britain who have been recipients of a Michelin Rising Star for two consecutive years. They love to draw on the West Country's bounteous larder and Combe's own kitchen garden. Ken maintains an exciting cellar where wines have been chosen for taste rather than name or vintage. Just a short drive to the coast and Dartmoor.

DEVON - ILSINGTON (DARTMOOR)

Ilsington Country House Hotel

ILSINGTON VILLAGE, NEAR NEWTON ABBOT, DEVON TQ13 9RR
Tel: 0845 365 1925 **International:** +44 (0)1364 661452 **Fax:** 01364 661307
Web: www.johansens.com/ilsington **E-mail:** hotel@ilsington.co.uk

Our inspector loved: *The overall warmth and welcome offered throughout this delightful country house.*

Price Guide: (including dinner)
single from £105
double from £154
suite from £184

Awards/Recognition: 2 AA Rosettes 2008-2009

Location: A38, 4 miles; M5 junction 30, 26 miles; Exeter Airport, 26 miles; Plymouth Airport, 31 miles

Attractions: Dartmoor; Numerous National Trust Properties; Buckfast Abbey; The Coast

If it's an idyllic country house break you're looking for, Ilsington certainly ticks all the right boxes with its warmth, charm, and great location, high on the rolling hills of Dartmoor National Park. The hosts, the Hassell family, provide a friendly service and offer standard and superior bedrooms as well as suites to suit families with up to 2 children. The hotel is rightly proud of its restaurant where menus of local, classic and contemporary dishes change daily to feature fresh market produce. An indoor pool and Health Club add to the year-round interest, but you'll inevitably be drawn to the outdoors with the abundance of National Trust properties in the area, as well as Dartmoor itself and the South Devon coastline.

DEVON - LEWDOWN (NEAR OKEHAMPTON)

Lewtrenchard Manor

LEWDOWN, NEAR OKEHAMPTON, DEVON EX20 4PN
Tel: 0845 365 2018 **International:** +44 (0)1566 783222 **Fax:** 01566 783332
Web: www.johansens.com/lewtrenchard **E-mail:** info@lewtrenchard.co.uk

Our inspector loved: The exciting launch of Purple Carrot, the chefs table - minimum 4 maximum 8 thought to be first in South West.

Price Guide:
single from £105
double/twin from £135
suite from £255

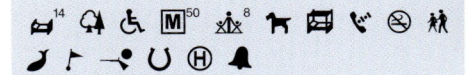

Awards/Recognition: 3 AA Rosettes 2008-2009

Location: A386, 6.6 miles; A30, 7 miles; M5 jct 31, 33.5 miles

Attractions: Exeter Cathedral; Dartmoor; Eden Project; Various Historic Houses, Castle & Gardens

Built in 1600 you can tell that this beautiful Jacobean manor has been well-loved, there is an unmistakeable warmth, and family antiques bump up against ornate ceilings, leaded windows and elegant carved oak staircases. Bedrooms look out over the valley, and another pretty impressive backdrop, the oak-panelled dining room, prepares you for an excellent dining experience with an emphasis on local, seasonal produce. For gourmands' there is an exciting new concept - Purple Carrot. Gather friends in a stunning private room to enjoy the interaction with the chef and his team. There's a birds eye view of the kitchen, a large flat screen relaying activity and a course cooked in front of you. The estate offers fishing, rough & clay pigeon shooting making this ideal for your weekend parties, as well as an idyllic setting for weddings and private functions. A von Essen hotel.

DEVON - LIFTON (NEAR LAUNCESTON)

The Arundell Arms

LIFTON, DEVON PL16 0AA
Tel: 0845 365 2394 **International:** +44 (0)1566 784666 **Fax:** 01566 784494
Web: www.johansens.com/arundellarms **E-mail:** reservations@arundellarms.com

Our inspector loved: *The restaurant, which is highly renowned for its creative use of delicious local ingredients.*

Price Guide:
single from £110
double/twin from £180
superior from £210

Awards/Recognition: 2 AA Rosettes 2007-2008

Location: A30, 2 miles; Plymouth, 27.5 miles; M5 jct 31, 40 miles; Exeter, 40 miles

Attractions: Eden Project; Various Historic Houses and Gardens; Tintagel

One of England's best-known sporting hotels for more than half a century, The Arundell Arms, a former coaching inn, dates back to Saxon times. Recommended by Condé Nast Johansens for over 25 years. The hotel boasts 20 miles of exclusive salmon and trout fishing on the Tamar and 5 of its tributaries, and a famous school of fly fishing. You can experience other country activities such as hill walking, shooting, riding and golf, or check out the surf on wonderful nearby Devon beaches. Alternatively just take some well earned time off and collapse into a comfortable armchair and enjoy the Old World charm of flagstone floors, fires, paintings, antiques and thoroughly delicious gourmet cooking.

DEVON - SALCOMBE (SOAR MILL COVE)

SOAR MILL COVE HOTEL

SOAR MILL COVE, SALCOMBE, SOUTH DEVON TQ7 3DS
Tel: 0845 365 2349 **International:** +44 (0)1548 561566 **Fax:** 01548 561223
Web: www.johansens.com/soarmillcove **E-mail:** info@soarmillcove.co.uk

Our inspector loved: *The beautifully refurbished lounge so very comfortable - striking fabrics and those magnificent coastal views.*

Price Guide:
single £75–£180
double/twin £150–£240
suite from £250

Awards/Recognition: 4 AA Rosettes 2006-2007

Location: A381, 1.5 miles; Salcombe, 4 miles; Plymouth, 24 miles; Exeter Airport, 30 miles

Attractions: Salcombe; Dartmoor; South West Coastal Park; Historic Barbican of Plymouth with famous Pilgrim steps

Strolling along golden sandy beaches, fishing in rock pools and exploring local caves – it all seems very 'Famous Five'. This family run, Devon hotel offers the right balance of attentive yet unobtrusive service. Nothing is too much trouble at Soar Mill Cove and there is plenty to keep you busy - take the hotels tandem for a spin, find a quiet corner by one of the two pools, enjoy a relaxing massage in "The Ocean Spa", or feast yourself on lobster and crab. Set within 2,000 acres of National Trust countryside between Dartmouth's historic port and The Pilgrim Steps of Plymouth, this is arguably the most dramatic seaside setting, with breathtaking views and coastal paths to die for. Dogs welcome too.

DEVON - SALCOMBE (SOUTH SANDS)

The Tides Reach Hotel

SOUTH SANDS, SALCOMBE, DEVON TQ8 8LJ
Tel: 0845 365 2713 **International:** +44 (0)1548 843466 **Fax:** 01548 843954
Web: www.johansens.com/tidesreach **E-mail:** enquire@tidesreach.com

Our inspector loved: Overlooking the Salcombe Estuary, enjoying the views of every season.

Price Guide: (including dinner)
single £78–£190
double/twin £146–£380

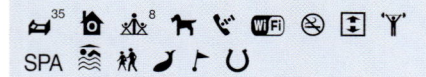

Awards/Recognition: 1 AA Rosette 2007-2008

Location: A381, 2 miles; M5, 43 miles; Salcombe, 1.7 miles; Exeter Airport, 30 miles

Attractions: Gardens of Overbecks; Plymouth Maritime Museum; South Devon Coastal Path; Dartmoor

A charming south-facing hotel sitting in a sandy cove just inside the mouth of the Salcombe Estuary. Over their 40 years of ownership the Edwards family have gained a reputation for warmth, hospitality and no-nonsense service. Chef Finn Ibsen creates menus with seasonal produce and makes the most of the morning catch from the local fishermen. Most of the immaculate bedrooms come with lovely sea views and offer plenty of flexibility for families. There's an indoor pool, sauna, spa, snooker table and for the very energetic a squash court. For sailing fans why not hire a Hobie Cat, sail into Salcombe for an ice-cream or spot of shopping and then happily retreat from the hordes to the comfort of Tides Reach.

DEVON - SALCOMBE ESTUARY

Buckland-Tout-Saints

GOVETON, KINGSBRIDGE, DEVON TQ7 2DS
Tel: 0845 365 3211 **International:** +44 (0)1548 853055 **Fax:** 01548 856261
Web: www.johansens.com/bucklandtoutsaints **E-mail:** buckland@tout-saints.co.uk

Our inspector loved: *This beautiful Sixteenth Century Manor House - loving to visit not enjoying to leave.*

Price Guide:
single from £90
double/twin £120-£180
suite £240–£280

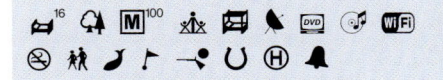

Awards/Recognition: 2 AA Rosettes 2007-2008

Location: A381, 2 miles; Totnes, 12 miles; Plymouth, 22 miles; M5 jct 29, 40 miles

Attractions: Various Historic Houses Castles & Gardens; National Marine Aquarium; Eden Project; Beautiful Coastal Walks and Beaches

Come and enjoy the hospitality of this elegant 300-year-old, AA 3 Red Star, country house nestled amidst 4 acres of landscaped gardens in idyllic Devon. If you're a nature lover you'll be in paradise, or you may just want to relax in tranquil surroundings. The 16 individually decorated bedrooms have wonderful views of the countryside, while a daily newspaper, mineral water and fluffy bathrobes are all complimentary. The restaurant has won accolades over the years and offers both local and exotic menus complemented by fine wines - take afternoon tea in front of a roaring wood fire or explore the local area with its castles and picturesque villages. You're very close here to the popular sailing and fishing towns of Salcombe and, Dartmouth.

87

DEVON - SIDMOUTH

HOTEL RIVIERA

THE ESPLANADE, SIDMOUTH, DEVON EX10 8AY
Tel: 0845 365 1904 **International:** +44 (0)1395 515201 **Fax:** 01395 577775
Web: www.johansens.com/riviera **E-mail:** enquiries@hotelriviera.co.uk

Our inspector loved: *The welcome from both the owners and staff.*

Price Guide: (including 6 course dinner):
single £114–£170
double/twin £228–£318
suite £348–£368

Awards/Recognition: 2 AA Rosettes 2008-2009

Location: A3052, 2.5 miles; M5 jct 30, 13 miles; Exeter Airport, 10 miles; Honiton/Exeter St Davids Railway Stations, 8/15 miles

Attractions: Killerton House and Gardens; Exeter Cathedral; Powderham Castle; Dartmoor

A warm welcome awaits you at this prestigious award-winning hotel. Peter Wharton's Hotel Riviera is arguably one of the most comfortable and most hospitable in the region. The exterior, with its fine Regency façade and bow fronted windows complements the elegance of the interior comprising handsome public rooms and beautifully appointed bedrooms, many with sea views. Perfectly located at the centre of Sidmouth's historic Georgian esplanade, and awarded 4 Stars by both the AA and Visit Britain, the Riviera is committed to providing the very highest standards of excellence, ensuring you a most enjoyable experience. Choose to dine in the attractive salon, with panoramic views across Lyme Bay, and indulge in the superb cuisine, prepared by English and French trained chefs. The exceptional cellar will please any wine connoisseur. Short breaks are available.

DEVON - TORQUAY (MAIDENCOMBE)

ORESTONE MANOR & THE RESTAURANT AT ORESTONE MANOR

ROCKHOUSE LANE, MAIDENCOMBE, TORQUAY, DEVON TQ1 4SX
Tel: 0845 365 2095 **International:** +44 (0)1803 328098 **Fax:** 01803 328336
Web: www.johansens.com/orestonemanor **E-mail:** enquiries@orestonemanor.com

Our inspector loved: Sitting on a beautiful terrace overlooking both Lyme Bay and Torbay whilst enjoying a leisurely lunch.

Price Guide:
single £99–£159
double/twin £150–£245

Awards/Recognition: 1 AA Rosettes 2008-2009

Location: On the A379; Torquay, 3 miles; Teignmouth, 4 miles; M5 jct 30, 19 miles

Attractions: Dartmoor; Cathedral City of Exeter; National Trust Houses & Gardens; Exmoor

With stunning views across the Torbay coastline and Lyme Bay this was formerly the home of painter John Calcott Horsley RA, renowned for painting the very first Christmas card, and whose celebrated portrait of his brother-in-law, Isambard Kingdom Brunel, hangs in the National Gallery. A colonial theme runs through the house and as expected an excellent afternoon tea is served on the terrace or in the conservatory. The lunch and dinner menu takes inspiration from local seasonal ingredients, with many of the herbs and vegetables coming from its own garden. There is plenty to do nearby, from National Trust properties to Dartmoor, Exmoor and stunning coastal walks.

DEVON - WEMBURY (SOUTH HAMS)

LANGDON COURT COUNTRY HOUSE HOTEL & RESTAURANT

DOWN THOMAS, SOUTH HAMS, PLYMOUTH, DEVON PL9 0DY
Tel: 0845 365 1985 **International:** +44 (0)1752 862358 **Fax:** 01752 863428
Web: www.johansens.com/langdon **E-mail:** enquiries@langdoncourt.com

Our inspector loved: *This delightfully tucked away country house hotel, yet only 6 miles from Plymouth and so very accessible.*

Price Guide:
single from £89
double from £139
suite from £179

Location: Plymouth, 6 miles; A38, 9 miles; M5 jct 31, 40 miles

Attractions: National Trust Coastal paths of Devon; Plymouth; Various National Trust Properties; Dartmoor; Yachting

Originally built for Katherine Parr, the sixth wife of Henry VIII, who would be no doubt impressed with today's modern incarnation of this Tudor manor and its Jacobean walled gardens. Behind the impressive façade lie tiled floors, warmly painted stone walls and a clever combination of the classic and contemporary. Bedrooms are well proportioned with gorgeous linen and welcoming touches. The bistro and bar menus are created using exceptional Devon produce and a combination of both simple and more adventurous cooking. A really exceptional area to explore; take the direct pathway to the beach at Wembury Cove or continue to picturesque villages that step up from the waterside where yachts moor and delightful pubs keep walkers entertained. Riding stables are across the road and historic Plymouth is an easy drive away. A magical place for a wedding or simply to take over for a house party.

DEVON - WOOLACOMBE

The Woolacombe Bay Hotel

SOUTH STREET, WOOLACOMBE, DEVON EX34 7BN
Tel: 0845 365 2819 **International:** +44 (0)1271 870388 **Fax:** 01271 870613
Web: www.johansens.com/woolacombebay **E-mail:** woolacombe.bayhotel@btinternet.com

Our inspector loved: The Chapel within the enclosed Victorian courtyard a must for Weddings.

Price Guide: (including dinner)
single £110–£137
double/twin £220–£274

Location: A361, 5 miles; Ilfracombe, 6 miles; Barnstaple, 11 miles; M5 jct 27, 46 miles

Attractions: Exmoor; National Trust Coastal Walks; Lynton; RHS Garden Rosemoor

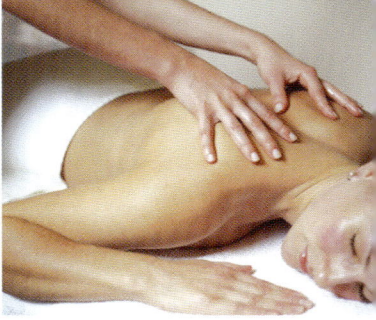

Always impressive at building fine hotels the Victorians also knew where to position them. Woolacombe Bay Hotel is testament to this, standing in 6 acres of grounds leading to 3 miles of golden Blue-flag sand. The beautifully presented new bedrooms and suites offer sea-facing views and some also have private balconies. The hotel is packed with activity both indoors and out, from unlimited use of tennis, squash, 2 pools, billiards, bowls and a health suite. Special rates are also available at nearby golf clubs. Being energetic is not a requirement however, and you can join others by relaxing in the grounds, which extend to the rolling surf of this magnificent bay.

DEVON - WOOLACOMBE (MORTEHOE)

WATERSMEET HOTEL

MORTEHOE, WOOLACOMBE, DEVON EX34 7EB
Tel: 0845 365 2793 **International:** +44 (0)1271 870333 **Fax:** 01271 870890
Web: www.johansens.com/watersmeet **E-mail:** info@watersmeethotel.co.uk

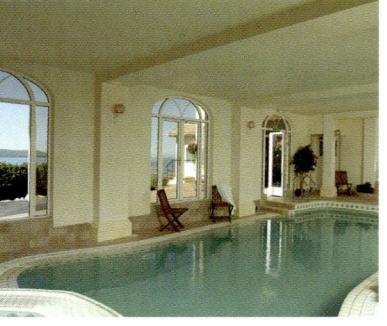

Our inspector loved: *The overall experience and the beautifully presented new suites.*

Price Guide: (including dinner)
single £98–£150
double/twin £150–£340
suite £220–£360

Awards/Recognition: 1 AA Rosette 2006-2007

Location: B3343, 2 miles; A361, 4 miles; M5 jct 27, 50 miles; Barnstaple, 15 miles

Attractions: Arlington Court; Saunton Sands Golf Course; National Trust Coastal Walks; Watermouth Castle

A dramatic and beautiful setting greets those arriving at Watersmeet just above Combesgate Beach. Steps lead down to the sandy shore and large picture windows in the reception rooms mean you never have to miss out on the ever-changing coastline. Bedrooms are in a classical style and all have the most wonderful views, some even have balconies. Quality local ingredients are used in the creative and thoughtfully balanced dishes in the Pavilion restaurant. Here you can marvel over sunsets by candlelight though on warm nights sitting on the terrace listening to the waves is also a tempting option. For those that like to be a bit more energetic there are a number of National Trust coastal walks nearby.

DORSET - EVERSHOT (NEAR DORCHESTER)

Summer Lodge Country House Hotel, Restaurant and Spa

9 FORE STREET, EVERSHOT, DORSET DT2 0JR
Tel: 0845 365 2381 **International:** +44 (0)1935 482000 **Fax:** +44 (0)1935 482040
Web: www.johansens.com/summerlodge **E-mail:** enquiries@summerlodgehotel.com

Our inspector loved: *The great attention to detail, sumptuous decor and relaxing spa.*

Price Guide:
single from £195
double/twin £225–£360
suite/master bedroom £425–£495

Awards/Recognition: Relais & Châteaux; 3 AA Rosettes 2007-2008; Dorset Business Awards – Restaurant of the Year 2007

Location: A37, 1.5 miles; M5 jct 25, 33.5 miles; Dorchester, 13 miles; Bournemouth, 46 miles

Attractions: Thomas Hardy Country; Cerne Abbas; Abbotsbury and Heritage Coast; Sherborne and Shaftesbury

Summer Lodge dates back to 1789. Built for the 2nd Earl of Ilchester, Thomas Hardy was commissioned to draw plans for a second floor by the 6th Earl in 1893. Impeccably restored with 24 gorgeous bedrooms, suites and cottages - many with fireplaces - it combines the finest English furnishings and classical art with the latest technology, including complimentary Wi-Fi. The award-winning restaurant, under Head Chef Steven Titman and Sommelier Eric Zwiebel is a delight and the Lodge's own vegetable garden and extensive wine cellar complement the culinary experience. Lighter meals are available in the well-stocked bar and sumptuous Dorset cream teas are served each afternoon. The spa treatment rooms offer Elemis products. Civil weddings, small business meetings and private dining are meticulously catered for.

DORSET - GILLINGHAM

Stock Hill Country House Hotel & Restaurant

STOCK HILL, GILLINGHAM, DORSET SP8 5NR
Tel: 0845 365 2371 **International:** +44 (0)1747 823626 **Fax:** 01747 825628
Web: www.johansens.com/stockhillhouse **E-mail:** reception@stockhillhouse.co.uk

Our inspector loved: *The true country house hospitality and ambience with great attention to detail.*

Price Guide: (including dinner)
single £145–£175
double £270–£335

Awards/Recognition: 3 AA Rosettes 2007-2008

Location: On the B3081; A303, 3 miles; Shaftesbury, 6 miles; Bristol, 47 miles

Attractions: Stonehenge; Stourhead House & Garden; Salisbury; Longleat

Set within 11 acres of attractive woodlands and beautiful gardens on the borders of 3 counties, this remarkable, 3 Red Star, late Victorian mansion exudes a relaxed charm. Impressive oak doors open to reveal a beautiful period interior which exudes comfort and is enhanced by personal touches. The bedrooms reflect the history and style of the house and the spacious rooms of Magnolia and Poesy have recently had a refurbishment in striking prints and tones. The restaurant with romantic candle-lit tables and attentive and friendly service is enhanced by antiques, curios and the lovely views of the gardens. The highly-acclaimed, creative award winning cuisine takes its innovation from European influences with ingredients sourced locally including fresh fish, shellfish and organic vegetables harvested from the walled kitchen garden. Sumptuous desserts are a perfect finish to a memorable evening.

DORSET - WAREHAM

The Priory Hotel

CHURCH GREEN, WAREHAM, DORSET BH20 4ND
Tel: 0845 365 2651 **International:** +44 (0)1929 551666 **Fax:** 01929 554519
Web: www.johansens.com/priorywareham **E-mail:** reservations@theprioryhotel.co.uk

Our inspector loved: *The beautiful setting and excellent care and attention.*

Price Guide:
single from £180
double/twin £225-£270
suite £315-£345

Location: A352, 1 miles; M27 jct 1, 32 miles; Poole, 9 miles; Southampton, 42 miles

Attractions: Corfe Castle; Lulworth Cove; Athelhampton House and Garden; Jurassic Coast

Since the 16th century, the one time Lady St Mary Priory has offered sanctuary to travellers. In Hardy's Dorset, "Far From the Madding Crowd", it placidly stands in immaculate gardens on the bank of the River Frome. The Priory underwent a sympathetic conversion, the result is an unpretentiously charming hotel. The bedrooms are distinctively styled and feature family antiques, many rooms have views of the Purbeck Hills. A 16th-century clay barn has been transformed into the Boathouse, creating 4 spacious luxury suites at the river's edge. The drawing room, residents' lounge and intimate bar create a convivial atmosphere. The Garden Room restaurant is open for breakfast and lunch, while splendid dinners are served in the vaulted stone cellars. There are moorings for guests arriving by boat.

DORSET - WEYMOUTH (FLEET)

Moonfleet Manor

FLEET, WEYMOUTH, DORSET DT3 4ED
Tel: 0845 365 2074 **International:** +44 (0)1305 786948 **Fax:** 01305 774395
Web: www.johansens.com/moonfleetmanor **E-mail:** info@moonfleetmanorhotel.co.uk

Our inspector loved: The great combination of being child friendly yet catering for the discerning family traveller.

Price Guide:
double/twin £160–£200
suite £285–£390
interconnecting £230–£390

Awards/Recognition: 2 AA Rosettes 2008-2009

Location: A354, 3 miles; M27 jct 1, 50 miles; Weymouth, 3 miles; Bournemouth, 42 miles

Attractions: Chesil Beach Jurassic Coast; Abbotsbury Swannery; Weymouth Town & Beaches; Portland Sailing Academy

Overlooking Chesil Beach, one of the finest barrier beaches in the world, Moonfleet Manor is both a country house hotel and a family resort. The use of a variety of unusual antiques and objets d'art from around the world lends a refreshing and individual style to this comfortable and attractive hotel. Colonial chic and grand Victoriana engage with contemporary spaces. Bedrooms are versatile; large family rooms, suites and interconnecting. Staff work hard to ensure that guests feel at home whatever their age. Moonfleet's dining room offers an excellent and varied menu based on fresh local produce and combines culinary styles from around the world. There are early supper menus for the younger guest giving adults the chance to enjoy fine dining in a more intimate atmosphere. Facilities at the hotel include an Ofsted registered nursery, baby sitting and listening services, indoor swimming pool, treatment rooms, squash and tennis courts. A von Essen Luxury Family Hotel.

DURHAM - SEAHAM

Seaham Hall Hotel & Serenity Spa

LORD BYRON'S WALK, SEAHAM, CO DURHAM SR7 7AG
Tel: 0845 365 4036 **International:** +44 (0)1915 161 400 **Fax:** 01915 161 410
Web: www.johansens.com/seahamhall **E-mail:** info@seaham-hall.co.uk

Our inspector loved: *The magical walkway to the Serenity Spa - oriental in design it gives you an intriguing and seamless transition from memorable service and hospitality in the Hall to pure relaxation and pampering in the Spa.*

Price Guide:
double/twin £250-£490
suite £550-£595

Awards/Recognition: 1 Star Michelin 2008 (The White Room) 4 AA Rosettes 2007-2008; 1 AA Rosette 2008-2009 (The Ozone)

Location: A19, 0.5 miles; A1M jct 62, 2 miles; Newcastle, 17 miles; Newcastle Airport, 24 miles

Attractions: Durham - World Heritage Site Castle and Cathedral; Newcastle; Beamish Museum; Hadrian's Wall

Seaham Hall is an unforgettable hotel set amongst 37 acres of landscaped clifftop grounds and twinned with the Feng Shui inspired Serenity Spa, it is a destination in it's own right. The two properties are joined by an impressive underground walkway and its not hard to see why they won awards for 'Best Spa for Style' by the Sunday Times and 'Best UK Spa Destination' by Condé Nast Traveller. Dining is taken seriously here. The White Room Restaurant deservedly holds a Michelin star for its innovative cuisine whilst The Ozone restaurant delights with a menu fusing the best of Asian with a western twist. The Ozone, awarded 1 AA rosette in May 2008, is for the exclusive use of guests and members during the day. Bedrooms have their own individual style and character with many boasting sea views or in the case of ground floor rooms private terraces. A von Essen hotel.

ESSEX - DEDHAM

Maison Talbooth

STRATFORD ROAD, DEDHAM, COLCHESTER, ESSEX CO7 6HN
Tel: 0845 365 4612 **International:** +44 (0)1206 322367 **Fax:** 01206 322752
Web: www.johansens.com/maisontalbooth **E-mail:** maison@milsomhotels.com

Our inspector loved: *The lovely new bedrooms at the top of the house.*

Price Guide:
single from £175
double from £195
suite from £225

Awards/Recognition: 2 AA Rosettes 2007–2008

Location: A12, 1 mile; Colchester, 9 miles; Ipswich, 12 miles

Attractions: Flatford Mill and Constable Country; Colchester Castle; Sailing on the Stour Estuary; Lavenham

A charming and luxurious former Victorian rectory overlooking the lush and tranquil Dedham Vale in the heart of Constable's picturesque Essex countryside. From the tall windows of beautifully furnished bedroom suites you can admire uninterrupted views of water meadows stretching away to the distant medieval church of Stratford St Mary. It is like an impressive English country house with all the right ingredients - peaceful surroundings, swimming pool and tennis court plus a team of staff ready to ensure you receive as much or as little attention as you wish. Five therapists oversee the new treatment rooms for that added element of pampering. Breakfast is taken in the Garden Restaurant and meals in the renowned, romantic riverside setting of Le Talbooth, located minutes away by courtesy car and who's popularly with locals speaks for itself. This would be wonderful for an exclusive house party or wedding setting

GLOUCESTERSHIRE - CHELTENHAM (SHURDINGTON)

The Greenway

SHURDINGTON, CHELTENHAM, GLOUCESTERSHIRE GL51 4UG
Tel: 0845 365 2514 **International:** +44 (0)1242 862352 **Fax:** 01242 862780
Web: www.johansens.com/greenway **E-mail:** info@thegreenway.co.uk

Our inspector loved: *The Oak room with it's beautiful four poster bed and the newly decorated sitting room and restaurant, stunning!*

Price Guide:
single from £130
double/twin £255–£315
suite from £345–£450

Awards/Recognition: 2 AA Rosettes 2008-2009

Location: A46, 0.5 miles; M5 jct 11a, 2.5 miles; Bristol Airport, 41.5 miles; Cheltenham, 10-min drive

Attractions: Cheltenham Racecourse; The Cotswolds; Shakespeare Country; Gloucester

Set in gentle parkland with the rolling Cotswold hills beyond, The Greenway manages to capture a unique style of its own. Elegant public rooms with their antique furniture, fresh flowers and roaring log fires in winter also have a welcoming sense of country house informality about them. 11 bedrooms in the main house, a further 10 in the converted Georgian coach house next door, are individually decorated. Some are more traditional whilst others have a fresh new English feel with striking fabrics and strong tones. Each room has outstanding views of the Cotswold Hills or gardens and bathrooms have indulgent Pascal Morabito products. The menus focus on local produce throughout the seasons and are complemented by an outstanding wine list. Not only in a beautiful location but just 10 minutes off the M5 making it an easy getaway. A von Essen hotel

GLOUCESTERSHIRE - CHIPPING CAMPDEN

Charingworth Manor

NR CHIPPING CAMPDEN, GLOUCESTERSHIRE GL55 6NS
Tel: 0845 365 3298 **International:** +44 (0)1386 593555 **Fax:** 01386 593353
Web: www.johansens.com/charingworthmanor **E-mail:** info.charingworthmanor@classiclodges.co.uk

Our inspector loved: *Sitting out on the terrace looking out over the beautiful rolling hills of the Cotswold countryside*

Price Guide:
single £125-£155
double £180-£210
suite £245-£295

Awards/Recognition: 2 AA Rosettes 2008-2009

Location: B4035, 1 miles; A429, 2.5 miles; Moreton-in-Marsh, 4.5 miles

Attractions: Chipping Campden; Cotswolds; Stratford-upon-Avon; Warwick Castle

A captivating 14th century manor house set in a 54 acre estate, with immaculate formal gardens and far-reaching views of the unmatchable Cotswold countryside. During the 1930s, the manor hosted several illustrious guests, including T.S.Eliot who wrote an ode to Charingworth. Individually designed guest rooms are furnished with antiques and fine fabrics, recreating the manor's original charm; two feature impressive four-poster beds and some offer private terraces from which to enjoy the beautiful grounds. The restaurant has a creative menu and offers a good selection of seasonally inspired dishes. On a mild evening you can enjoy strolling through the extensive gardens or during the winter months log fires warm the series of intimate, tapestry-hung public rooms which are inviting retreats from inclement weather.

GLOUCESTERSHIRE - LOWER SLAUGHTER

Lower Slaughter Manor

LOWER SLAUGHTER, GLOUCESTERSHIRE GL54 2HP
Tel: 0845 365 2047 **International:** +44 (0)1451 820456 **Fax:** 01451 822150
Web: www.johansens.com/lowerslaughtermanor **E-mail:** info@lowerslaughter.co.uk

Our inspector loved: *The stunningly decorated restaurant, particularly the area which was once a chapel, great for a small party.*

Price Guide:
single from £215
double £295–£400
suite £450–£850

Awards/Recognition: Relais & Châteaux; 3 AA Rosettes 2008-2009

Location: A429, 0.5 miles; Stow-on-the-Wold, 4 miles; M5 jct 10, 20 miles; Cheltenham, 21 miles

Attractions: Stratford-upon-Avon; Warwick Castle; Sudeley Castle; The Cotswolds

At the heart of the incredible picturesque cotswold village of Lower Slaughter, this beautifully restored Grade II listed country manor house positively oozes style. A contemporary feel teases the house's historic character and its "designer" bedrooms are chic and continental in flavour. Here detail is exceptional with beautiful linen, eclectic pieces of art and wall mounted ipod docking stations. Enjoy the exquisite cuisine alongside a well balanced list of specially selected wines from the Old and New Worlds. The wonderful grounds feature a croquet lawn and, within the delightful walled garden, a unique 2-storey dovecote that dates back to the 15th century. This is a wonderful setting for private parties, business meetings, weddings and civil partnership ceremonies. A von Essen hotel.

GLOUCESTERSHIRE - LOWER SLAUGHTER

WASHBOURNE COURT

LOWER SLAUGHTER, GLOUCESTERSHIRE GL54 2HS
Tel: 0845 365 2791 **International:** +44 (0)1451 822143 **Fax:** 01451 821045
Web: www.johansens.com/washbournecourt **E-mail:** info@washbournecourt.co.uk

Our inspector loved: *Modern and traditional meet in the fabulous new style after a complete refurbishment.*

Price Guide: (including dinner)
single from £205
double/twin from £225
suite from £355

Awards/Recognition: 2 AA Rosettes 2008-2009

Location: A429, 0.5 miles; Bourton-on-the-Water, 2 miles

Attractions: Cheltenham Race Course; Batsford Arboretum; Cotswold Wildlife Park; Sudley Castle

Washbourne Court offers a unique refreshing twist on a luxury country house hotel. Situated right in the heart of the beautiful village of Lower Slaughter this truly splendid 17th century hotel stands in four acres of beautiful grounds alongside the River Eye. An inspired mix of exciting contemporary design and handsome historic features include Traditional beamed ceilings, stone mullioned windows and the most magnificent fireplace in the lounge. The "uber" cool Etons Restaurant, luxuriously relaxing Scholars Lounge or the beautiful riverside terrace, offers a choice for the discerning diner to sample the modern British cuisine with an emphasis on the best local ingredients and seasonally changing menus. The 30 "designer" bedrooms are sophisticated yet informal incorporating flat screen tvs, ipod docking stations and dvd players, an understated blend of traditional and funky creating the ultimate Cotswold retreat. A von Essen hotel.

GLOUCESTERSHIRE - MINCHINHAMPTON

BURLEIGH COURT

BURLEIGH, MINCHINHAMPTON, NEAR STROUD, GLOUCESTERSHIRE GL5 2PF
Tel: 0845 365 3217 **International:** +44 (0)1453 883804 **Fax:** 01453 886870
Web: www.johansens.com/burleighgloucestershire **E-mail:** burleighcourt@aol.com

Our inspector loved: *The beautiful well-maintained gardens and Victorian plunge pool together with lovely spacious bedrooms.*

Price Guide:
single £85-£105
double £130-£150
suite £190

Awards/Recognition: 2 AA Rosettes 2007-2008

Location: A419, 0.5 miles; M4 jct, 28.5 miles; Cirencester, 11.5 miles; Cheltenham, 16 miles

Attractions: Cotswolds; Bath; Slimbridge Wildfowl Trust; Westonbirt Arboretum

Journey through honey-stoned Cotswold villages to reach this 18th-century former gentleman's manor. Nestling on a steep hillside overlooking the Golden Valley its relaxed atmosphere and acres of beautifully tended gardens featuring terraces, ponds, pools, hidden pathways and Cotswold stone walls create an idyllic setting. Many bedrooms in the main house have garden views though for families we recommend the coach house rooms, located by a Victorian plunge pool as well as those within the courtyard gardens which offer flexible accommodation. The restaurant has a reputation for classical dishes and a wine cellar to satisfy the most demanding drinker. From here you can easily explore the market towns of Minchinhampton, Tetbury, Cirencester, Painswick and Bibury.

GLOUCESTERSHIRE - STONEHOUSE

STONEHOUSE COURT HOTEL

BRISTOL ROAD, STONEHOUSE, GLOUCESTERSHIRE GL10 3RA
Tel: 0845 365 2378 **International:** +44 (0)1453 794950 **Fax:** 0871 871 3241
Web: www.johansens.com/stonehousecourt **E-mail:** info@stonehousecourt.co.uk

Our inspector loved: *The spacious rooms overlooking the lovely gardens in the manor house.*

Price Guide:
single from £75
double/twin £90–£140
four poster £180

Awards/Recognition: 2 AA Rosettes 2008–2009

Location: Off the A419; M5 jct 13, 1.7 miles; Stroud, 3.2 miles; Bristol, 29 miles

Attractions: Slimbridge Wildfowl Trust; Gloucester Cathedral; Westonbirt Arboretum; Cheltenham Racecourse

Overlooking the Cotswold landscape and built in 1601, this outstanding Grade II listed manor house is set in 6 acres of private grounds and offers the largest conference and meeting venue in the area. Comprehensive facilities are available for up to 150 guests, intimate civil wedding ceremonies can be held in the picturesque outdoor pagoda and marquees on the lawn. Relaxation and comfort extend into the individually decorated bedrooms, some located in the original Tudor manor house have fireplaces and mullioned windows with views of the mature gardens. Dinner is served in the lounge or on the terrace, and Henry's restaurant creates delicious dishes using fine local ingredients. Menus include fillet of line caught sea bass, duet of spring lamb, carrot infused pannacotta and apple and lavender mousse.

GLOUCESTERSHIRE - TETBURY

Calcot Manor Hotel & Spa

NEAR TETBURY, GLOUCESTERSHIRE GL8 8YJ
Tel: 0845 365 3220 **International:** +44 (0)1666 890391 **Fax:** 01666 890394
Web: www.johansens.com/calcotmanor **E-mail:** reception@calcotmanor.co.uk

Our inspector loved: Sitting in the outdoor hot tub on a chilly day with the open fire burning, then having a wonderful massage in the fabulous spa.

Price Guide:
double/twin £220–£275
family room from £275
family suite from £320

Awards/Recognition: 2 AA Rosettes 2007-2008; Condé Nast Johansens Most Excellent Meeting Venue 2007

Location: On the A4135; Tetbury, 3.5 miles; M5 jct 13, 11 miles; M4 jct 18, 12.5 miles

Attractions: Westonbirt Arboretum; Bath; Cotswolds; Cirencester

For excellent family facilities look no further! The delightful family suites feature bunk beds and baby listening devices, while a play area to keep older children entertained has Playstations, Xboxes and a small cinema. The Ofsted registered crèche means you can enjoy quality time away from your little ones in the spa with its 16m pool, steam room, gym, outdoor hot tub and beauty treatments. A farmhouse until 1983, the Manor's stone barns and stables include one of the oldest tithe barns in England. The Barn features the Thomas Suite with digital state-of-the-art audio-visual equipment for conferences. Dinner in the elegant conservatory restaurant is memorable while the ever popular Gumstool Bistro and Bar offers simpler food and local ales.

GLOUCESTERSHIRE - TEWKESBURY (CORSE LAWN)

Corse Lawn House Hotel

CORSE LAWN, NR TEWKESBURY, GLOUCESTERSHIRE GL19 4LZ
Tel: 0845 365 3249 **International:** +44 (0)1452 780479/771 **Fax:** 01452 780840
Web: www.johansens.com/corselawn **E-mail:** enquiries@corselawn.com

Our inspector loved: *As friendly and comfortable as ever with fabulous food too.*

Price Guide:
single £95
double/twin £150
four-poster/suite £170-£185

Just 6 miles from the M5 and M50, Corse Lawn occupies 12 acres of an unspoilt, typically English hamlet in a peaceful Gloucestershire backwater. The hotel, an elegant Queen Anne listed building set back from the village green offers you charm, history and very good food. As well as the renowned restaurant, there are 3 comfortable drawing rooms, a large lounge bar, and two private dining-cum-conference rooms which can accommodate up to 45 and a smaller room for up to 20. A tennis court, heated indoor swimming pool and croquet lawn adjoin the hotel and most sports and leisure activities can be arranged by prior request. You'll find it ideal for exploring the Cotswolds, Malverns and Forest of Dean. Short breaks are available on request.

Awards/Recognition: 2 AA Rosettes 2007-2008

Location: On the B4211; A438, 1 1/2 miles; A417, 1 1/2 miles; Cheltenham, 12 miles

Attractions: Cotswolds; Malverns; Forest of Dean

SOUTH GLOUCESTERSHIRE - BRISTOL (THORNBURY)

THORNBURY CASTLE

THORNBURY, SOUTH GLOUCESTERSHIRE BS35 1HH
Tel: 0845 365 2749 **International:** +44 (0)1454 281182 **Fax:** 01454 416188
Web: www.johansens.com/thornburycastle **E-mail:** info@thornburycastle.co.uk

Our inspector loved: *A unique experience, fabulous rooms and great food. You feel royal in the most relaxed way!*

Price Guide:
single from £125
double/twin £250–£360
suite from £450

Awards/Recognition: 2 AA Rosettes 2008-2009; AA Notable wine list award 2007/2008; Wine spectator award of Excellence 2008/2009; No. 4 Condé Nast Traveller Gold List of Top 26 English Hotels

Location: B4061, 0.5 miles; A38, 2 miles; M5 jct 14, 5 miles; M5 jct 16, 6 miles

Attractions: Bath; Cardiff; The Cotswolds; Bristol

Built in 1511 by Edward Stafford, third Duke of Buckingham. Thornbury Castle was once owned by Henry VIII, who stayed there in 1535 with Anne Boleyn. You can now enjoy the colourful history, rich furnishings, ornate oriel windows, suits of armour, panelled walls and large open fireplaces, and sleep comfortably in one of the 27 carefully restored bedchambers that retain many period details. The castle is acclaimed for its food, which features dishes such as Gloucestershire Old Spot pork, fresh south coast fish, local seasonal vegetables and cheeses and organic free-range eggs. A good wine cellar also includes its own wine from grapes grown in the grounds. You'll often see the chef picking herbs from the garden. Personally guided tours will introduce you to little-known areas of this magnificent building as well as the famous places nearby. A von Essen hotel.

HAMPSHIRE - ANDOVER (HURSTBOURNE TARRANT)

Esseborne Manor

HURSTBOURNE TARRANT, ANDOVER, HAMPSHIRE SP11 0ER
Tel: 0845 365 3284 **International:** +44 (0)1264 736444 **Fax:** 01264 736725
Web: www.johansens.com/essebornemanor **E-mail:** info@esseborne-manor.co.uk

Our inspector loved: *The peaceful location and "at home feel" of the Manor House.*

Price Guide:
single £98–£130
double/twin £125–£180
suite £250

Awards/Recognition: 1 AA Rosettes 2008-2009

Location: Just Off A343; M4 jct 13, 13 miles; Andover, 7 miles; Heathrow Airport 55 miles

Attractions: Salisbury and Winchester Cathedrals; Stonehenge; Highclere Castle; Newbury Racecourse

Esseborne Manor is small, unpretentious yet stylish. The present house was built at the end of the 19th century and carries the name used to record details of the local village in the Domesday Book. It is set in a pleasing garden amid the rich farmland and natural beauty of the North Wessex Downs. Owners Ian and Lucilla Hamilton have established the restful atmosphere of a private country home. The bedrooms include a luxurious suite with a giant sunken Jacuzzi bath; some bedrooms are reached via a courtyard and others are delightful cottage rooms with their own patios overlooking the garden. Head Chef Anton Babarovic's fine AA Rosette-awarded cooking can be fully appreciated in the elegant fabric-lined dining room. Meetings and private parties can also be accommodated.

HAMPSHIRE - BASINGSTOKE

Oakley Hall

RECTORY ROAD, OAKLEY, BASINGSTOKE RG23 7EL
Tel: 0845 365 4628 **International:** +44 (0)1256 783 350 **Fax:** 01256 783 351
Web: www.johansens.com/oakleyhall **E-mail:** enquiries@oakleyhall-park.com

Our inspector loved: The 2 new guest cottages and stable block rooms that will be opening in early 2009.

Price Guide:
single £260–£298
double £260–£298
suite £392–£1,176

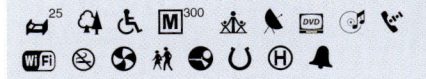

Location: Just off B3400; M3 jct 6/7, 0.75 miles; Basingstoke, 6 miles; Heathrow Airport, 45 miles

Attractions: On-site Clay Pigeon Shoots; Willis Museum; Marwell Zoological Park; The Watercress lIne

A long, winding driveway leads up to this stunningly elegant Georgian mansion, which is set amidst 315 acres of wooded rural grounds, perfect for outdoor activities and corporate or private events. There is a strong link to Jane Austen, who was friends with the Bramstons, its former owners, and it is rumoured that she based her novel Mansfield Park on Oakley Hall. The interior is beautiful, with a pretty tiled hallway and an impressive oak-panelled library overlooking the large south-facing terrace and lawns. Corniced ceilings adorn the dining room, where you can peruse a mouth-watering menu based on fresh local produce, also served as a barbecue, picnic and al fresco. Accommodation can be found in 2 cottages, East Lodge and The Gardners Cottage, and in 20 new Courtyard Rooms in the old stable block.

HAMPSHIRE - BROCKENHURST

New Park Manor and Bath House Spa

LYNDHURST ROAD, BROCKENHURST, NEW FOREST, HAMPSHIRE SO42 7QH
Tel: 0845 365 2084 **International:** +44 (0)1590 623467 **Fax:** 01590 622268
Web: www.johansens.com/newparkmanor **E-mail:** info@newparkmanorhotel.co.uk

Our inspector loved: *The incredibly comfortable Rufus Lounge and fantastic spa.*

Price Guide:
double/twin £155–£285
suite £295–£315

Awards/Recognition: 2 AA Rosettes 2008-2009

Location: A337, 0.5 mile; M27 jct 1, 6.5 miles; Brockenhurst, 1 mile; Southampton, 18 miles

Attractions: Beaulieu; Riding; Sailing Isle of Wight

New Park Manor Hotel and Spa is set in the heart of Hampshire's National Park, The New Forest, and is today one of the very few hotels set within its own grounds offering magnificent views over the untouched ancient Forest. The award winning Spa, The Bath House Spa is all about your enjoyment time and total relaxation and really does take its inspiration from nature with a fabulous array of treatments with natural orientation and offers a multitude of massage therapies to nurture, calm and revitalise. Enjoy the tranquil serenity of the spa garden, unwind in the Canadian hot tub and be up close and personal to roaming deer and New Forest ponies with magnificent 270° panoramic views. The traditional English hotel combined with a modern day luxurious spa makes this a truly unique experience you won't want to miss. A von Essen hotel.

HAMPSHIRE - LYMINGTON (MILFORD ON SEA)

WESTOVER HALL

PARK LANE, MILFORD-ON-SEA, HAMPSHIRE SO41 0PT
Tel: 0845 365 3425 **International:** +44 (0)1590 643044 **Fax:** 01590 644490
Web: www.johansens.com/westoverhall **E-mail:** info@westoverhallhotel.com

Our inspector loved: *The gorgeous new beach retreat cottage adjacent to the hotel.*

Price Guide:
double from £206
superior from £266
suite from £256

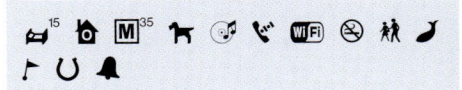

Awards/Recognition: 2 AA Rosettes 2008-2009

Location: A337, 3 miles; M27 jct 1, 17 miles; Lymington, 3 miles; Bournemouth, 13 miles

Attractions: New Forest; Lymington; Beaulieu and Exbury; Hurst Castle

Westover Hall effortlessly combines stately grandeur with a home-from-home atmosphere. Use the hotel as a base for local excursions, or stroll down to the private beach hut on the pebble sea front and watch the yachts on the Solent. The main hall is encircled with oak panelling and illuminated through pre-Raphaelite stained glass windows. Guestrooms boast high ceilings and period features, offset by elegant furnishings and individual touches, most enjoy views of the Solent and the Isle of Wight. The oak-panelled dining room, showcasing a collection of art and photography, is at once impressive and intimate. The daily menu comprises Modern European dishes, all artistically presented and using local produce. Wile away the rest of the evening in the contemporary bar, or in a well-padded, fireside armchair in the lounge. The new beach retreat cottage adjacent to the hotel has 2 double bedrooms and own private terrace.

HAMPSHIRE - NEW MILTON

Chewton Glen

NEW MILTON, NEW FOREST, HAMPSHIRE BH25 6QS
Tel: 0845 365 3233 **International:** +44 (0)1425 275341 **US toll free:** US toll free 1 800 344 5087 **Fax:** 01425 272310
Web: www.johansens.com/chewtonglen **E-mail:** reservations@chewtonglen.com

Our inspector loved: *The sheer elegance of this classic country hotel with it's wonderful spa.*

Price Guide:
double £299–£485
suites £485–£1,250

Awards/Recognition: 3 AA Rosettes 2008-2009; Condé Nast Traveller Gold List 2006; Relais & Châteaux

Location: A35, 2 miles; M27 jct 1, 14 miles; Highcliffe, 1 mile; Heathrow, 85 miles

Attractions: New Forest; Bournemouth; Lymington; Isle of Wight

Arrive with high expectations and you certainly won't be disappointed. Chewton Glen is set in 130 acres of gardens and parkland on the edge of the New Forest, not far from the sea. Bedrooms are the ultimate in luxury, with marble bathrooms, cosy bathrobes and views over the grounds . Head chef Luke Matthews creates suprising and innovative dishes using fresh local produce, and the wine list is impressive. You'll be tempted to spend much of your time in the stunning spa, with its magnificent 17 metre swimming pool, steam, sauna, treatment rooms, gym and hydrotherapy pool. Outside there's another pool, sun terrace, croquet lawn, tennis and a 9-hole par 3 course. What more could you really want?

HAMPSHIRE - ROTHERWICK

Tylney Hall

ROTHERWICK, HOOK, HAMPSHIRE RG27 9AZ
Tel: 0845 365 2782 International: +44 (0)1256 764881 Fax: 01256 768141
Web: www.johansens.com/tylneyhall E-mail: reservations@tylneyhall.com

Our inspector loved: *The impeccable service and glorious afternoon tea.*

Price Guide:
single from £155
double/twin from £205
suite from £335

Awards/Recognition: 2 AA Rosettes 2008-2009

Location: A30, 1 mile; M3 jct5, 3 miles; Basingstoke, 6.5 miles; Heathrow, 32 miles

Attractions: Watercress Line steam railway; Antiques at Hartley Wintney; West Green House and Gardens; Milestones Museum

Arriving there in the evening, with floodlights and the forecourt fountain, it is easy to imagine partying in a private stately home. Set in 66 acres of ornamental gardens and parkland, Tylney Hall typifies the great houses of another era. Apéritifs are taken in the panelled library bar; haute cuisine is served in the glass-domed award winning Oak Room restaurant. The health and leisure facilities include 2 heated pools and whirlpool, solarium, fitness studio, spa, sauna, tennis, croquet and snooker. Surrounding the hotel are wooded trails ideal for jogging. Functions for up to 120 people are catered for in the Tylney Suite or Chestnut Suite; there are a further 10 private banqueting rooms. Tylney Hall is licensed to hold wedding ceremonies and civil partnerships on-site

HAMPSHIRE - SOUTHAMPTON (CHILWORTH)

Chilworth Manor

CHILWORTH, SOUTHAMPTON, HAMPSHIRE SO16 7PT
Tel: 0845 365 3234 **International:** +44 (0)23 8076 7333 **Fax:** 023 8076 6392
Web: www.johansens.com/chilworth **E-mail:** sales@chilworth-manor.co.uk

Our inspector loved: *The new leisure centre.*

Price Guide:
single £55-£150
double £110-£165
deluxe £185-£195

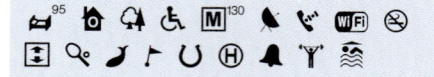

Location: Off the A27; M3 jct 14, 1 mile; Southampton, 4 miles; Southampton International Airport, 4 miles.

Attractions: New Forest; National Motor Museum Beaulieu; Cathedral City of Winchester; Marwell Zoo.

An imposing Edwardian manor house, set in 12 landscaped acres of glorious Hampshire countryside, this mellow, cream-coloured stone exterior is highlighted by tall, sparkling sash windows and heavy, dark oak front doors that open out onto an bright and airy galleried hall. All bedrooms are well furnished with every comfort, including 24-hour room service. You can dine leisurely on imaginative cuisine while enjoying views over manicured lawns, or if you're feeling more energetic there's a jogging route and hard tennis court within the grounds and new leisure centre with well-equipped gym and indoor pool. Southampton's shopping and night-life are in easy reach, as is cathedral city of Winchester. Perfect for weddings and conferences, there are extensive purpose-built conference and meeting facilities available.

HEREFORDSHIRE - HEREFORD

Castle House

CASTLE STREET, HEREFORD, HEREFORDSHIRE HR1 2NW
Tel: 0845 365 3225 **International:** +44 (0)1432 356321 **Fax:** 01432 365909
Web: www.johansens.com/castlehse **E-mail:** info@castlehse.co.uk

Our inspector loved: *The lovely terrace right on the moat. An ideal spot for a snack and a glass of wine.*

Price Guide:
single £120
double £175
suite £185–£220

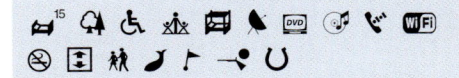

Awards/Recognition: 3 AA Rosettes 2008-2009

Location: Off the A438; A49, 0.8 miles; M4 jct 20, 43 miles

Attractions: Mappa Mundi & Chained Library at Hereford Cathedral; Ludlow; Hay on Wye; Cheltenham

Hard to believe this peaceful hotel is in the heart of a city and just 100m from Hereford cathedral. As soon as you step though the door of its immaculate Georgian façade you find yourself in a bright lobby area dominated by the grand staircase. You'll be warmly greeted and taken up to comfortable bedrooms which offer personal touches of fresh flowers, bowls of fruit and a decanter filled with a complimentary tipple. The Castle House Restaurant serves carefully presented English dishes with a European twist, such as fillet of Hereford beef with sweet potato dauphinoise, caramelised shallots and wild mushroom compote. The bar area is the place for those who prefer a lighter lunch or snacks. A beautifully landscaped garden runs down to the old castle moat and is a wonderful place to enjoy afternoon tea after a day exploring this historic area.

HERTFORDSHIRE - BISHOP'S STORTFORD

GREAT HALLINGBURY MANOR HOTEL

GREAT HALLINGBURY, BISHOP'S STORTFORD, HERTFORDSHIRE CM22 7TJ
Tel: 0845 365 4629 **International:** +44 (0)1279 506475 **Fax:** 01279 505523
Web: www.johansens.com/greathallingburymanor **E-mail:** info@greathallingburymanor.com

Our inspector loved: *The spacious bedrooms with huge walk-in showers.*

Price Guide:
single from £95
double £130-£220

Awards/Recognition: 3 AA Rosettes 2007–2008

Location: M11 J8, ½ mile; Bishop Stortford, 3-min drive; Stansted Airport, 5-min drive; Cambridge, 20-min drive

Attractions: Mountfitchet Castle; Audley End House; Cambridge; Constable Country

This Tudor-style manor house is nestled amidst 9 acres of landscaped gardens in the picturesque village of Great Hallingbury and has had a total refurbishment to transform it into a true 21st-century gem. The hotel is aiming to be totally carbon neutral: heating, air conditioning and hot water are all ground sourced, and there is dual plumbing with recycled filtered water. Currently, bio-diesel is used for electricity, however, a photovoltaic farm will soon be installed to create electricity. The spacious de luxe and superior bedrooms and suites all have high ceilings and offer attractive contemporary décor and scenic views of the surroundings. Not to be missed is a visit to Anton's Restaurant and Champagne Barn, where renowned chef Anton Edelmann creates culinary delights from home-grown produce. A real treat for parties of up to 10 is the Laurent Perrier "Chefs Table".

HERTFORDSHIRE - ST ALBANS

St Michael's Manor

ST MICHAEL'S VILLAGE, FISHPOOL STREET, ST ALBANS, HERTFORDSHIRE AL3 4RY
Tel: 0845 365 2359 **International:** +44 (0)1727 864444 **Fax:** 01727 848909
Web: www.johansens.com/stmichaelsmanor **E-mail:** reservations@stmichaelsmanor.com

Our inspector loved: *The elegant modern interpretation of traditional decor.*

Price Guide:
manor from £125
premier from £185
luxury from £250

Awards/Recognition: AA 2 Rosettes 2007-2008

Location: A5183, 1.5 miles; A405, 2 miles; M25, 4 miles; Luton Airport, 11.7 miles; London - St Pancras Station 20-mins train

Attractions: St Albans Roman Remains; St Albans Abbey; Hatfield House; London

Everyone loves a rare gem and this is certainly one of them! The hospitable Newling Ward family have owned and run St Michael's Manor for over 40 years, and in that time have created a place of peaceful elegant charm. Many of the bedrooms - some with four-poster beds, some sitting-room suites - overlook the picturesque grounds with wide sweeping lawns and beautiful lake. If you tip-toe quietly you'll see all manner of wildlife, or you can enjoy garden views from the conservatory dining room. Dinners are tantalisingly tasty, and if you're a vegetarian you'll be very happy with the excellent selection of dishes. The Roman remains of Verulamium and Verulam golf course - Home of the Ryder Cup - are within easy reach.

HERTFORDSHIRE - NEAR STANSTED (HATFIELD HEATH)

Down Hall Country House Hotel

HATFIELD HEATH, NEAR BISHOP'S STORTFORD, HERTFORDSHIRE CM22 7AS
Tel: 0845 365 3271 **International:** +44 (0)1279 731441 **Fax:** 01279 730416
Web: www.johansens.com/downhall **E-mail:** sales@downhall.co.uk

Our inspector loved: *The wonderful high ceilings and elegant proportions.*

Price Guide:
single from £74
double from £109
suite from £179

Awards/Recognition: 2 AA Rosettes 2007–2008

Location: M11 J7, 6 miles; M11 J8, 5 miles; Stansted Airport, 15-min drive

Attractions: Cambridge; Newmarket; Audley End House

Surrounded by a staggering 110 acres of woodland and gardens, Down Hall is just 30 minutes from central London and surprisingly close to Stansted Airport. This beautiful building's history dates back to the 13th century and today, proudly stands as a magnificent example of Italianate design featuring tall, narrow windows that bring in floods of natural daylight into the lofty, spacious interior. The décor is very much of the classic English country house style with beautiful drapes, sparkling chandeliers and elegant bedrooms accompanied by marble bathrooms. The hotel is commendably becoming carbon neutral, supporting local suppliers and growing its own fruit and vegetables, and also maintains a natural habitat pond area, a project supported by Essex Wildlife Trust. The great British pastime of afternoon tea by a roaring log fire can be enjoyed before experiencing the offerings of the fine dining restaurant or a more informal meal at the bistro-style Grill Room.

KENT - ASHFORD (BOUGHTON LEES)

EASTWELL MANOR

BOUGHTON LEES, NEAR ASHFORD, KENT TN25 4HR
Tel: 0845 365 3279 **International:** +44 (0)1233 213000 **Fax:** 01233 635530
Web: www.johansens.com/eastwellmanor **E-mail:** enquiries@Eastwellmanor.co.uk

Our inspector loved: *The gracious and comfortable interiors enhanced by wonderful flower arrangements.*

Price Guide:
single £110–£280
double/twin £140–£310
suites £270–£445

Awards/Recognition: 2 AA Rosettes 2007-2008

Location: A251, 0.5 miles; M20 jct 9, 2.5 miles; Ashford International Station, 4.5 miles; Gatwick Airport, 55 miles

Attractions: Canterbury Cathedral; Leeds Castle; Rye - Ancient Town, Port Lympne Wildlife Park

Come to the "Garden of England", and stay at historical Eastwell Manor, dating back to the 16th century when Richard Plantagenet, son of Richard III, lived on the estate. The impressive grounds are perfectly matched by rather splendid interiors, featuring exquisite plasterwork, carved oak panelling and antiques adorning public rooms. Some bedrooms and suites, have fine views across the gardens and meet all your creature comforts and there are 19 courtyard apartments giving 39 more bedrooms. Outside, is a formal Italian garden, scented rose gardens and attractive lawns and parkland, as well as the smart new health and fitness spa with indoor and outdoor pools, hydrotherapy pool, sauna, steam room, technogym and 15 treatment rooms. The new 9 hole golf course is proving very popular with guests.

LANCASHIRE - PRESTON (CHIPPING)

The Gibbon Bridge Hotel

NEAR CHIPPING, FOREST OF BOWLAND, LANCASHIRE PR3 2TQ
Tel: 0845 365 2501 **International:** +44 (0)1995 61456 **Fax:** 01995 61277
Web: www.johansens.com/gibbonbridge **E-mail:** reception@gibbon-bridge.co.uk

Our inspector loved: *Dining in the conservatory overlooking the award winning gardens and Longridge Fell.*

Price Guide:
single £90–£120
double/twin £130
suite £150–£250

Now officially recognised as the Centre of the Kingdom, this area, in the heart of Lancashire, is a favourite of the Queen, and where proprietor Janet Simpson and her late mother Margaret have created a welcoming, peaceful retreat. The buildings combine traditional architecture and interesting Gothic masonry, a theme that has been carried into the well-appointed bedrooms with their four-posters, half-testers and Gothic brass beds. Overlooking the garden, the restaurant is renowned for its imaginative dishes using home-grown vegetables and herbs, and alfresco dining can be enjoyed in one of the 3 Julian & Christian designed thatched pergolas perfect for an informal, unique experience. If you're seeking a venue for business meetings and conferences, the hotel can offer that "something a bit different", and the garden bandstand is perfect for musical repertoires or civil wedding ceremonies.

Location: Chipping, 1 mile; Longridge, 5 miles; M6 jct 31a, 7.5 miles; Preston, 12 miles

Attractions: Historic Market Towns and Villages; Clitheroe Castle; Pendle Witches Trail; Forest of Bowland - AONB

LEICESTERSHIRE - MELTON MOWBRAY

Stapleford Park Country House Hotel & Sporting Estate

STAPLEFORD, NEAR MELTON MOWBRAY, LEICESTERSHIRE LE14 2EF
Tel: 0845 365 2367 **International:** +44 (0)1572 787 000 **Fax:** 01572 787 001
Web: www.johansens.com/staplefordpark **E-mail:** reservations@stapleford.co.uk

Our inspector loved: *The total grandeur of the place - outside and in.*

Price Guide:
double/twin from £199
suites from £400

Awards/Recognition: 2 AA Rosettes 2008-2009

Location: B676, 1 mile; M1 jct 21a, 40-min drive; Melton Mowbray, 12-min drive; East Midlands Airport, 40-min drive

Attractions: Belvoir Castle; Rutland Water; Burghley House; Stamford

Following a multi million pound refurbishment, casual luxury is the byword at this 16th-century stately home and sporting estate. Once coveted by Edward, Prince of Wales, his mother Queen Victoria forbade him to buy it for fear that his morals would be corrupted by the Leicestershire hunting society! You can only live in hope, because today its "lifestyle experience" is more to do with superb comfort than potential corruption. Voted Top UK Hotel for Leisure Facilities by Condé Nast Traveller and with innumerable awards for style and hospitality, its bedrooms and 2 self-contained cottages have been created by famous names such as Mulberry, Wedgwood, Zoffany and Crabtree & Evelyn. The Dining Room offers British with European influenced menus carefully prepared to the highest standards and matched by an excellent wine list.

LINCOLNSHIRE - STAMFORD

The George Of Stamford

ST MARTINS, STAMFORD, LINCOLNSHIRE PE9 2LB
Tel: 0845 365 3295 **International:** +44 (0)1780 750750 **Fax:** 01780 750701
Web: www.johansens.com/georgeofstamford **E-mail:** reservations@georgehotelofstamford.com

Our inspector loved: *Everything about this excellent welcoming hotel.*

Price Guide:
single from £90
double from £130
suite from £175

Awards/Recognition: Condé Nast Johansens Taittinger Wine List Awards, Best Value Wine List, Hotels & Spas Category Winner and Overall Winner 2008; 1 AA Rosette 2006-2007

Location: A1, 1 mile; Peterborough, 10 miles; London 60 min train

Attractions: Burghley House; Rutland Water;

Historic Stamford was described by Walter Scott as the finest view between London and Edinburgh and as a well travelled man he was probably right. He was a frequent visitor to this engaging coaching Inn whose own history as a hostelry goes back some 900 years. Plenty of deep wood panelling and high wood beamed ceilings tell of an intriguing and fascinating past. Guest rooms retain traditional charms and are decorated with pretty floral fabrics and individual touches. The Restaurant serves a formidable menu using the best of local produce (complemented by an excellent wine cellar) whilst on warm nights you can enjoy the informal Garden Lounge. Afternoon tea is a delight and a very good idea after taking a long stroll around Burghley House just a short walk away.

LONDON - BUCKINGHAM PALACE

41

41 BUCKINGHAM PALACE ROAD, LONDON SW1W 0PS
Tel: 0845 365 3601 **International:** +44 (0)20 7300 0041 **Fax:** +44 (0)20 7300 0141
Web: www.johansens.com/41buckinghampalaceroad **E-mail:** book41@rchmail.com

Our inspector loved: *This hotel really sets the benchmark for service - everything is just for you!*

Price Guide:
king bedded from £345
junior suite from £495
master suite from £695

Location: Victoria station, 5-min walk; St Pancras/Eurostar, 3.6 miles; Heathrow Airport, 15 miles; Gatwick Airport, 23 miles; Stansted Airport, 37 miles

Attractions: Buckingham Palace; London Eye; Houses of Parliament; Hyde Park

Adjacent to St James's Park, overlooking the Royal Mews and Buckingham Palace, 41 offers guests a discreet and secluded retreat cosseted in magnificent architectural features, beautiful furniture and club-like qualities. Its the high standards of bespoke service that really make this property standout. There are no arbitrary rules about breakfast times, a turndown menu that fits around you and a trusting honesty bar. 30 bedrooms and suites, some split level are furnished with traditional mahogany and black leather decor which are exquisite and original. All feature an iPod docking station, movies, music and Wi-Fi broadband. Extremely comfortable, English mattresses have been handmade to order. You can enjoy round the clock informal personalised dining and from 8 o'clock each evening you are invited to 'Plunder the Pantry' - take your pick of complimentary snacks in the Executive Lounge. There are excellent local restaurants and several can be billed directly to your room.

LONDON - CHELSEA HARBOUR

The Wyndham Grand London Chelsea Harbour

CHELSEA HARBOUR, LONDON SW10 0XG
Tel: 0845 365 3786 **International:** +44 (0)20 7823 3000 **Fax:** 020 7352 8174
Web: www.johansens.com/wyndhamlondon **E-mail:** wyndhamlondon@wyndham.com

Our inspector loved: *The staggering views! The whole of London stretches before you as you look out from this wonderfully stylish hotel.*

Price Guide:
suite £190
penthouse from £2,500

Awards/Recognition: 1 AA Rosette 2007–2008

Location: London St Pancras, 7 miles; London Heathrow Airport, 14 miles

Attractions: Chelsea Harbour Design Centre; Harrods; Harvey Nichols; King's Road

A unique hotel for London, The Wyndham Grand is an impressive all suite property that sits proudly overlooking the boats moored in exclusive Chelsea Harbour, an area now considered to be the hub of the capitals interior design. The suites are spacious, immaculate and the detail reflects thoughtful consideration for the seasoned traveller. There is something incredibly relaxing about dining at the award-wining harbour-side Aquasia Bar & Restaurant that on warm days extends outside. You get a feeling that you are anywhere other than a city centre, yet a short ride in the river launch will take city travellers right to the centre of the docklands, whilst the more fashion conscious will enjoy the chauffeur service to the heart of Knightsbridge.

LONDON - EARLS COURT

The Mayflower Hotel

26-28 TREBOVIR ROAD, LONDON SW5 9NJ
Tel: 0845 365 2591 **International:** +44 (0)20 7370 0991 **Fax:** 020 7370 0994
Web: www.johansens.com/mayflower **E-mail:** info@mayflower-group.co.uk

Our inspector loved: *The new upstairs bedrooms are surprisingly spacious and are beautifully light and fresh!*

Price Guide:
double £120-£155
suite £130-£195

Awards/Recognition: 4 AA Rosettes 2007-2008

Location: Earl's Court Underground Station, 2-min walk; M4 jct1, 8 miles; Heathrow Airport, 14 miles; Waterloo International, 5 miles

Attractions: Buckingham Palace; Harrods; Victoria and Albert Museum; Hyde Park

A sleek fusion of Eastern influences in the centre of London, The Mayflower is perfect if you're travelling alone or on business. The guest rooms on the ground floor are small, yet stylish and rich in pale stone, vibrant fabrics and Indian and Oriental antiques. Johansens guests preferring more space however, should ask for one of the new first floor bedrooms - newly refurbished in light, fresh colours with sparkling glass lighting and mirrors. Stylish bathrooms sparkle with slate and chrome and have walk in showers. A continental buffet breakfast is served in the downstairs dining room, or when the weather is fine, in the new extended patio garden. You can grab a caffeine or vitamin C fix in the coffee and juice bar before heading out to Knightsbridge, Chelsea and surrounding attractions such as the Victoria & Albert, Natural History and Science Museums. The hotel is close to the Earl's Court Exhibition Centre.

LONDON - EARLS COURT

Twenty Nevern Square

20 NEVERN SQUARE, LONDON SW5 9PD
Tel: 0845 365 2769 **International:** +44 (0)20 7565 9555 **Fax:** 020 7565 9444
Web: www.johansens.com/twentynevernsquare **E-mail:** hotel@twentynevernsquare.co.uk

Our inspector loved: *The large new Ottoman Suite is stunning - and has french windows overlooking leafy Nevern Square.*

Price Guide:
double/twin £130–£165
suite £275

Awards/Recognition: 4 AA Rosettes 2007-2008

Location: Earl's Court Underground, 2-min walk; M4, 8 miles; Heathrow Airport, 14 miles; Gatwick Airport, 35 miles

Attractions: Victoria and Albert Museum; Natural History Museum; Harrods; Hyde Park

To say that a unique hospitality experience awaits you at this elegant 4-star townhouse hotel wouldn't be overselling it, as it's sumptuously restored, compact bedrooms emphasise natural materials, hand-carved beds and white marble. Choose the delicate silks of the Chinese Room or a touch of opulence in the Rococo Room, and if you want to spoil someone the grandeur and style of the new Ottoman Suite is a perfect treat! Breakfast is served in the light, bright Conservatory opening onto a decked balcony area, and gym facilities are available by arrangement. You're close to Earl's Court and Olympia Exhibition Centres, and a mere 10 minutes from some of London's finest shops, restaurants, theatres and attractions such as the V&A and Science Museums.

LONDON - KENSINGTON

Kensington House Hotel

15-16 PRINCE OF WALES TERRACE, KENSINGTON, LONDON W8 5PQ
Tel: 0845 365 1936 **International:** +44 (0)20 7937 2345 **Fax:** 020 7368 6700
Web: www.johansens.com/kensingtonhouse **E-mail:** reservations@kenhouse.com

Our inspector loved: *The atmosphere - it's just so friendly and relaxed here!*

Price Guide: (including continental breakfast)
single £155
double/twin £180-£200
junior suites £230

Location: High Street Kensington Underground, 0.3 miles; M4, 8 miles; Heathrow, 14 miles; Gatwick, 37 miles

Attractions: Kensington Palace; Harrods; Hyde Park; London Eye

This charming townhouse located just off Kensington High Street, looks out over delightful mews houses, leafy streets and City rooftops. The atmosphere is relaxed, service informal yet professional, and bright, airy bedrooms with tall, ornate windows and modern furnishings add freshness to classic design. You can slip between crisp linen sheets and snuggle up in cosy bathrobes, and for those travelling en famille, 2 junior suites convert into a family room. The Tiger Bar is a perfect venue for coffee and pre dinner drinks, where menus of traditional and modern dishes have a range of influences. The serenity of Kensington Gardens is just a gentle stroll away, while some of the capital's most fashionable shops, restaurants and cultural attractions are within walking distance.

LONDON - KENSINGTON

MILESTONE HOTEL

1 KENSINGTON COURT, LONDON W8 5DL
Tel: 0845 365 2594 **International:** +44 (0)20 7917 1000 **US toll free:** 1 877 955 1515 **Fax:**+44 (0)20 7917 1010
Web: www.johansens.com/milestone **E-mail:** bookms@rchmail.com

A beautifully appointed property located opposite Kensington Palace and Gardens and Hyde Park. The Milestone will give you an education in Victorian splendor as well as the utmost in comfort and service. Its apartments, bedrooms and suites, all with complimentary WiFi, are individually designed with antiques - some with private balconies. You can relax in the panelled Park Lounge or dine in Cheneston's restaurant, which bears the original spelling of Kensington. The Stables bar is perfect for evening drinks and the fitness centre, with it's resistance pool and spa treatments, is a great place to unwind. The Milestone is a short walk from Kensington and Knightsbridge, and a brief taxi ride to the London's West End. The Royal Albert Hall and all the museums in Exhibition Road are also just a stroll away.

Our inspector loved: The stunning new suites and the immaculate attention to detail in all areas.

Price Guide: (Room only, excluding VAT)
double £310-£490
suite £570-£910

Awards/Recognition: Voted no.1 British Hotel, Condé Nast Traveler Gold List World's Best Hotels 2008;2 AA Rosettes 2007-2008

Location: Kensington High Street, 5-min walk; Paddington Heathrow Express, 2.18 miles; Heathrow Airport, 13.6 miles; Gatwick Airport, 37 miles

Attractions: Kensington Palace and Gardens; Portabello Road; Harrods; Buckingham Palace

LONDON - KENSINGTON

THE PARKCITY HOTEL

18-30 LEXHAM GARDENS, KENSINGTON, LONDON W8 5JE
Tel: 0845 365 4031 **International:** +44 (0)20 7341 7091 **Fax:** 0870 7657 555
Web: www.johansens.com/theparkcity **E-mail:** reservations@theparkcity.com

Our inspector loved: *The Park City Hotel is one of Kensington's 'best kept secrets'. Located just off the Cromwell Road.*

Price Guide:
single from £200
double from £200
suite from £200

Location: Earls Court Underground, 5-min walk; Gloucester Road Underground, 5-min walk; Heathrow Airport, 12 miles; Gatwick Airport, 35 miles

Attractions: Earl's Court and Olympia Exhibition Halls; Shopping in Kensington and Knightsbridge; British Museum; Natural History Museum; Royal Albert Hall

The Parkcity is a great find for those wanting to be in the heart of Kensington with plenty of fast links across London. The 62 beautifully appointed rooms are styled in simple, modern schemes with an excellent finish. This hotel offers a high level of service and luxury with well thought out modern facilities. You will find a small gym, perfect for an early morning work out before enjoying breakfast in Lessandro's restaurant. Dine here for lunch or dinner and be impressed with the Classic Mediterranean cuisine inside or outside on the terrace. Pop in to Ruby's cocktail bar for pre-drinks and prepared to be impressed with the business facilities and meeting rooms for up to 50 people. Lessandro's is also available for private parties and functions, overlooking the hotel's private garden.

LONDON - KNIGHTSBRIDGE

BEAUFORT HOUSE

45 BEAUFORT GARDENS, KNIGHTSBRIDGE, LONDON SW3 1PN
Tel: 0845 365 3029 **International:** +44 (0)20 7584 2600 **US toll free:** US toll free: 1 800 23 5463 **Fax:** 020 7584 6532
Web: www.johansens.com/beauforthouseapartments **E-mail:** info@beauforthouse.co.uk

Our inspector loved: *What a great refurbishment! The location is just superb and now the apartments are as stunning as their surroundings!*

Price Guide: (per apartment excluding VAT)
£210–£810

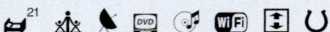

Location: Knightsbridge Underground, 3-min walk; Victoria Station, 2 miles; Heathrow, 14 miles; Gatwick, 28 miles

Attractions: Harrods; Hyde Park; Buckingham Palace; Victoria and Albert Museum

On a quiet and exclusive, tree-lined Regency cul-de-sac, are 21 self-contained luxury apartments, ranging in size from an intimate one Bedroom to a spacious four bedroom apartment. A major refurbishment of the property has resulted in light, fresh, modish interiors decorated in neutral tones that are complemented by stylish accents of colour. Kitchens are bright, crisp white spaces, most condusive to culinary creativity! Enjoy the privacy and comfortable atmosphere of your own home together with the benefits of a first-class hotel. All apartments have direct dial telephones with voice mail, safes, iPod connectors and Wireless Internet Access. Some benefit from balconies or patios. The apartments are serviced daily at no additional charge, and full laundry/dry cleaning services are available. The 24-hour Guests Services team are happy to organise your theatre tickets, restaurant bookings or chauffeur.

LONDON - KNIGHTSBRIDGE

The Capital Hotel & Restaurant

22 BASIL STREET, KNIGHTSBRIDGE, LONDON SW3 1AT
Tel: 0845 365 2413 **International:** +44 (0)20 7589 5171 **Fax:** 020 7225 0011
Web: www.johansens.com/capital **E-mail:** reservations@capitalhotel.co.uk

Our inspector loved: Exceptional, from the decor and antique furniture of this small and perfectly formed hotel right up to the mouthwatering two Michelin star restaurant with equally faultless service.

Price Guide:
single £175–£210
double/twin £215–£365
suite £390–£850

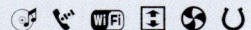

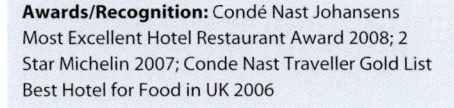

Awards/Recognition: Condé Nast Johansens Most Excellent Hotel Restaurant Award 2008; 2 Star Michelin 2007; Conde Nast Traveller Gold List Best Hotel for Food in UK 2006

Location: Knightsbridge Underground, 2-min walk; Victoria Station, 2 miles; Heathrow, 14 miles; Gatwick, 28 miles

Attractions: Harrods; Hyde Park; Buckingham Palace; Victoria and Albert Museum

Established in 1971 at its exclusive Knightsbridge address, The Capital remains the only hotel restaurant in London to hold 2 coveted Michelin Stars. Head Chef Eric Chavot's French inspired cuisine is acclaimed as 'faultlessly assured' by even the most discriminating critics. The London bakery owned by the Capital Group, supplies all the bread and pastries for the restaurant and a mouth-watering afternoon tea in the Sitting Room. The excellent wine list features wine from the Hotel's own vineyard in the Loire Valley in France. The 49 individually designed bedrooms are the height of luxury and comfort with their super king-sized beds, handmade mattresses, Egyptian cotton sheets and marble bathrooms. Three stunning event spaces, The Cadogan Suite, The Eaton Suite and The Sitting Room, are available for private dining.

LONDON - KNIGHTSBRIDGE

The Egerton House Hotel

17-19 EGERTON TERRACE, KNIGHTSBRIDGE, LONDON SW3 2BX
Tel: 0845 365 2483 **International:** +44 (0)20 7589 2412 **Fax:** +44 (0)20 7584 6540
Web: www.johansens.com/egertonhouse **E-mail:** bookeg@rchmail.com

Our inspector loved: *You would be hard-pressed to better a stay at the Egerton House - the location is simply stunning and nothing is too much trouble for the friendly and welcoming staff!*

Price Guide:
double/queen £255–£275
deluxe/suite £315–£495
garden suite £850

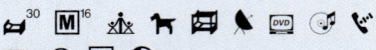

This quiet townhouse hotel's owners have restyled it to suit the 21st century without abandoning its Victorian roots. Rooms and suites are individually designed with an eclectic mix of Italian Rococo and contemporary furnishings. All offer 24 hour service. Original artworks and antiques complete the look, while sleek accessories include flat-screen TVs, WiFi and specially programmed Video iPods. Breakfast is served in the lower ground floor dining room, a stunning space full of glass and light with ivory leather banquette, and in the cosy, muted drawing room and bar you might feel like you've joined a discreet private club. For martini lovers, Head Barman, Antonio Pizzuto is renowned for serving the best in London. Set on a residential Knightsbridge street, you can walk a leafy 3-minutes to Harrods and venture further to all of central London's attractions.

Location: Knightsbridge Underground, 5-min walk; Victoria Station, 2 miles; Heathrow, 14 miles; Gatwick, 28 miles

Attractions: Harrods; Victoria and Albert Museum; Hyde Park; Buckingham Palace

LONDON - KNIGHTSBRIDGE

JUMEIRAH CARLTON TOWER

ON CADOGAN PLACE, LONDON SW1X 9PY
Tel: 0845 365 1932 **International:** +44 (0)20 7235 1234 **Fax:** +44 (0)20 7235 9129
Web: www.johansens.com/carltontower **E-mail:** JCTinfo@jumeirah.com

Our inspector loved: *This luxurious hotel in the heart of Knightsbridge, perfect for business and pleasure. Relax in the Spa after shopping or try the golf simulator and health club!*

Price Guide: (excluding VAT)
double from £239
suite from £349

Awards/Recognition: Condé Nast Traveller Gold List 2007 – Voted one of the best hotels in the world for service; Condé Nast Traveller (UK) Reader Awards 2008 – Voted "Top Ten UK Day Spa"; Condé Nast Johansens Most Excellent London Hotel Award 2006

Location: Knightsbridge Underground, 5-min walk; Heathrow, 15 miles; Gatwick, 30 miles

Attractions: Harrods; Harvey Nichols; Hyde Park; Buckingham Palace

Situated in fashionable Knightsbridge and only moments from the exclusive boutiques on Sloane Street, the Jumeirah Carlton Tower features 220 rooms, including 59 suites. With stunning views over London's skyline and the private gardens of Cadogan Place, the hotel offers three restaurants serving a wide range of mouth-watering cuisine, including the renowned Rib Room. Alternatively, you can visit the GILT Champagne Lounge for the ultimate in sophistication and glamour. Guests can enjoy the luxurious Peak Health Club & Spa, offering a fully equipped gymnasium, a state-of-the-art golf simulator, aerobics studio, sauna, steam room, and a 20 metre stainless steel heated indoor pool.

LONDON - KNIGHTSBRIDGE

Jumeirah Lowndes Hotel

21 LOWNDES STREET, KNIGHTSBRIDGE, LONDON SW1X 9ES
Tel: 0845 365 1934 **International:** +44 (0)20 7823 1234 **Fax:** 020 7235 1154
Web: www.johansens.com/lowndes **E-mail:** JLHinfo@jumeirah.com

Our inspector loved: *The ambience of the exquisite Mimosa Bar & Restaurant, sampling the speciality cocktails and dining on the terrace.*

Price Guide: (room only, excluding VAT)
double from £199
suite from £299

Location: Knightsbridge Underground, 5-min walk; Heathrow, 15 miles; Gatwick, 30 miles

Attractions: Harrods; Harvey Nichols; Hyde Park; Buckingham Palace

This chic, contemporary boutique hotel, overlooking leafy Lowndes Square in Belgravia, offers 87 sumptuous bedrooms, including 14 spacious suites on the dedicated all-suite 6th floor. All rooms feature marble bathrooms with luxurious Temple Spa toiletries and other amenities including plasma-screen TVs, internet access and iPod docks. Distinguished by its originality and style, the Mimosa Bar & Restaurant offers delectable modern European cuisine all day with al fresco dining on the terrace during the Summer months. Weekend brunch is also a top favourite at Mimosa. Guests have complimentary access to all facilities at nearby sister hotel, the Jumeirah Carlton Tower, including the renowned Peak Health Club & Spa.

LONDON - KNIGHTSBRIDGE

No.11 London

CADOGAN GARDENS, SLOANE SQUARE, KNIGHTSBRIDGE, LONDON SW3 2RJ
Tel: 0845 365 3926 **International:** +44 (0)20 7730 7000 **Fax:** 020 7730 5217
Web: www.johansens.com/numbereleven **E-mail:** info@number-eleven.co.uk

Our inspector loved: *The new style of No 11! It has to be one of the most exciting refurbishments!*

Price Guide: (excluding VAT)
single from £145
double/twin from £185
suite from £425

Location: Sloane Square Underground Station, 2-min walk; London Waterloo, 10-min train/metro; London King's Cross Eurotunnel, 20-min train/metro; A3, 5-min drive

Attractions: Sloane Square Shopping; Harrods; Buckingham Palace; London Eye

Coming out of an extensive renewal and restoration, this hotel fully lives up to its luxurious iconic status. Overlooking leafy gardens in an enviable corner of Knightsbridge, it is an idyllic preference for all of you wishing to stay in an impressive design-led property. Behind a classical Victorian façade, No 11 is very high-end and ultra contemporary with town house character that includes turning staircases, oil paintings, photographs and a tranquil courtyard garden. Furnishings are often theatrical and shout texture and colour. Schemes go from the dark and dramatic to the ice-blue accented conservatory and crisp white and cream dining room. Bedrooms are the height of comfortable elegance and all with great individual character. A haven for an end of day cocktail is the sophisticated No 11 Bar.

135

LONDON - MAYFAIR

The Mandeville Hotel

MANDEVILLE PLACE, LONDON W1U 2BE
Tel: 0845 365 2589 **International:** +44 (0)20 7935 5599 **Fax:** 020 7935 9588
Web: www.johansens.com/mandeville **E-mail:** info@mandeville.co.uk

Our inspector loved: *The home made ice cream in the exquisite deVille Restaurant in the heart of Marylebone Village.*

Price Guide: (Room only, excluding VAT)
single from £306
superior from £380
deluxe from £428

Awards/Recognition: 1 AA Rosette 2008–2009

Location: Bond Street Underground, 0.2 miles; Heathrow Airport, 15 miles; Victoria Station, 2 miles

Attractions: The Wallace Collection; Selfridges; Wigmore Hall; Bond Street

An exciting hotel with a generous helping of opulence and luxury enhanced with a very personalised service; nothing is too much trouble for their exemplary team. Style and sophistication runs throughout the hotel from the delicious penthouse suite with its indulgent bathroom to decadent features and lighting in the lobby. The bedrooms are exquisitely furnished with fabrics of striking textures and tones from some of the leading London design houses. The deVigne Bar at The Mandeville Hotel, is a beautifully sophisticated cocktail bar, great for meeting friends in the heart of London and now serving new organic cocktails as well as an extensive martini and mojito list. The perfect location, minutes from Oxford Street, Bond Street and Mayfair.

LONDON - MAYFAIR

Westbury Hotel

BOND STREET, MAYFAIR, LONDON W1S 2YF
Tel: 0845 365 4028 **International:** +44 (0)20 7629 7755 **Fax:** 020 7499 1270
Web: www.johansens.com/westburymayfair **E-mail:** enquiries@westburymayfair.com

Our inspector loved: *The location, decor and the eclectic luxurious design of the bedrooms, especially the rooftop patio overlooking Bond Street!*

Price Guide: (room only)
single £399
double £439
suite from £1099

Location: Oxford Street Underground, 5-min walk; St Pancras - Eurostar, 4 miles; Heathrow Airport, 18 miles; Gatwick Airport, 30 miles

Attractions: Perfect shopping in the heart of Mayfair; West End Theatre's; National Gallery; London Eye

The Westbury sits proudly in an enviable location just off Bond Street in the heart of London's fashionable Mayfair. The excellent personalized service reflects the staff's passion to ensure every guest has a memorable stay. Complete with expert concierge and extremely adept and mulit-lingual staff, this is the ideal choice for discerning guests from around the world. Bedrooms are luxuriously designed in warm tones and offer the utmost in comfort and style. Sample the mouth-watering delights from the simple yet inspired menu in the Artisan restaurant, offering delicious modern European cuisine. A great way to start the evening is in the sophisticated Polo Bar with its impressive cocktail list and bar menu. You can see why this is popular with guests and Londoners alike.

LONDON - NOTTING HILL

THE NEW LINDEN HOTEL

58 - 60 LEINSTER SQUARE, NOTTING HILL, LONDON W2 4PS
Tel: 0845 365 3915 **International:** +44 (0)20 7221 4321 **Fax:** 020 7727 3156
Web: www.johansens.com/newlindenhotel **E-mail:** newlindenhotel@mayflower-group.co.uk

Our inspector loved: The hotel's modern, stylish and unpretentious atmosphere within this lively area.

Price Guide:
double £120-£155
suite £130-£195

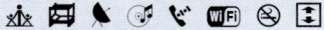

Location: Notting Hill / Bayswater Tube, 5-min walk; Paddington Station, 1 mile; London Heathrow, 15 miles

Attractions: Madame Tussauds; Whiteleys of Bayswater; Hyde Park; Kensington Palace Gardens

The New Linden Hotel is a little gem with instant appeal. This pretty, white town house is discovered in a peaceful residential street, within the heart of London's cosmopolitan Notting Hill, just a short walk from Portobello Market and within easy reach of tourist hot spots. The hotel's owners have transformed the building to suit the times without losing any of its Victorian charm. Once past the ornate entrance pillars you will find stylish bedrooms in colours of cream, brown, red and black, trendy minimal furnishings, high-tech entertainment units and stunning marble bathrooms. Not large, but with everything you could wish for. The lower ground breakfast room with its zebra wallpaper and limestone floor particularly impressed our inspector.

LONDON - PICCADILLY

Sofitel London St James

6 WATERLOO PLACE, LONDON SW1Y 4AN
Tel: 0845 365 2351 **International:** +44 (0)20 7747 2200 **Fax:** +44 (0) 20 7747 2210
Web: www.johansens.com/stjames **E-mail:** H3144@accor.com

Our inspector loved: *The sophistication of the St James Bar is perfect for meeting friends or colleagues before dining in the stunning Brasserie Roux.*

Price Guide: (room only, excluding VAT)
single from £275
double from £320
suite £430-£1,200

Awards/Recognition: Condé Nast Johansens Most Excellent London Hotel Award 2008

Location: Piccadilly underground, 5-min walk; St Pancras - Eurostar, 5 miles; Heathrow, 16 miles; Gatwick, 28 miles

Attractions: Trafalgar Square; Buckingham Palace; London Eye; National Gallery

Standing proudly and perfectly placed, on the corner of Waterloo Place and Pall Mall, this is the former home of Cox's and King's bank whose original artwork is still on display and is now cleverly balanced with more recent contemporary interiors. The well appointed bedrooms and suites continue in this vain with a generous sprinkling of state-of-the-art technology. This is a hotel that wants you to feel at home and depending on the time of day or your mood there are plenty of corners to retreat to. The handsome St James bar for a cocktail or post dinner cognac, the Rose lounge with its large sofas and vivid prints tempting you to afternoon tea and the stylish Brasserie Roux overseen by renowned chef Albert Roux is open throughout the day.

LONDON - WESTMINSTER

51 BUCKINGHAM GATE, TAJ SUITES AND RESIDENCES

51 BUCKINGHAM GATE, WESTMINSTER, LONDON SW1E 6AF
Tel: 0845 365 2653 **International:** +44 (0)20 7769 7766 **Fax:** 020 7828 5909
Web: www.johansens.com/buckinghamgate **E-mail:** info@51-buckinghamgate.co.uk

Our inspector loved: *Going for dinner at Quilon and letting the chef choose what to eat, simply divine after the Anne Semonin treatment in the Spa at 51!*

Price Guide:
suites £385–£975
prime ministers suite p.o.a

This is an exquisite Victorian town house in the heart of Westminster minutes from Buckingham Palace, complete with an award-winning, magical courtyard garden. The contemporary design combines subtle, state of the-art-technology with impeccable service. The rooms are equally impressive and range from junior to the impressive Prime Minister's Suite. You can indulge in the Spa at 51 exclusively offering Anne Semonin treatments or use the many other wonderful amenities including the gymnasium, saunas and steam rooms. The room service is 24 hour and nothing is too much trouble for the highly trained staff. Try the mouth watering Michelin Star rated, Quilon Restaurant and Bar for a unique and delicious dining experience. Be brave and let the chef choose for you.

Awards/Recognition: 5 AA Rosettes 2006-2007; 1 Star Michelin 2008

Location: Victoria station, 10-min walk; St Pancras, Eurostar, 5 miles; Heathrow Airport, 16 miles; Gatwick Airport, 28 miles

Attractions: Houses of Parliment; Buckingham Palace; St James Park; London Eye

NORFOLK - BURNHAM MARKET

The Hoste Arms

THE GREEN, BURNHAM MARKET, KING'S LYNN, NORFOLK PE31 8HD
Tel: 0845 365 2536 **International:** +44 (0)1328 738777 **Fax:** 01328 730103
Web: www.johansens.com/hostearms **E-mail:** reception@hostearms.co.uk

Our inspector loved: *The pure comfort, hospitality and 'buzz'!*

Price Guide:
single from £95
double from £125
suite from £166

Awards/Recognition: 2 AA Rosettes 2008-2009

Location: On the B1155; King's Lynn, 24 miles; Cromer, 27.5 miles; Norwich, 32 miles

Attractions: Holkham Hall; Houghton Hall; Sandringham; North Norfolk Coast

This 17th-century coaching inn, situated on the green, is very much the hub of the pretty village of Burnham Market. Its relaxed and welcoming atmosphere is hard to beat with its put-your-feet-up-by-the-fire front bar and 36 beautifully styled bedrooms and suites, located in the main building and the Zulu wing. Owner Paul Whittome, prides himself on providing his guests with the highest standards of service and dining, be it for afternoon tea, a light lunch in the conservatory or dinner. The Hoste chefs create exciting modern dishes using fresh local produce, taking advantage of the seafood sourced along the North Norfolk coast. Wonderfully located, this is the perfect base from which to enjoy stunning beaches and wild salt marshes; an area of outstanding natural beauty.

NORFOLK - KING'S LYNN (GRIMSTON)

Congham Hall

GRIMSTON, KING'S LYNN, NORFOLK PE32 1AH
Tel: 0845 365 3244 **International:** +44 (0)1485 600250 **Fax:** 01485 601191
Web: www.johansens.com/conghamhall **E-mail:** info@conghamhallhotel.co.uk

Our inspector loved: *Dining in the Orangery restaurant over-looking peaceful parkland watched only by grazing horses.*

Price Guide:
single from £110
double/twin from £195
suite from £335

Awards/Recognition: 2 AA Rosettes 2008–2009

Location: A148, 2 miles; M11, 55 miles; King's Lynn, 6 miles; Norwich, 38 miles

Attractions: Fakenham Racecourse; Sandringham; Houghton Hall; Holkham Hall

This handsome cream-coloured Georgian country house epitomises the best of country living. Classic interiors, fresh flowers, homemade pot-pourri and roaring log fires blend in to a welcome, warm atmosphere. The hotel's famous herb garden grows over 700 varieties of herbs, many of which are used by the chef's in preparing the modern English dishes using locally sourced seasonal produce from Norfolk markets. Take in panoramic views of the Norfolk countryside from the terrace adjoining the Orangery restaurant, or find a cosy corner to enjoy an English cream tea in the delightful drawing room. The 14 rooms are individually decorated with floral prints and views overlooking the walled garden or mown lawns and parkland. This is the ideal base for a tour of the spectacular north Norfolk coastline with its' sandy beaches and teeming wildlife. A von Essen hotel.

NORTHAMPTONSHIRE - KETTERING (RUSHTON)

Rushton Hall Hotel & Spa

RUSHTON, NEAR KETTERING, NORTHAMPTONSHIRE NN14 1RR
Tel: 0845 365 2316 **International:** +44 (0)1536 713001 **Fax:** 01536 713010
Web: www.johansens.com/rushtonhall **E-mail:** enquiries@rushtonhall.com

Our inspector loved: The so relaxing spa and stunning pool.

Price Guide:
superior from £150
state room from £170
four poster from £260

Awards/Recognition: 2 AA Rosettes 2008-2009

Location: A6003, 3 miles; M1 jct 19, 20 miles; Kettering, 5 miles; Birmingham International, 48 miles

Attractions: The Triangular Lodge; Rockingham Castle; Althorp; Rockingham Motor Racing Circuit

It is an exciting feeling to pass through the imposing iron gates, up the sweeping drive and catch sight of this stunning, 4 Star, Grade I listed hall. An elegant hotel with high levels of service. Beautiful linen fold panelling and original 16th-century floors are adorned by stylish, comfortable furnishings and rich drapes. There is the spectacular great hall with vaulted ceiling, an intimate library and a most charming drawing room. Bedrooms include four-posters and spacious state rooms which delight with a mix of sumptuous furnishings, antiques and eccentricities. Led by Adrian Coulthard the Brasserie and Restaurant serve imaginative seasonal menus. The tempting smells from the kitchen include the daily baking of breads, cakes and pastries. The Stableyard Spa opened its doors in 2008 and includes a level deck swimming pool, an integral spa pool, a sauna and if you like the idea of getting back to nature you can relax in the outdoor spa pool.

NORTHAMPTONSHIRE - NORTHAMPTON (SILVERSTONE)

WHITTLEBURY HALL

WHITTLEBURY, NEAR TOWCESTER, NORTHAMPTONSHIRE NN12 8QH
Tel: 0845 365 2804 **International:** +44 (0)1327 857857 **Fax:** 01327 858987
Web: www.johansens.com/whittleburyhall **E-mail:** sales@whittleburyhall.co.uk

Our inspector loved: *The dual aspect Emperor Suite and its sweeping views over the golf course.*

Price Guide:
single £150
double/twin £175
suite £290

Awards/Recognition: 2 AA Rosettes 2007-2008

Location: A143, 1 miles; A5, 2 miles; M1 jct 15, 11 miles; Towcester, 4 miles

Attractions: Silverstone Motor Racing Circuit; Towcester Racecourse; Oxford; Althorp

Few hotels could boast about such a good location close to both the M1 and M40 but perhaps more impressive for some is the direct pedestrian access to international Silverstone Racing Circuit . Whittlebury Hall is a modern hotel in Georgian style and understands personalised and flexible service for both those visiting for a much needed break or on business. Inside rich furnishings and fabrics create a truly impressive hotel and the ambience is relaxed with staff offering a warm, genuine, welcoming yet unobtrusive service. The dedicated Management Training Centre will offer all you need for a successful meeting or conference. From small intimate gatherings to grand affairs, Private Dining and Banqueting under the profession eye of a dedicated team will leave you to enjoy your celebration.

NOTTINGHAMSHIRE - NOTTINGHAM

Hart's Hotel

STANDARD HILL, PARK ROW, NOTTINGHAM, NOTTINGHAMSHIRE NG1 6GN
Tel: 0845 365 3826 **International:** +44 (0)115 988 1900 **Fax:** 0115 947 7600
Web: www.johansens.com/hartsnottingham **E-mail:** reception@hartsnottingham.co.uk

Our inspector loved: *Enjoying a quiet breakfast outside one of the Garden rooms with their amazing views over the city.*

Price Guide:
single £120
double £120–£140
garden £170
suite £260

Awards/Recognition: 2 AA Rosettes 2007-2008

Location: A52, 1 mile; M1 jct 25, 10-min drive; Nottingham, 5-min walk; Nottingham East Midlands Airport, 13 miles

Attractions: Nottingham Castle; Lace Market; Sherwood Forest; Nottingham Ice Centre

Built in 2002 on the former ramparts of Nottingham's medieval castle, Harts Hotel is a quiet haven with a secluded garden offering glorious views over the city. It's just five minutes to Nottingham's bustling central market square. Tim Hart, who also owns the eminent Hambleton Hall in Rutland, has created a sophisticated, comfortable and affordable environment with light and airy bedrooms, chic décor and the best of 21st-century facilities. The elegant Park Bar is a great spot to enjoy breakfast, tea or a light snack, whilst dinner is served in the colourful setting of Hart's Restaurant in its own building just 20m away. Head Chef, Gareth Ward creates modern British cuisine that plays on the seasons and also oversees the catering of the impressive private room aptly named Hart's Upstairs.

NOTTINGHAMSHIRE - NOTTINGHAM

LACE MARKET HOTEL

29-31, HIGH PAVEMENT, THE LACE MARKET, NOTTINGHAM, NOTTINGHAMSHIRE NG1 1HE
Tel: 0845 365 1973 **International:** +44 (0)115 852 3232 **Fax:** 0115 852 3223
Web: www.johansens.com/lacemarkethotel **E-mail:** stay@lacemarkethotel.co.uk

Our inspector loved: The impeccable standard of housekeeping.

Price Guide:
single £99-£129
standard double £129-£159
king double £149-£179
superior £209-£239
suite £249-£279

Just yards from Nottingham's most fashionable shops and the National Arena, this privately-owned town house hotel has a loyal following from music industry and A-list celebrities and you'll see why. Join them in their appreciation of its luxurious accommodation, gastro-pub, upmarket brasserie and chic cocktail bar - all under one roof! Bedrooms are individually designed with unique artwork, and superior rooms and studios have eye-catching views from bed and bath. Recently licensed for weddings, the hotel is perfect for an intimate ceremony with loved ones and there are four venue rooms to choose from. Newlyweds can also use the beautiful grounds of St. Mary's Church next door for photographs. You can obtain complimentary access to the nearby Virgin Active Health Club, complete with indoor pool, full gym facilities and fitness classes.

Awards/Recognition: Condé Nast Johansens Most Excellent City Hotel 2007

Location: City Centre; M1 jct 26, 5 miles; Nottingham East Midlands Airport, 15 miles

Attractions: Nottingham Castle; Theatre Royal; National Ice Centre

NOTTINGHAMSHIRE - RETFORD

Ye Olde Bell Hotel & Restaurant

BARNBY MOOR, RETFORD, NOTTINGHAMSHIRE DN22 8QS
Tel: 0845 365 3457 **International:** +44 (0)1777 705121 **Fax:** 01777 860424
Web: www.johansens.com/yeoldebell **E-mail:** enquiries@yeoldebell-hotel.co.uk

Our inspector loved: *The impeccable taste shown in the choice of furniture and furnishings epitomised by the Bowness Suite.*

Price Guide:
single from £90
double from £125
suite from £225

Awards/Recognition: 1 AA Rosette 2006-2007

Location: On A638; M1 jct 30, 18 miles; Retford, 3 miles; Robin Hood Airport, 11 miles

Attractions: Sherwood Forest; Historic City of Lincoln; Chatsworth House; Doncaster Racecourse

This cosy family-run hotel, formerly a 16th century farm and one of England's oldest coaching inns, is brimming with quality, character and a history of hospitality. The distinguished visitors book with names including Charlie Chaplin, Oliver Reed and, more recently, Louis Theroux, illustrates the many people who have been charmed by this hotel's warm and welcoming atmosphere. All the bedrooms have undergone a sympathetic re-design and refurbishment and have been completed in a fresh, classic style introducing warm and neutral colours. Inside, a homely feeling is created in the lounge with open fires. The 'St Leger Bar' is great for a light snack whilst the pretty wood panelled "Restaurant 1650" is ideal for intimate meals or can be taken over for receptions and civil ceremonies. Lovely gardens can be used for weddings and events.

OXFORDSHIRE - OXFORD

Old Bank Hotel

92/94 HIGH STREET, OXFORD, OXFORDSHIRE OX1 4BN
Tel: 0845 365 4608 **International:** +44 (0)1865 799599 **Fax:** 01865 799598
Web: www.johansens.com/oldbankhotel **E-mail:** info@oldbank-hotel.co.uk

Our inspector loved: *The sophistication and buzz of this contemporary hotel in the heart of Oxford.*

Price Guide: (room only, complimentary car parking is available)
single from £170
double from £185
suite from £220

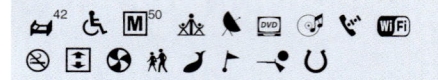

Location: Oxford City Centre; A34, 5 miles; M40, 8 miles; Heathrow Airport, 60 miles

Attractions: Oxford Colleges; Ashmoleum/Pitt Rivers Museum; Cotswold Villages; Blenheim Palace

This fantastic Georgian building, formerly a bank, has gained renown as one of the most exciting places to stay in Oxford city. Modern, comfortable and sophisticated, the atmosphere is lively and informal. This is especially evident in the Quod Brasserie where an all-day collection of Mediterranean influenced cuisine is served. Guest rooms combine style and comfort with sumptuous beds fitted with rich throws and cushions, and suites have beautifully upholstered window seats that line the original leaded light windows allowing you to admire views of the city spires. Art lovers will delight in the owner's collection of 20th-century paintings carefully acquired over the last 35 years. Some of which is on display in the meeting rooms that are perfect for hosting interviews, private dinners, conferences and social events alike. Venture out and explore the city on one of the hotel's complimentary bicycles or use the hotel punt for free and spend an afternoon on the river.

OXFORDSHIRE - OXFORD

The Old Parsonage Hotel

1 BANBURY ROAD, OXFORD, OXFORDSHIRE OX2 6NN
Tel: 0845 365 4607 **International:** +44 (0)1865 310210 **Fax:** 01865 311262
Web: www.johansens.com/oldparsonage **E-mail:** info@oldparsonage-hotel.co.uk

Our inspector loved: *Stepping back in time into this cosy yet stylish hotel that offers just the right touch of contemporary glamour.*

Price Guide: (room only)
double/twin £170–£185
deluxe double/twin £210–£225
junior suite £235–£250

Location: A34, 4 miles; M40, 7 miles; Oxford City Centre, 0.5 mile; Heathrow Airport, 59 miles

Attractions: Ashmoleum and Pitt Rivers Museum; Oxford Colleges; Blenheim Palace; Cotswolds

Walk through the heavy oak door and you will instantly be amazed by the sense of history here. A beautiful wisteria-clad hotel dating back to the 17th century, it has numerous quirky passageways and low ceilings throughout. Its intimate, romantic atmosphere is enhanced by the refreshingly chic and fashionable décor that is not only modern but also warm and welcoming. Bedrooms feature neutral colours with touches of bold accents, and are filled with hand-made beds and intriguing pieces of art. Enjoy drinks in the main bar with its Russian red walls covered in original cartoons and portraits or privately dine or attend a meeting in The Pike Room. There are fantastic jazz evenings every Friday that are held within the famous walled terrace during the summer. Explore the surrounding area on a complimentary hotel bike or take to the river on the hotel's very own punt, which is also free to guests. No fee is charged to guests visiting the nearby Esporta Health & Racquets Club.

OXFORDSHIRE - OXFORD (GREAT MILTON)

Le Manoir Aux Quat' Saisons

GREAT MILTON, OXFORDSHIRE OX44 7PD
Tel: 0845 365 2014 **International:** +44 (0)1844 278881 **Fax:** 01844 278847
Web: www.johansens.com/lemanoirauxquatsaisons **E-mail:** lemanoir@blanc.co.uk

Our inspector loved: *The anticipation of a wonderful experience at Le Manoir which never disappoints.*

Price Guide: (including French breakfast)
double/twin £395–£590
suites £600–£1200

Awards/Recognition: Condé Nast Johansens Taittinger Wine List Award, Innovation 2008; 2 Star Michelin 2008; 5 AA Rosettes 2007-2008; Relais & Châteaux

Location: A329, 0.20 miles; M40 J7/8a, 2 miles; Oxford, 8 miles; Heathrow Airport, 40 miles

Attractions: Oxford; Blenheim Palace; Cotswolds; Henley

This beautiful 15th-century, golden stone house is the culmination of Chef Patron, Raymond Blanc's vision to create a hotel and restaurant where guests find perfection in food, comfort and service, and it's the only country house to have retained 2 Michelin Stars for 25 years. Set in 7 acres of stunning grounds, with its own organic herb and vegetable gardens, there are 32 beautifully designed suites and bedrooms. If you're really passionate about food, why not enjoy a course at The Raymond Blanc Cookery School, which in summer runs a series of Junior Chef days to inspire young talent. An array of fabulous experiences and organised breaks can be enjoyed here, whether you consider yourself a gourmand, hopeless romantic or garden lover. Chocolate tastings, organic wine tastings and a music festival are amongst the events to enjoy. Corporate and private dining can also be arranged and the entire property is available for exclusive use.

OXFORDSHIRE - WALLINGFORD (NORTH STOKE)

THE SPRINGS HOTEL & GOLF CLUB

NORTH STOKE, WALLINGFORD, OXFORDSHIRE OX10 6BE
Tel: 0845 365 2697 **International:** +44 (0)1491 836687 **Fax:** 01491 836877
Web: www.johansens.com/springshotel **E-mail:** info@thespringshotel.com

Our inspector loved: *The traditional and welcoming atmosphere not to mention glorious grounds and golf course.*

Price Guide:
single from £95
double/twin from £110
suite from £155

Awards/Recognition: 1 AA Rosette 2007-2008

Location: A4074, 0.1 miles; M40, 15 miles; Wallingford, 2 miles; Heathrow, 40 miles

Attractions: Oxford; Blenheim Palace; Henley; Basildon Park (NT)

Dating from 1874 this very early English Mock Tudor style house is set in 6 acres within the heart of the Thames Valley. Large south-facing windows overlook a spring-fed lake, from which the hotel takes its name. Many of the bedrooms and suites share this lake view; others overlook the quiet woodland that surrounds the hotel and those with private balconies have patios. The subject of recent refurbishment, each bedroom is in a contemporary-style decorated in neutral tones with dark chocolate and cappuccino accents. Public areas and meeting rooms are also benefiting from an ongoing refreshing "facelift" whilst retaining their traditional features. The Lakeside Restaurant's menu offers fresh local produce and a great cellar filled with fine international wines. Leisure facilities include an 18-hole par 72 golf course, clubhouse and putting green, outdoor pool, sauna and bicycles. Enjoy these facilities for business or pleasure or even participate in a themed weekend.

RUTLAND - OAKHAM

Hambleton Hall

HAMBLETON, OAKHAM, RUTLAND LE15 8TH
Tel: 0845 365 1809 **International:** +44 (0)1572 756991 **Fax:** 01572 724721
Web: www.johansens.com/hambletonhall **E-mail:** hotel@hambletonhall.com

Our inspector loved: *The dual aspect Fern room - if you tire of the fantastic views of the gardens and Rutland Water you can always lie in the bath to watch TV!*

Price Guide:
single from £175
double/twin £205–£375
suite £500–£600

Awards/Recognition: 1 Star Michelin 2008; Relais & Châteaux; 4 AA Rosettes 2008-2009

Location: A606, 2 miles; Oakham, 2 miles; A1(M), 10 miles; East Midlands International Airport, 40 miles

Attractions: Rutland Water; Burghley House; Rockingham Castle; Barnsdale Gardens

Originally a Victorian mansion, Hambleton Hall celebrated its 25th year as a hotel in 2005, and continues to attract acclaim for achieving near perfection. Artful blends of flowers from local hedgerows and London flower markets add splashes of colour to the bedrooms. The Croquet Pavilion a 2 bedroom suite with living and breakfast rooms is a luxurious additional option. In the Michelin-starred restaurant, chef Aaron Patterson and his team offer strongly seasonal menus - Grouse, Scottish ceps, chanterelles, partridge and woodcock all appear when they're supposed to, accompanied by vegetables, herbs and salads from the Hall's garden. If you're feeling energetic you can embark on walks around the lake and there are opportunities for tennis, swimming, golf, cycling and sailing, otherwise you can browse for hidden treasures in Oakham's antique shops.

SOMERSET - BATH (STON EASTON)

STON EASTON PARK

STON EASTON, BATH, SOMERSET BA3 4DF
Tel: 0845 365 2376 **International:** +44 (0)1761 241631 **Fax:** 01761 241377
Web: www.johansens.com/stoneastonpark **E-mail:** info@stoneaston.co.uk

Our inspector loved: *The feeling of staying in a fine country mansion in a bygone era, with every modern comfort.*

Price Guide:
single from £220
double/twin £250–£400
suite £410–£550

Awards/Recognition: 2 AA Rosettes 2008-2009

Location: just off A37 miles; Bath, 14 miles; Brsitol Airport 19 miles

Attractions: Thermae Bath Spa; Wells Cathedral; Glastonbury Tor and Abbey; Cheddar Gorge and caves

Recently refurbished yet retaining the superb Palladian details this is one of the West Country's most romantic estates. Log fires burn, comfortable antique furniture and exquisite paintings beckon, evoking memories of a more leisured age and providing a welcome you might associate with a magnificent private country house. The Library and the magnificent State Rooms are exceptional and will impress even the untrained eye though it is the warm and unobtrusive service that really makes you feel at home. Herbs and vegetables are grown in the Victorian kitchen garden and are present in creating the English inspired dishes. If you are really in need of peaceful solitude then book a private suite in the 17th-century Gardener's Cottage, on the wooden banks of the River Norr. A von Essen hotel.

SOMERSET - SHEPTON MALLET

Charlton House Hotel & The Sharpham Park Restaurant

CHARLTON ROAD, SHEPTON MALLET, SOMERSET BA4 4PR
Tel: 0845 365 2876 **International:** +44 (0)1749 342008 **Fax:** 01749 346362
Web: www.johansens.com/charltonhouse **E-mail:** enquiry@charltonhouse.com

Our inspector loved: *The very attentive service and the irresistible spa treatments.*

Price Guide:
single from £140
double £180-£375
suite £465-£565

An early 17th century country house that combines the grandeur of a country retreat with inviting homeliness. The owners, Roger and Monty Saul, know a thing or two about creativity having founded Mulberry Design Company. Every where you look there are luxurious fabrics, eclectic touches and a sense of the elegant yet informal. Several bedrooms feature grand bathrooms, striking four-poster beds and working fireplaces; others offer a particularly intimate atmosphere with private gardens. The Sharpham Park Restaurant uses organic ingredients from its own farm; organic spelt, White Park Beef and Vension. For a bit of heavenly nurturing Monty's spa makes its own products freshly by hand, with ingredients chosen for their purity and therapeutic values.

Awards/Recognition: 2 AA Rosettes 2007-2008

Location: Off the A361; A303, 28 miles

Attractions: Bath; Longleat House; Stourhead; Wells Cathedral

SOMERSET - TAUNTON

The Castle at Taunton

CASTLE GREEN, TAUNTON, SOMERSET, TA1 1NF
Tel: 0845 365 2415 **International:** +44 (0)1823 272671 **Fax:** 01823 336066
Web: www.johansens.com/castleattaunton **E-mail:** Reservations@the-castle-hotel.com

Our inspector loved: *The eclectic mix of the traditional and modern decor and the wonderful cuisine.*

Price Guide:
single from £140
double from £230
garden rooms from £335

Awards/Recognition: 1 Star Michelin 2007; 3 AA Rosettes 2006-2007

Location: Town Centre; M5 jct 25, 3 miles

Attractions: Exmoor; Somerset Levels; Wells Cathedral; Hestercombe Gardens

In the heart of the West Country, The Castle at Taunton has been welcoming travellers to explore the region's plethora of attractions since the 12th century. Run by the Chapman family for over 60 years, this former Norman fortress serves as a convivial gateway to the land of King Arthur and features 44 bedrooms, all of which are individually appointed. Gastronomes will be delighted with the award-winning restaurant whose Head Chef Richard Guest has won a Michelin star. Ambitious dishes include Brixham crab cakes with marinated cauliflower, red mullet minestrone and a celebration of British beef comprising steamed oxtail pudding, roast fillet of South Devon beef and ox tongue sauce. Alternatively, there is the more informal BRAZZ, The Castle's contemporary brasserie, where delicious food created from fresh local produce is served. Conference planners should note that meetings for up to 100 delegates can be accommodated.

SOMERSET - TAUNTON (LOWER HENLADE)

Mount Somerset Country House Hotel

LOWER HENLADE, TAUNTON, SOMERSET TA3 5NB
Tel: 0845 365 2076 **International:** +44 (0)1823 442500 **Fax:** 01823 442900
Web: www.johansens.com/mountsomerset **E-mail:** info@mountsomersethotel.co.uk

Our inspector loved: *The grand entrance to this fine country house; the welcoming staff and grand yet comfortable surroundings.*

Price Guide:
single from £130
double/twin from £155
suite from £230

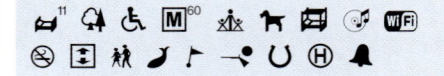

Awards/Recognition: 2 AA Rosettes 2007-2008; Condé Nast Johansens Most Excellent Country Hotel 2006

Location: A358, 1 mile; M5 jct 25, 3 miles; Taunton, 6 miles

Attractions: Glastonbury; Wells Cathedral; Exmoor; Various National Trust Properties

This elegant Regency residence sits high on the slopes of the Blackdown Hills, overlooking miles of lovely countryside. The hotel is rich in intricate craftsmanship and displays fine original features. The team have committed themselves to creating an atmosphere where you can relax, confident that your needs are taken care of. The bedrooms are very comfortable and many offer views across the Quantock Hills, all have luxurious bathrooms some with spa baths. Light lunches, teas, coffees and home-made cakes draw you into the beautifully furnished drawing room. The restaurant offers excellent menus and fine wines supported by a team of chefs working together to create dishes that will exceed your expectations. Nearby places of interest include Glastonbury Abbey and Wells Cathedral. Enjoy special breaks throughout the year. A von Essen hotel.

STAFFORDSHIRE - LICHFIELD (HOAR CROSS)

Hoar Cross Hall Spa Resort

HOAR CROSS, NEAR YOXALL, STAFFORDSHIRE DE13 8QS
Tel: 0845 365 1864 **International:** +44 (0)1283 575671 **Fax:** 01283 575652
Web: www.johansens.com/hoarcrosshall **E-mail:** info@hoarcross.co.uk

Our inspector loved: *This excellent fully inclusive spa resort with all its facilities and treatments.*

Price Guide: (fully inclusive of spa treatment, breakfast, lunch and dinner)
single £175-£195
double/twin £320-£370
single/double/twin suite £230–£494

Location: A515, 2 miles; A50, 8 miles; Lichfield, 8 miles; M6 jct 12 or 15, 22 miles

Attractions: In the heart of The National Forest; Historic Lichfield

The only stately home spa resort in England and winner of England's Leading Resort at the World Travel Awards 2005, 2006 & 2007. Surrounded by 100 acres of beautiful landscaped grounds. Oak panelling, tapestries, rich furnishings and paintings adorn the interior. A Jacobean staircase leads up to the bedrooms, all with crown tester or four-poster beds. Penthouses have private saunas and balconies overlooking the treetops. Gilded ceilings and William Morris wallpaper in the ballroom set the scene for the dining room, where a superb à la carte menu is offered. Trained professionals are ready to assist with yoga, meditation, tai chi, pilates, dance classes and aqua-aerobics. The spa features salt water and hydrotherapy swimming pools, baths, flotation therapy, saunas, a 4000 sq ft gymnasium, steam rooms, water grottos, saunariums, aromatherapy room, aerobics and yoga suites. A PGA golf academy is also available.

SUFFOLK - BURY ST. EDMUNDS (THE ICKWORTH ESTATE)
The Dower House Apartments & Aquae Sulis Retreat

HORRINGER, BURY ST. EDMUNDS, SUFFOLK IP29 5QE
Tel: 0845 365 4037 **International:** +44 (0)1284 735350 **Fax:** 01284 736300
Web: www.johansens.com/dowerhousebury **E-mail:** info@ickworthhotel.co.uk

Our inspector loved: *The beautiful parkland setting and the combination of privacy and hotel facilities.*

Price Guide:
1-bed apartment £165-£365
2-bed apartment £365-£570
interconnecting £480–£700

The Dower House shares 1800 acres of National Trust parkland on the Ickworth Estate in Suffolk with its sister property The Ickworth Hotel. Here you experience a relaxed atmosphere, privacy and flexibility over your own time combined with all the facilities of a country house hotel. Each of the 11 apartments (one and two bedrooms) is individually styled creating a unique feeling of comfort and space. Nearly all have a specially designed dresser base with small dishwasher, fridge and convection/microwave oven. No need to eat in though as just a short bicycle or walk away at The Ickworth Hotel is a choice of two super restaurants. Take advantage of the Ofsted Registered Four Bear's Den, at the hotel, a safe haven for babies and young children, the indoor heated pool & Aquae Sulis Retreat or for those older kids Club Blu. Guests at the Dower House can also utilise baby sitting and food take away services. A von Essen Luxury Family Hotel.

Awards/Recognition: 2 AA Rosettes 2008-2009

Location: A143, 0.5 miles; A14 jct 42, 2.7 miles; Bury St. Edmunds, 5-min drive

Attractions: Jimmy's Farm; Duxford Air Museum; Banham Zoo; Go Ape

SUFFOLK - BURY ST EDMUNDS (ICKWORTH ESTATE)

The Ickworth Hotel & Aquae Sulis Retreat

HORRINGER, BURY ST EDMUNDS, SUFFOLK IP29 5QE
Tel: 0845 365 2539 **International:** +44 (0)1284 735350 **Fax:** 01284 736300
Web: www.johansens.com/ickworth **E-mail:** info@ickworthhotel.com

Our inspector loved: *The magnificence of staying in a stately home and the stunning grounds.*

Price Guide:
double/twin £160–£400
suite £350–£470
interconnecting £365–£580

Awards/Recognition: 2 AA Rosettes 2008-2009

Location: A143, 0.5 miles; A14 jct 42, 2.7 miles; Bury St Edmunds, 5-min drive

Attractions: Jimmy's Farm; Duxford Air Museum; Banham Zoo; Go Ape

A great retreat for families, where children are special guests and you can happily leave them in the safe hands of the Ofsted registered nursery while you head off to ride, cycle, swim or indulge in extreme pampering at the Aquae Sulis Retreat. Older children will love Club Blu – a funky room with table football, table tennis and computer games. The hotel's airy rooms have been decorated in a delightful mix of classic, traditional and contemporary furnishings, all adding a dash of style and warmth. Bedrooms are diverse in size and design. There are early supper menus for the younger guests and baby sitting and listening services giving adults the chance to enjoy fine dining in the more intimate atmosphere of Fredericks restaurant or more informally in the Grand Conservatory. Sitting in 1800 acres of National Trust Parkland on the Ickworth Estate, this is a great place for children to be children and adults to unwind. A von Essen Luxury Family Hotel.

SUFFOLK - IPSWICH (HINTLESHAM)

HINTLESHAM HALL

HINTLESHAM, IPSWICH, SUFFOLK IP8 3NS
Tel: 0845 365 1857 **International:** +44 (0)1473 652334 **Fax:** 01473 652463
Web: www.johansens.com/hintleshamhall **E-mail:** reservations@hintleshamhall.com

Our inspector loved: *The luxurious comfort of the garden room lounge.*

Price Guide:
single from £120
double/twin £140–£280
suite £350–£495

Awards/Recognition: 3 AA Rosettes 2007-2008

Location: A1071, 1 mile; Ipswich, 4 miles; Lavenham, 13.5 miles; Bury St Edmunds, 30 miles

Attractions: Constable Country; Newmarket Racecourse; Aldeburgh

You'll be constantly surprised by this house and its evolving styles. A splendid Georgian façade hides its 16th-century origins to which the Tudor red-brick at the back of the hall is a clue. The Stuart period is evoked by the magnificent carved oak staircase leading to the hall's north wing. This mix works well, with lofty Georgian reception rooms contrasting with timbered Tudor rooms. Complimentary Wi-Fi is available throughout the hall. The well-balanced menus will appeal to every taste. Whether feeling decadent or health-conscious why not play at the associated championship size golf course or take time out in the Health Club with state-of-the-art gym and beauty/sport treatment rooms.

SUFFOLK - KESGRAVE (IPSWICH)

Kesgrave Hall

HALL ROAD, KESGRAVE, IPSWICH, IP5 2PU
Tel: 0845 365 4613 **International:** +44 (0)1473 333741 **Fax:** 01473 617614
Web: www.johansens.com/kesgravehall **E-mail:** reception@kesgravehall.com

Our inspector loved: The "wow factor" of the interior design.

Price Guide:
single £90-£160
double £110-£195

Location: On the B1214; A12, 5-min drive

Attractions: Woodbridge; Constable Country; Aldeburgh and Snape Maltings; East Coast

As welcoming as it is attractive, this splendid Georgian mansion has been transformed into a stylish boutique hotel filled with calming furnishings and décor that blends beautifully with its indulgent early 19th-century features. Kesgrave's interior has been creatively influenced by its diverse history as a family home, shooting lodge, wartime RAF and US Air Force base, school and corporate headquarters. Bedrooms are individual & for those who like open living some come with free standing baths. The hotel buzzes around the innovative "gastro bar" restaurant, which spills onto a terrace where summertime diners can enjoy creative dishes showcasing all that is great about suffolk produce. Special for private dinners and meetings is "The Mess" which, like all the imaginative interiors, is reminiscent of bygone days. All this is set in 38 acres of scenic parkland, complete with bluebell wood.

SUFFOLK - NEWMARKET

BEDFORD LODGE HOTEL

BURY ROAD, NEWMARKET CB8 7BX
Tel: 0845 365 3785 **International:** +44 (0)1638 663175 **Fax:** 01638 667391
Web: www.johansens.com/bedfordlodge **E-mail:** info@bedfordlodgehotel.co.uk

Our inspector loved: *The library that can be used to host executive meetings and private dinners.*

Price Guide:
single £145-£220
double/twin £185-£325

Awards/Recognition: 2 AA Rosettes 2007–2008

Location: Just off the A1304; A14, 2 miles; A11, 3 miles; Stansted Airport, 45-mins drive

Attractions: Horse Racing in Newmarket; The National Stud; Horse Racing Museum; Cambridge; Ely

Bedford Lodge Hotel, originally an 18th century lodge owned by the 5th Duke of Bedford, is located in the heart of Newmarket, and is the ideal setting for horse lovers and countryphiles alike who can admire the elegant racehorses pass by on their morning gallops. The property, which has recently undergone an extensive refurbishment, is surrounded by a well-tended rose garden and boasts 55 beautifully appointed bedrooms and suites, The Edge health and fitness club, 8 contemporary event spaces and the award-winning Orangery Restaurant renowned for its fine seasonal cuisine. The inviting Roxanna Bar offers a convivial, sophisticated atmosphere where you can recline by the log fire - one of the hotel's many original features. During the summer months, enjoy the quintessential English pastime of an afternoon tea served al fresco. The Spa at Bedford Lodge Hotel is due to open soon, offering luxury treatments and packages.

SUFFOLK - WOODBRIDGE

SECKFORD HALL

WOODBRIDGE, SUFFOLK IP13 6NU
Tel: 0845 365 2319 **International:** +44 (0)1394 385678 **Fax:** 01394 380610
Web: www.johansens.com/seckfordhall **E-mail:** reception@seckford.co.uk

Our inspector loved: The lovely gardens and lake.

Price Guide:
single £85–£145
double/twin £140–£225
suite £180–£225

Awards/Recognition: 2 AA Rosettes 2007-2008

Location: Off the A12; Woodbridge, 2 miles; Ipswich, 9.5 miles

Attractions: Suton Hoo; Constable Country; Aldeburgh; Snape Maltings

Seckford Hall dates from 1530 and it is said that Elizabeth I once held court here. Set in 34 acres of parkland with sweeping lawns and a willow fringed lake the house is furnished as a private residence with many fine period pieces. The panelled rooms, beamed ceilings, carved doors and great stone fireplaces are set against the splendour of English oak. Local delicacies such as the house speciality, lobster, feature on the à la carte menu. The courtyard area was converted from a giant Tudor tithe barn, dairy and coach house and now incorporates 10 charming cottage-style suites and a leisure complex, which includes a heated swimming pool, exercise machines, spa bath and beauty salon. You may also use the fully equipped Business Lounge.

163

SURREY - EGHAM

GREAT FOSTERS

STROUDE ROAD, EGHAM, SURREY TW20 9UR
Tel: 0845 365 1793 **International:** +44 (0)1784 433822 **Fax:** 01784 472455
Web: www.johansens.com/greatfosters **E-mail:** enquiries@greatfosters.co.uk

Our inspector loved: *The tiny ancient doorway that leads into the beautiful great hall.*

Price Guide:
single from £125
double/twin from £170
suite from £245

Awards/Recognition: 2 AA Rosettes 2008-2009

Location: Off the B3376; Egham, 1 mile; M25, 7 miles; Heathrow Airport, 6 miles

Attractions: Wentworth; Hampton Court Palace; Windsor Castle; Horse-racing at Ascot

This is where you come for a true taste of luxury, excellence and history: this is absolute grandeur. Great Fosters is an immaculately preserved, 16th-century stately home with impressive oak beams, wood panelling, Jacobean chimney features, superb tapestries and a rare oakwell staircase. There are mullioned windows, a moat with Japanese bridge and 50 acres of parkland and gardens – once the heart of Royal Windsor Forest – to wander around prior to or after enjoying inspired modern English cuisine in the elegant restaurant. Guest rooms are magnificent and a "step back in time" experience. The Orangery and Tithe Barn offer wonderful event space and would impress any wedding guest or client lucky enough to be invited. Simply stunning, this is a great place for that well-earned escape.

SURREY - HASLEMERE

Lythe Hill Hotel & Spa

PETWORTH ROAD, HASLEMERE, SURREY GU27 3BQ
Tel: 0845 365 2052 **International:** +44 (0)1428 651251 **Fax:** 01428 644131
Web: www.johansens.com/lythehill **E-mail:** lythe@lythehill.co.uk

Our inspector loved: *The clever mix of old and new styles...The beautiful Tudor restaurant sits comfortably with the contemporary new lounge*

Price Guide: (including use of the spa)
double £160–295
suite £260–350

Location: B2131; A3, 5.2 miles; Guildford, 19 miles; London Waterloo, 50-min train/metro

Attractions: Petworth House; Lurgashall Winery; Ramster Gardens; Haslemere Museum

Cradled by the Surrey foothills is Lythe Hill Hotel & Spa, comprising of an unusual cluster of ancient buildings – parts of which date from the 14th century. While most of the well appointed accommodation is in the more recently converted part of the hotel, 5 rooms can be found in the Tudor House, including the Henry VIII room with a four-poster bed dated 1614. There are 2 restaurants: the Auberge de France and the 'Dining Room' with a choice of imaginative English dishes. Complemented by over 200 international wines. The Amarna leisure facility has a 16 x 8 metre swimming pool, steam room and sauna, gym, hairdressing, treatment rooms and a nail bar. National Trust hillside adjoining the hotel grounds provides interesting walks and views over the surrounding countryside.

165

SURREY - RICHMOND-UPON-THAMES

The Richmond Gate Hotel and Restaurant

RICHMOND HILL, RICHMOND-UPON-THAMES, SURREY TW10 6RP
Tel: 0845 365 2674 **International:** +44 (0)20 8940 0061 **Fax:** 020 8332 0354
Web: www.johansens.com/richmondgate **E-mail:** richmondgate@foliohotels.com

Our inspector loved: *There is something so welcoming about this beautiful building - and the new bedrooms are simply stunning - I can think of few nicer places to wake up!*

Price Guide:
double/twin from £135
four poster from £195

Awards/Recognition: 2 AA Rosettes 2007-2008

Location: On the B353; Richmond Underground Station, 1 mile; Central London, 7 miles; Heathrow Airport, 7 miles

Attractions: Hampton Court Palace; Kew Gardens; Richmond Hill

A completed multi-million pound refurbishment has put The Richmond Gate Hotel firmly back at the top of the luxury marketplace. Even though you're on the edge of London you could imagine you were in the country as this Georgian house, with its Victorian walled garden, stands on the crest of Richmond Hill with commanding views of the River Thames. The newly designed bedrooms are fantastic, vast spaces decorated in beautiful colour schemes. And although they exude a contemporary feel, they remain in-keeping with the original Georgian routes of the building. Space for weddings, meetings, parties and private dining is very flexible, and the award-winning 2 AA Rosette-awarded restaurant, Gates on the Park, offers imaginative menus complemented by an exciting range of over 60 worldwide wines. Cedars Leisure Club has a beautiful 20m indoor pool, which can be a welcome retreat after a day spent shopping in Richmond or walking through the park.

EAST SUSSEX - ALFRISTON

Deans Place Hotel

SEAFORD ROAD, ALFRISTON, EAST SUSSEX BN26 5TW
Tel: 0845 365 3264 **International:** +44 (0)1323 870248 **Fax:** 01323 870918
Web: www.johansens.com/deansplacehotel **E-mail:** mail@deansplacehotel.co.uk

Our inspector loved: *This very popular and welcoming hotel in its edge of historic village setting.*

Price Guide:
single from £75
double/twin from £110
four poster from £150

Awards/Recognition: 1 AA Rosette 2008-2009

Location: A27, 1 mile; M23 (A23), 15 miles; Lewes, 10 miles; Gatwick Airport, 40 miles

Attractions: Wonderful walking country; Seven Sisters Country Park; Beachy Head; Glyndebourne Opera

On the edge of one of England's prettiest villages, Deans Place with its origins in the 14th Century offers guests a wonderful retreat from modern life. Set in 4 acres of beautiful gardens, with a back drop of the South Downs the hotel is the perfect location from which to visit Glyndebourne, Charleston or simply enjoy leisurely strolls or longer walks in some of the South East's finest scenery encompassing river, forest and the sea. Many of the bedrooms have fine views over the wedding garden or the South Downs. Fine international cuisine, using fresh local produce is served in the award winning dining room or alfresco on the terrace overlooking the croquet lawn. Boules and putting are also available and in summer the heated swimming pool is a great place to relax.

EAST SUSSEX - BATTLE

The PowderMills

POWDERMILL LANE, BATTLE, EAST SUSSEX TN33 0SP
Tel: 0845 365 2648 **International:** +44 (0)1424 775511 **Fax:** 01424 774540
Web: www.johansens.com/powdermills **E-mail:** powdc@aol.com

Our inspector loved: *The delightful dining room with crisp linen, sparkling glass and warm home-made breads.*

Price Guide:
single from £105
double/twin from £130
suites from £195

Awards/Recognition: 1 AA Rosette 2007-2008

Location: A21 (A2100), 3 miles; M25 jct5, 50 miles; Battle, 1 mile; Gatwick Airport, 48 miles

Attractions: Battle Abbey; Cinque Port Rye; Bodiam Castle; Hastings Old Town, Beautiful Gardens

The PowderMills, once the site for the production of the finest gunpowder in Europe is now an 18th-century listed country house skilfully converted into an elegant hotel. The beautiful grounds encompass 150 acres of parks, woodland and a 7-acre specimen fishing lake. Close to the historic town of Battle, the hotel adjoins the famous battlefield of 1066 and has been thoughtfully furnished with locally acquired antiques and paintings. On cooler days welcoming log fires burn in the entrance hall and drawing room. Many of the individually decorated bedrooms and junior suites have four-poster beds. Fine classical cooking by chef James Penn is served in the award winning Orangery Restaurant, whilst light meals and snacks are available in the library and conservatory.

EAST SUSSEX - BRIGHTON

Lansdowne Place, Boutique Hotel & Spa

LANSDOWNE PLACE, BRIGHTON, EAST SUSSEX BN3 1HQ
Tel: 0845 365 1987 **International:** +44 (0)1273 736266 **Fax:** 01273 729802
Web: www.johansens.com/lansdowneplace **E-mail:** info@lansdowneplace.co.uk

Our inspector loved: *The larger sumptuous bedrooms, and the friendly staff.*

Price Guide:
single from £90
double £130–£320

Location: On the A259; A23, 1.5 miles; Brighton Railway Station, 1.3 miles; Gatwick Airport, 40 miles

Attractions: Town Centre; The Royal Pavilion; Brighton Racecourse; Lewes

Describing itself as "touch of a class", Lansdowne Place doesn't disappoint. As soon as you enter its spacious lobby you're enveloped by a stylish blend of classic and contemporary. Rooms pay homage to the grandeur of Regency Brighton, with rich fabrics, elegant wallpaper and period lamps, and after a day exploring the south coast you can chill out in the spa before indulging in an Espa treatment inspired by the sea - salt and oil scrubs, aromatherapy facials and detoxifying algae wraps. The Grill's Restaurant uses locally sourced and organic produce where possible, and afterwards you can head to the lounge bar, glass of champagne firmly in hand, and settle yourself on a leopard print bar stool.

EAST SUSSEX - BRIGHTON

ROYAL YORK HOTEL

OLD STEINE, BRIGHTON BN1 1NP
Tel: 0845 365 4619 **International:** +44 (0)1273 766 700 **Fax:** 01273 766 707
Web: www.johansens.com/royalyorksussex **E-mail:** reservations@royalyorkbrighton.co.uk

As unique and vibrant as Brighton itself, the Royal York Hotel is perfect if you're looking for an opulent, cosmopolitan base for exploring the city's sea front, Lanes area and night-life. However, the hotel itself has plenty to offer. The restaurant can cook your food to order and invites you to select from the day's freshest available produce, including seafood and locally farmed poultry. Fine wines, champagne cocktails and great martinis are shaken and stirred at the contemporary-styled Cocktail Bar and should you fancy belting out a few tunes in the company of friends, you could hire a state-of-the-art karaoke suite! The selection of rooms and suites are all luxurious and the bright apartments come with kitchenettes. Meeting and private rooms have plenty of flexibility for working or entertaining space. The new Spa Treatment room offers a full range of beauty, spa and massage therapies in central Brighton.

Our inspector loved: The innovative and quirky elements in this historic Brighton property. Look out for the fish counter in the restaurant!

Price Guide:
queen/king double from £130
suites from £240
apartments from £300

Location: Central Brighton, Old Steine; A23, 2 yards; M23, 30-mins drive; Gatwick Airport, 38 miles

Attractions: The Lanes; Royal Pavilion; Horse Racing; Brighton Pier & Aquarium

EAST SUSSEX - EASTBOURNE

The Grand Hotel

KING EDWARD'S PARADE, EASTBOURNE, EAST SUSSEX BN21 4EQ
Tel: 0845 365 2504 **International:** +44 (0)1323 412345 **Fax:** 01323 412233
Web: www.johansens.com/grandeastbourne **E-mail:** reservations@grandeastbourne.com

Our inspector loved: *The newly landscaped forecourt with additional guest parking.*

Price Guide:
single £160–£505
double/twin £190–£535
suite £405–£535

Awards/Recognition: 2 AA Rosettes 2007-2008

Location: On the Seafront; A22, 7.5 miles; M23 jct 11, 40 miles; Gatwick Airport, 48 miles

Attractions: Beachy Head; Sovereign Harbour; Three Theatres; Glyndebourne Opera

A grand old dame of the Victorian era, the Grand's majestic façade conceals reception rooms adorned with rich fabrics, and many of the 152 bedrooms have vast proportions, all recently refurbished to include every comfort with attractive bathrooms. There are numerous places in which to relax, and a good choice of restaurants and bars - the Mirabelle in particular achieves exceptional standards of fine dining. Leisure facilities include indoor and outdoor pools, gym, sauna, spa bath, steam room, snooker tables, a hair salon and 8 beauty rooms. If you are seeking a peaceful retreat you'll be more than happy with the tranquil atmosphere at The Grand Hotel with its impeccably delivered standards of traditional service. Pastimes include golf at a nearby club, walks along the downs, sea fishing and visits to nearby theatres.

EAST SUSSEX - FOREST ROW

ASHDOWN PARK HOTEL AND COUNTRY CLUB

WYCH CROSS, FOREST ROW, EAST SUSSEX RH18 5JR
Tel: 0845 365 2896 **International:** +44 (0)1342 824988 **Fax:** 01342 826206
Web: www.johansens.com/ashdownpark **E-mail:** reservations@ashdownpark.com

Our inspector loved: *The open fires and masses of fresh flowers throughout the public rooms.*

Price Guide:
single £160–£340
double/twin £190–£390
suite £305–£420

Awards/Recognition: 2 AA Rosettes 2007-2008

Location: A22, 0.5 miles; M25 jct 6, 15 miles; East Grinstead, 5 miles; Gatwick Airport, 16 miles

Attractions: Ashdown Forest; Bluebell Railway; Wakehurst Place Gardens; Lingfield Park Racecourse

A grand, rambling 19th-century mansion overlooking nearly 200 acres of landscaped gardens, Ashdown Park is ideally situated to satisfy the needs of escapees from urban stress. You can amble through the grounds and nearby woodland paths, retire to the indoor pool, steam room and sauna or pamper yourself with a visit to the beauty salon. The more energetic among you can indulge in a game of tennis or croquet, and for golfers who cannot survive a weekend without a round, there is an indoor and outdoor driving range and 18-hole par 3 golf course. The Anderida restaurant's menu and wine list are well constructed, with a service that is discreet and attentive.

EAST SUSSEX - LEWES

PELHAM HOUSE

ST ANDREW'S LANE, LEWES, EAST SUSSEX BN7 1UN
Tel: 0845 365 2098 **International:** +44 (0)1273 488 600 **Fax:** 01273 470 371
Web: www.johansens.com/pelhamhouse **E-mail:** reservations@pelhamhouse.com

Our inspector loved: *Taking lunch on the terrace at this delightful contemporary town house.*

Price Guide:
single from £95
standard £130
standard garden view £170
club £220

Location: A27, 1 mile; M23 jct 11, 30 miles; Lewes, on-site; Gatwick, 38 miles

Attractions: Glyndebourne Opera; Regency Brighton; Glynde Place and Firle House; Charleston Farmhouse

When you arrive at this Georgian town house hotel, you will be immediately struck by the stylish, yet seemingly effortless, refurbishment that combines both contemporary and historic features. Stripped floors, carved panelled walls, a cosy atmosphere and chic interior design will ensure a comfortable few days. All members of the staff are extremely welcoming, and everything seems to have been thought of already. Bedrooms are gorgeous; not only do they have views over the gardens and South Downs beyond, but also hand-made oak furniture and luxury bathrooms. And as for the restaurant, you are in for a treat! Mouth-watering modern British cuisine is the theme, prepared from locally sourced ingredients served in an elegant room that dates back to the 16th century.

EAST SUSSEX - LEWES (LITTLE HORSTED)

Horsted Place Country House Hotel
LITTLE HORSTED, EAST SUSSEX TN22 5TS
Tel: 0845 365 1893 **International:** +44 (0)1825 750581 **Fax:** 01825 750459
Web: www.johansens.com/horstedplace **E-mail:** hotel@horstedplace.co.uk

Our inspector loved: *The always splendid dining experience in a lovely Pugin setting.*

Price Guide:
double/twin from £130
suite from £220

Awards/Recognition: 2 AA Rosettes 2007-2008

Location: On the A26; M23 jct 10, 20 miles; Lewes, 6 miles; Gatwick, 25 miles

Attractions: Glyndebourne Opera; Sheffield Park Gardens; Bluebell Railway; Regency Brighton

Horsted Place sits amidst the peace of the Sussex Downs. This splendid Victorian Gothic Mansion, built in 1851, features an interior predominantly styled by the celebrated Victorian architect, Augustus Pugin. In former years the Queen and Prince Philip were frequent visitors. Guests today are invited to enjoy the excellent service offered by a committed staff. Chef Allan Garth offers a daily fixed price menu as well as the seasonal à la carte menu. The Terrace Room is an elegant and airy private function room, licensed for weddings for up to 100 guests. The smaller Morning Room and Library are ideal for boardroom-style meetings and intimate dinner parties, and the self-contained management centre offers privacy and exclusivity for business meetings in a contemporary setting.

EAST SUSSEX - LEWES (NEWICK)

NEWICK PARK

NEWICK, NEAR LEWES, EAST SUSSEX BN8 4SB
Tel: 0845 365 2085 **International:** +44 (0)1825 723633 **Fax:** 01825 723969
Web: www.johansens.com/newickpark **E-mail:** bookings@newickpark.co.uk

Our inspector loved: *The impressive standards of fine dining presented in a delightful setting.*

Price Guide:
single from £125
double/twin from £165

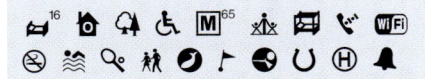

Awards/Recognition: Condé Nast Johansens Readers' Award 2008; 3 AA Rosettes 2007-2008

Location: A272, 1 mile; M23 jct 11, 18 miles; Lewes, 8 miles; Gatwick Airport, 28 miles

Attractions: Sheffield Park Garden and Wakefield Place; Opera at Glyndebourne; Regency Brighton; Bluebell Railway

This magnificent Grade II listed Georgian country house is set in 200 acres of beautiful parkland and landscaped gardens overlooking the Longford River and South Downs. Whilst situated in a convenient location near to the main road and rail routes and only 30 minutes from Gatwick Airport the hotel maintains an atmosphere of complete tranquility and privacy. Bedrooms are decorated in a classic style featuring elegant antiques and friendly staff ensure that you receive a warm welcome. The exquisite dining room offers culinary delights carefully prepared by Head Chef, Chris Moore. The house and grounds are ideal for weddings, conferences and private parties and The Dell gardens primarily planted in Victorian times include a rare collection of Royal Ferns. Exclusive use can be arranged by appointment.

EAST SUSSEX - TICEHURST (NEAR TUNBRIDGE WELLS)

Dale Hill

TICEHURST, NEAR TUNBRIDGE WELLS, EAST SUSSEX TN5 7DQ
Tel: 0845 365 3259 **International:** +44 (0)1580 200112 **Fax:** 01580 201249
Web: www.johansens.com/dalehill **E-mail:** info@dalehill.co.uk

Our inspector loved: *The spacious and quiet bedrooms - wonderful for a little "me time".*

Price Guide:
single £110–£130
double/twin £120–£250

Awards/Recognition: 1 AA Rosette 2008-2009

Location: A21, 1 mile; M25 jct 5, 26 miles; Tunbridge Wells, 11 miles; Gatwick Airport, 57 miles

Attractions: Bewl Water; Tunbridge Wells Pantiles; Lamberhurst Vineyard; Bedgebury Pinetum

This stylish, hotel offers you the best of all worlds. Comfortable rooms, award-winning dishes and a fully-equipped health club are an impressive start. Keen golfers can choose between two 18-hole courses, a gently undulating 6,093 yards par 70 and a new, challenging championship standard course designed by former US Masters champion Ian Woosnam. Just a 20-minute drive away, under the same ownership as the hotel, is the Nick Faldo designed Chart Hills course hailed as "the best new course in England". Packages allow you to play both championship courses. You can enjoy glorious views from a choice of restaurants where delicious dishes are complemented by an excellent wine list. If you like fly-fishing then Bewl Water is nearby.

WEST SUSSEX - AMBERLEY

Amberley Castle

AMBERLEY, NEAR ARUNDEL, WEST SUSSEX BN18 9LT
Tel: 0845 365 3612 **International:** +44 (0)1798 831992 **Fax:** 01798 831998
Web: www.johansens.com/amberleycastle **E-mail:** info@amberleycastle.co.uk

Our inspector loved: *This magical world of peace and tranquility.*

Price Guide: (room only)
double/twin £200–£345
suite £295–£450

Awards/Recognition: Relais & Châteaux; 3 AA Rosettes 2008-2009

Location: A29, 3 miles; M23 jct 11, 30 miles; Arundel, 5 miles; Gatwick Airport, 34 miles

Attractions: Goodwood Estate; Petworth House; Polo at Cowdray Park; Antiques at Arundel

At 900 years Amberley Castle is almost as old as time itself. Set between the rolling South Downs and the calming expanses of the Amberley Wildbrooks. The massive 14th century curtain walls, battlements and mighty portcullis were once built to withstand unwelcome visitors! The opposite is true today, as you will receive a warm and personal welcome and the ultimate in classic luxury. 5 distinctive suites have been added in the Bishopric by the main gateway. Each room is individually designed and has its own whirlpool bath. The exquisite 12th-century Queen's Room is the perfect setting for the creative cuisine of the head chef and his team. Amberley Castle is a natural first choice for romantic or cultural weekends, sporting breaks or confidential executive meetings. A von Essen hotel.

WEST SUSSEX - ARUNDEL (CLIMPING)

BAILIFFSCOURT HOTEL & SPA

CLIMPING, ARUNDEL, WEST SUSSEX BN17 5RW
Tel: 0845 365 3025 **International:** +44 (0)1903 723511 **Fax:** 01903 723107
Web: www.johansens.com/bailiffscourt **E-mail:** bailiffscourt@hshotels.co.uk

Our inspector loved: *The stunning architectural detail of the spa - wonderful use of space and light.*

Price Guide: (including dinner)
single from £170
double from £250
feature from £425

Awards/Recognition: 2 AA Rosettes 2007-2008

Location: A259, 1 mile; M27 jct 1, 30 miles; Arundel, 6 miles; Gatwick Airport, 44 miles

Attractions: Arundel Castle; Goodwood Estate; Chichester Festival Theatre; The Beach

Feel that you've stepped back in time at this perfectly preserved "medieval" manor and out-buildings built in the 1930s using authentic material salvaged from historic old buildings. Gnarled 15th-century beams and gothic mullioned windows recreate the Middle Ages, and many luxurious rooms offer four-poster beds, open log fires and beautiful views across the surrounding countryside. Menus are varied, and in summer you can eat out in the rose-clad courtyard or walled garden. The award-winning health spa features an outdoor Californian hot tub, indoor spa pool, sauna, gym, hammocks and 6 beauty rooms. 2 tennis courts and a croquet lawn complete the on-site leisure facilities, while a private pathway leads 100yds down to Climping beach, ideal for your morning walk.

WEST SUSSEX - CHICHESTER (GOODWOOD)

The Goodwood Park Hotel

GOODWOOD, CHICHESTER, WEST SUSSEX PO18 0QB
Tel: 0845 365 4632 **International:** +44 (0)1243 775537 **Fax:** 01243 520125
Web: www.johansens.com/thegoodwoodparkhotel **E-mail:** reservations@thegoodwoodparkhotel.co.uk

Our inspector loved: *The newly refurbished comfortable and stylish public areas and restaurants.*

Price Guide:
standard from £100
character from £150
suite from £175

Awards/Recognition: 2 AA Rosettes 2008–2009

Location: A27, 3 miles; A3(M) / M27 jct 12, 13 miles; Gatwick Airport, 49 miles; London, 60 miles

Attractions: Goodwood Estate, horseracing and motor events; Chichester Festival Theatre and harbour; Arundel, antiques and castle; West Wittering, beaches

Built around an 18th-century coaching inn, this luxury hotel has been sensitively and beautifully refurbished. Within such vast Estate grounds, 12,000 acres in total, you will find pretty much everything you could possibly desire. The Estate has its own airfield, horseracing, motor sports and 2 stunning 18 hole golf courses. Décor is modern and discreet; the essence of elegance. If you feel like treating yourself, don't miss out on a visit to the health club with its extensive range of treatments and 14m indoor pool. A whole variety of dining options range from award-winning cuisine in The Richmond Arms to summer barbecues on the terrace overlooking the golf course in the Goodwood Bar and Grill. The creative menus are inspired by the best, seasonal ingredients and feature beef, lamb and pork from the organic Goodwood Farm. This is a practical and inspirational choice for a business meeting, celebration or wedding with 8 air-conditioned spacious private rooms.

WEST SUSSEX - CUCKFIELD (NEAR GATWICK)

Ockenden Manor

OCKENDEN LANE, CUCKFIELD, WEST SUSSEX RH17 5LD
Tel: 0845 365 2093 **International:** +44 (0)1444 416111 **Fax:** 01444 415549
Web: www.johansens.com/ockendenmanor **E-mail:** reservations@ockenden-manor.com

Our inspector loved: *The dining room with its stylish presentation and superb cuisine.*

Price Guide:
single from £110
double £175–£324
suite £288–£360

Awards/Recognition: 3 AA Rosettes 2008-2009; 1 Star Michelin 2008

Location: A272, 0.5 mile; M23 jct 10, 4 miles; Haywards Heath, 2 miles; Gatwick Airport, 18 miles

Attractions: Wakehurst and Nymans Gardens; Glyndebourne Opera; Regency Brighton; Bluebell Railway

Discover Sussex and Kent, The Garden of England from Ockendon Manor, first recorded in 1520 and now a hotel of great character, charm and hospitality. Rooms are all highly individual, you can climb your private staircase to Thomas or Elizabeth, gaze out across the glorious Sussex countryside from Victoria's bay window or choose Charles, with its handsome four-poster bed. This highly seductive romantic ambience reaches into the wood-panelled restaurant with its beautiful handpainted ceiling, where you can enjoy innovative cooking and an extensive wine list which includes a splendid choice of first-growth clarets. A lovely conservatory, part of the Ockendon Suite, opens onto the lawns where marquees can be set up for summer celebrations. Private dining can be arranged subject to availability.

WEST SUSSEX - MIDHURST

The Spread Eagle Hotel & Spa

SOUTH STREET, MIDHURST, WEST SUSSEX GU29 9NH
Tel: 0845 365 2695 **International:** +44 (0)1730 816911 **Fax:** 01730 815668
Web: www.johansens.com/spreadeaglemidhurst **E-mail:** reservations@spreadeagle-midhurst.com.

Our inspector loved: *The new guest provision in their already excellent Spa.*

Price Guide:
single £90-£206
double £115-£315
suite from £395

Awards/Recognition: 2 AA Rosettes 2008-2009

Location: Town Centre; Just off A272/286, 0.2 miles; M25 jct 9, 31 miles; Gatwick Airport, 38 miles

Attractions: Petworth; Cowdray Park; Goodwood House and Estate; Chichester Cathedral

Although it's one of England's oldest hotels, dating from 1430 and is rich in charms and period features, The Spread Eagle boasts an outstanding modern Health Spa – with an impressive vaulted glass ceiling and plenty of wet areas. In the restaurant Gary Morton-Jones creates a modern classic menu using seasonal flavours and plenty of local ingredients. The bedrooms are delightful, many with antiques and some with four-posters. The White Room contains a 'secret passage' and is said to have been used by smugglers in their attempt to evade the King's men. This is a great area to explore, after which a cream tea at the Spread Eagle will be well deserved. Childrens high-teas can be arranged and well-behaved dogs are allowed in some bedrooms.

TYNE & WEAR - NEWCASTLE-UPON-TYNE

The Vermont Hotel

CASTLE GARTH, NEWCASTLE-UPON-TYNE, TYNE & WEAR NE1 1RQ
Tel: 0845 365 2714 **International:** +44 (0)191 233 1010 **Fax:** 0191 233 1234
Web: www.johansens.com/vermont **E-mail:** info@vermont-hotel.co.uk

Our inspector loved: *The combination of classical and modern in this luxury city centre hotel. Dining high in the hotel's restaurant and admiring spectacular views of the famous Tyne Bridge.*

Price Guide:
single/double £130
suites from £240

Awards/Recognition: 1 AA Rosette 2006-2007

Location: A1 M, 2 miles; Newcastle International. Airport, 7 miles

Attractions: Newcastle Cathedral; Castle Keep; Durham

The Vermont is Newcastle's only 4-star independent hotel, located next to the Castle, overlooking the Cathedral and the Tyne and Millennium Bridges and adjacent to the renovated High Bridge that has excellent pedestrian access with unique views of the Tyne. This impressive 12 storey, Manhattan-style tower is close to the shops, theatres, galleries, universities and railway station and has direct access to the Quayside and on site free car parking. The 101 bedrooms and suites are a combination of classical and modern design with i-Pod docking stations and 24-hour service. 7 meeting rooms are available for special occasions and private dining. The Bridge Restaurant affords spectacular views of the Tyne Bridge, alternatively there is the Redwood Bar, open until late. For those wishing to sample the atmosphere of the famous Quayside, go to Martha's Bar & Courtyard on the ground floor.

WARWICKSHIRE - COVENTRY (BERKSWELL)

Nailcote Hall

NAILCOTE LANE, BERKSWELL, NEAR SOLIHULL, WARWICKSHIRE CV7 7DE
Tel: 0845 365 2078 **International:** +44 (0)2476 466174 **Fax:** 02476 470720
Web: www.johansens.com/nailcotehall **E-mail:** info@nailcotehall.co.uk

Our inspector loved: *The enchanting and so relaxing Cherry Suite.*

Price Guide:
single £185
double/twin £200
suite £200–£305

Awards/Recognition: 2 AA Rosettes 2006-2007

Location: A452, 2 miles; M42 jct 5, 7 miles; Balsall Common, 3 miles; Birmingham International, 9 miles

Attractions: Warwick Castle; Kenilworth Castle; Royal Leamington Spa; Coventry Cathedral

Located in the heart of England, Nailcote Hall is a charming Elizabethan country house built in 1640 and used by Oliver Cromwell and his troops during the Civil War. In more peaceful times and fully restored today, it not only tempts you into the intimate Tudor surrounds of the Oak Room restaurant and offers luxury accommodation, it also boasts impressive leisure facilities. These include a swimming pool, gym, solarium and sauna, outside all-weather tennis courts, pétanque, croquet, a challenging 9-hole par-3 golf course and putting green - host to the British Championship Professional Short Course Competition. Right in the heart of England, Nailcote Hall is within 15 minutes' drive of the castle towns of Kenilworth and Warwick, Coventry Cathedral, Birmingham International Airport/Station and the NEC.

WARWICKSHIRE - ROYAL LEAMINGTON SPA

Mallory Court

HARBURY LANE, BISHOPS TACHBROOK, LEAMINGTON SPA, WARWICKSHIRE CV33 9QB
Tel: 0845 365 2053 **International:** +44 (0)1926 330214 **Fax:** 01926 451714
Web: www.johansens.com/mallorycourt **E-mail:** reception@mallory.co.uk

Our inspector loved: *The Ashorne Suite and its views over the immaculate gardens and topiary.*

Price Guide:
double (single occupancy) from £115
double from £145
master rooms from £325

Surrounded by 10 acres of attractive gardens Mallory Court boasts a stunning backdrop across the beautiful Warwickshire countryside, a stone's throw from Stratford-upon-Avon and Warwick Castle. Sip champagne on the terrace before heading off to the Royal Shakespeare Theatre, and for those who don't wish to venture far, cosy up beside log fires. Tailor-made menus are available at the restaurant, however, why not simply put your diet on hold for an evening and enjoy the roasted Skye scallops, chicken with Avruga caviar, braised shoulder and roasted fillet of Lighthorne lamb follwed by hot passion fruit soufflé! Alternatively, there is the more informal, yet excellent brasserie where a lighter menu awaits. This is a truly ravishing venue for weddings and business events with 30 luxuriously appointed bedrooms that look out to stunning views across the grounds.

Awards/Recognition: 1 Star Michelin 2008; 3 AA Rosettes 2008-2009 (Main Restaurant); 1 AA Rosette 2008-2009 (Brasserie); Relais & Châteaux

Location: A452, 1 mile; M40 jct 14 (North) & jct 13 (South), 2 miles; Royal Leamington Spa, 2 miles; Birmingham International, 23 miles

Attractions: Warwick Castle; Blenheim Palace; Kenilworth Castle; Packwood House

WARWICKSHIRE - WARWICK (CLAVERDON)

Ardencote Manor Hotel, Country Club & Spa

THE CUMSEY, LYE GREEN ROAD, CLAVERDON, NEAR WARWICK, WARWICKSHIRE CV35 8LT
Tel: 0845 365 3615 **International:** +44 (0)1926 843111 **Fax:** 01926 842646
Web: www.johansens.com/ardencote **E-mail:** hotel@ardencote.com

Our inspector loved: The impressive marbled reception area, staircase and chandeliers in the original mansion.

Price Guide:
single from £90
double from £130
suite from £240

Awards/Recognition: 2 AA Rosettes 2006-2007

Location: A4189, 1 mile; Warwick, 5-min drive; M40 exit 16, 12-min drive; Birmingham International, 20-min drive

Attractions: Warwick Castle; Stratford-upon-Avon; Kenilworth; Hatton Locks

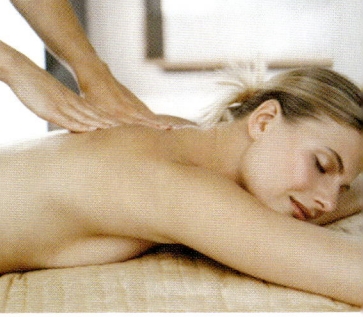

Built as a Gentleman's residence in 1860, and now under private ownership, the house has been sympathetically refurbished and substantially extended to create a luxury hotel retaining its traditional elegance and appealing intimacy. Make the most of the well appointed bedrooms – many with views over the lake and gardens – and extensive sports and leisure facilities, including an indoor pool, spa bath, outdoor whirlpool, sauna and steamrooms. Squash and tennis courts, fully equipped gymnasia and 9-hole golf course are also provided. The spa offers an extensive choice of relaxing, holistic treatments. And dinner at the award-winning lakeside Lodge restaurant is a treat. Visits to Warwick Castle are available (at special rates) through the hotel, and you can brush up on your Shakespeare in Stratford-upon-Avon.

WARWICKSHIRE - WARWICK (WROXALL)

WROXALL ABBEY ESTATE

BIRMINGHAM ROAD, WROXALL, NEAR WARWICK, WARWICKSHIRE CV35 7NB
Tel: 0845 365 2835 **International:** +44 (0)1926 484470 **Fax:** 01926 485206
Web: www.johansens.com/wroxallabbey **E-mail:** reservation@wroxall.com

Our inspector loved: *The amazing diversity of the bedrooms. Try "Love" with its dual aspect or "Romance" with its super-sized double bathtub*

Price Guide:
single from £89
double from £109
suite from £249

Location: On the A4141; M42 jct 5, 12 miles; Warwick, 5 miles; Birmingham International Airport, 16 miles

Attractions: Warwick Castle; Stratford-upon-Avon; NEC; Kenilworth Castle

This recently restored and impressive listed building, set in 27 acres of landscaped gardens, features comfortable public rooms and a beautiful chapel that define the character of this country estate, once the home of Sir Christopher Wren. A spacious marquee situated in the grounds will accommodate all your entertainment needs, whether a wedding or a special anniversary party. You'll find that this is a romantic place for the perfect escape, where each bedroom is different - many have four-poster beds and original marble fireplaces, whilst bathrooms have separate walk-in showers and whirlpool baths. Whatever the occasion, you'll find a choice of menus to suit your mood, from the á la carte to the informal bistro menu, which are both served in the elegant Sonnets restaurant, next to the classic Broadwood Bar and Garden Lounge.

WILTSHIRE - BATH (COLERNE)

LUCKNAM PARK, BATH

COLERNE, CHIPPENHAM, WILTSHIRE SN14 8AZ
Tel: 0845 365 2048 **International:** +44 (0)1225 742777 **Fax:** 01225 743536
Web: www.johansens.com/lucknampark **E-mail:** reservations@lucknampark.co.uk

Our inspector loved: *The stunning view of the driveway and surrounding countryside from the luxurious and elegant Grand Master Suites*

Price Guide: (room only)
single/double/twin from £265
suite from £585

Awards/Recognition: 1 Star Michelin 2008; Relais & Châteaux; 3 AA Rosettes 2007-2008

Location: A420, 1.5 miles; M4 jct 18, 9 miles; Bristol, 20 miles

Attractions: Bath; Lacock; Castle Combe; Westonbirt Arboretum

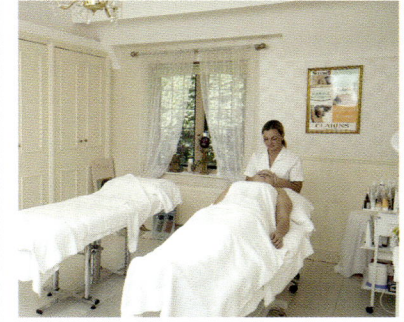

Built in 1720 at the end of a mile long beech and lime tree lined avenue, this magnificent Palladian mansion, with its 5 AA red stars has always been host to fine society and sophisticated living. The delicate aura of historical context is reflected in fine art and antiques dating from the late Georgian and early Victorian periods. Award winning cuisine can be enjoyed in the elegant Park Restaurant, where tables are laid with exquisite porcelain, silver and glassware, accompanied with excellent wines from an extensive cellar. Set within the gardens of the hotel is the beauty salon offering an impressive range of treatments. A new "world class"spa will open Autumn 2008. The Equestrian Centre welcomes complete beginners, experienced riders and also accepts liveries. Winners in 2007 of the Andrew Harper Grand Hideaway of the year award and the Relais & Châteaux Welcome Trophy.

WILTSHIRE - BRADFORD-ON-AVON

WOOLLEY GRANGE

WOOLLEY GREEN, BRADFORD-ON-AVON, WILTSHIRE BA15 1TX
Tel: 0845 365 2831 **International:** +44 (0)1225 864705 **Fax:** 01225 864059
Web: www.johansens.com/woolleygrange **E-mail:** info@woolleygrangehotel.co.uk

Our inspector loved: *The lovely outdoor swimming pool, heated all year round and with beautiful views of the surrounding countryside.*

Price Guide:
double/twin £190–£410
suite £190–£410
interconnecting £300–£410

Awards/Recognition: 2 AA Rosettes 2008-2009

Location: Just off B3105; M4 jct 18, 16 miles; Bath, 8 miles

Attractions: Bowood House, Gardens & Adventure Playground; Wookey Hole Caves; Stourhead House & Gardens; The EGG Children's Theatre.

Gorgeous views, slightly eclectic, warm and very homey. This quintessentially English 17th-century Jacobean manor manages to be both luxurious and extremely accommodating to its younger guests. The Victorian coach house is home to a well-equipped nursery, full-time nannies look after children for 2 hours at a time from 10am-4.45pm every day. Older children (and parents!) will love 'The Hen House' – a quirky games room. With the children entertained, parents can head out to explore the region or indulge in an in-room massage before lying in a cosy corner with a good book. 'Woolley's' reputation for food is outstanding, largely thanks to the chef who creates sophisticated country house food using local farm produce and organically grown fruit and vegetables from the Victorian kitchen gardens. With baby sitting & listening services available, dinner is an informally elegant affair. A children's lunch and tea are provided daily. A von Essen Luxury Family Hotel.

WILTSHIRE - MALMESBURY

WHATLEY MANOR

EASTON GREY, MALMESBURY, WILTSHIRE SN16 0RB
Tel: 0845 365 2801 **International:** +44 (0)1666 822888 **Fax:** 01666 826120
Web: www.johansens.com/whatley **E-mail:** reservations@whatleymanor.com

Our inspector loved: *A very relaxing and spoiling experience. Gorgeous bedrooms, an amazing spa and great food.*

Price Guide: (including full English breakfast, use of spa facilities)
standard from £290
superior/deluxe £340-£490
suite £650-£850

Awards/Recognition: Condé Nast Johansens Taittinger Wine List Award, Best Wine Promotions 2008; 1 Star Michelin 2007; 3 AA Rosettes 2006-2007; Relais & Châteaux

Location: Off the B4040; A429, 3 miles; M4 jct 17, 8 miles; London, 75-min train

Attractions: The Cotswolds; Bath; Malmesbury House; Westonbirt Arboretum

Very careful attention to detail has created this beautifully designed stylish and sophisticated retreat that never quite stops feeling like a family owned country home. The 15 bedrooms and 8 suites are furnished with Italian furniture and handmade French wallpaper, and are equipped with sound and vision systems to keep you blissfully occupied. There are 2 gastronomic experiences on offer: "The Dining Room", echoing the sumptuousness of the hotel, and the more informal brasserie "Le Mazot" with its refreshingly alternative Swiss interior. The highly acclaimed spa, Aquarias, includes one of the UK's largest hydrotherapy pools as well as a La Prairie "Art of Beauty" centre. A private cinema can accommodate up to 40 people, and the encompassing gardens have plenty of spaces for you to escape to.

WILTSHIRE - SALISBURY (TEFFONT EVIAS)

Howard's House

TEFFONT EVIAS, SALISBURY, WILTSHIRE SP3 5RJ
Tel: 0845 365 1905 **International:** +44 (0)1722 716392 **Fax:** 01722 716820
Web: www.johansens.com/howardshouse **E-mail:** enq@howardshousehotel.co.uk

Our inspector loved: *This is such a pretty house in a beautiful little village. Peaceful and relaxing, a perfect getaway.*

Price Guide:
single £105
double/twin £165–£185

Location: Just off B3089; A303, 3 miles; Salisbury, 10 miles

Attractions: Salisbury Cathedral; Stonehenge; Stourhead Gardens; Longleat

Tucked away in the depths of rural Wiltshire you can easily be persuaded to curl up by the fire in winter with a good book and glass of port, or listen to the tinkling of the fountain in the lily pond while inhaling fragrant jasmine through open windows in summer. Howard's House in the quintessential English hamlet of Teffont Evias is a charming small country house hotel, with thoughtful touches of fresh fruit, homemade biscuits and glossy mags in the bedroom. Home-grown and local produce is transformed into modern British cuisine with flair and imagination in the award-winning restaurant. An ideal escape, the hotel is 9 miles from Stonehenge, and ideally situated for visiting Salisbury Cathedral, Wilton House and Stourhead Gardens.

WILTSHIRE - SWINDON (PURTON)

The Pear Tree At Purton

CHURCH END, PURTON, SWINDON, WILTSHIRE SN5 4ED
Tel: 0845 365 2635 **International:** +44 (0)1793 772100 **Fax:** 01793 772369
Web: www.johansens.com/peartree **E-mail:** relax@peartreepurton.co.uk

Our inspector loved: *The extensive, well-kept gardens, including a wetland area and vineyard*

Price Guide:
single £110
double/twin £110–£135
suite £135

Awards/Recognition: 2 AA Rosettes 2007-2008

Location: B4534, 2.3 miles; A3102, 3.3 miles; M4 jct 16, 3.7 miles; Swindon, 5 miles

Attractions: Avebury; Bowood House; Bath; Cirencester

Owners Francis and Anne Young are justly proud of their achievements at this lovely honey-coloured stone hotel, nestling in the Vale of the White Horse between the Cotswolds and Marlborough Downs. It has received many awards for excellence and you will understand why as you enjoy good English food in the conservatory restaurant overlooking beautiful gardens or rest in the well-appointed bedrooms and suites with digital TV, safe and other little essential luxuries. Each bedroom is named after a character associated with the Saxon village of Purton, such as Anne Hyde, mother of Queen Mary II, and Queen Anne. Explore some of the history for yourself at the unique twin-towered Parish Church and the ancient hill fort of Ringsbury Camp.

WILTSHIRE - WARMINSTER

Bishopstrow House & Spa

WARMINSTER, WILTSHIRE BA12 9HH
Tel: 0845 365 3038 **International:** +44 (0)1985 212312 **Fax:** 01985 216769
Web: www.johansens.com/bishopstrowhouse **E-mail:** info@bishopstrow.co.uk

Our inspector loved: *A peaceful setting with good service and relaxing atmosphere.*

Price Guide:
single from £125
double/twin £170–£280
suite £330–£395

Awards/Recognition: 2 AA Rosettes 2008-2009

Location: On the B3414; A303, 10 miles; Bristol International Airport, 38 miles; M3 jct 8, 40 miles

Attractions: Bath; Longleat; Stourhead; Stonehenge;

This ivy-clad, Grade II listed Georgian mansion is an intimate country retreat with comfortable contemporary elements and the not to be missed Bishopstrow Spa. Attention to detail is uppermost in the library, drawing room and conservatory with their beautiful antiques and Victorian oil paintings. Bedrooms are individual, some with classical fabrics and tones whilst others contrast with striking contemporary furnishings. Skilfully prepared modern British food is served in the Mulberry Restaurant, alternatively a good selection of lighter meals can be enjoyed in the bar and conservatory with views overlooking 27 acres of gardens. There is an indoor and outdoor heated swimming pool, gym and sauna, fly fishing on the hotel's private stretch of the River Wylye, golf at 5 nearby courses, riding, game and clay pigeon shooting. A von Essen hotel

WORCESTERSHIRE - ABBERLEY

The Elms Hotel & Aquae Sulis Spa

STOCKTON ROAD, ABBERLEY, WORCESTERSHIRE WR6 6AT
Tel: 0845 365 2485 **International:** +44 (0)1299 896666 **Fax:** 01299 896804
Web: www.johansens.com/elmsworcester **E-mail:** info@theelmshotel.co.uk

Our inspector loved: *The welcoming family-friendly feel and the beautifully furnished bedrooms.*

Price Guide:
double/twin £145–£325
suite £245–£345
interconnecting £265–£595

Awards/Recognition: 2 AA Rosettes 2008-2009; Restaurant of the Year – Worcestershire Food & Drink Awards 2007

Location: On the A443; M5 jct 5/ 6, 11.5 miles; Birmingham International Airport, 29 miles

Attractions: West Midlands Safari Park; Severn Valley Railway, Cadbury World; Witley Court

This fine Queen Anne mansion sits between Worcester and Tenbury Wells, surrounded by beautiful meadows, woodland, hop fields and orchards of the Teme Valley. There's a very friendly country house party feel to The Elms, which recently underwent a complete refurbishment. 17 charming bedrooms are in the main building and 6 in the characterful coach-house. The new Aquae Sulis Spa follows a concept of fun and shared experiences from learning to swim to full body pampering, adding a great new dimension to family holidays. Ofsted registered nursery/playroom, babysitting, listening services and an outdoor play area are all available. With younger guests eating early, adults can enjoy time to themselves in the award-winning Brooke Room Restaurant or in the more informal and new Pear Terrace Brasserie; both serve sophisticated, imaginative dishes prepared by Head Chef Daren Bale. A von Essen Luxury Family Hotel.

WORCESTERSHIRE - BUCKLAND (NEAR BROADWAY)

BUCKLAND MANOR

BUCKLAND, NEAR BROADWAY, WORCESTERSHIRE WR12 7LY
Tel: 0845 365 3210 **International:** +44 (0)1386 852626 **Fax:** 01386 853557
Web: www.johansens.com/bucklandmanor **E-mail:** info@bucklandmanor.co.uk

Our inspector loved: *Breakfast on the terrace by the lovely gardens.*

Price Guide:
double/twin £265-£350
suite £385-£460

Awards/Recognition: Relais & Châteaux; Condé Nast Johansens Taittinger Wine List Award, Best Selection of Champagne 2008; 3 AA Rosettes 2008-2009

Location: A44, 3 miles; M40 jct 8, 45 miles; Broadway, 2.5 miles; Birmingham International Airport, 45 miles

Attractions: Sudeley Castle; Snowshill Manor; Cotswolds; Stratford-upon-Avon

You can almost feel the warm glow of Buckland Manor's golden Cotswold stone, and willl be dying to get to the luxury and history behind its weather-beaten walls. First mentioned in the records of Gloucester Abbey in 600AD, the Abbot received it as a gift from Kynred, ruler of Mercia and chief king of the 7 kingdoms of England. Buckland Manor remains gracious and traditional, and glorious grounds reveal small waterfalls, tennis courts, putting green and croquet lawns. Relax before log fires in 3 delightfully decorated drawing rooms, one with wood panelling and a beamed ceiling. Elegant bedrooms with lovely furnishings and bathrooms that use water from the Manor's own spring. General Manager, Nigel Power ensures guests recieve the highest level of discreet service and Chef, Matt Hodgkins creates impressive cuisine for his award-winning restaurant. A von Essen hotel.

WORCESTERSHIRE - CHADDESLEY CORBETT (NEAR KIDDERMINSTER)

BROCKENCOTE HALL

CHADDESLEY CORBETT, NR KIDDERMINSTER, WORCESTERSHIRE DY10 4PY
Tel: 0845 365 3204 **International:** +44 (0)1562 777876 **Fax:** 01562 777872
Web: www.johansens.com/brockencotehall **E-mail:** info@brockencotehall.com

Our inspector loved: *The great combination of French "chateau" and cuisine set in 70 acres of classic English parkland.*

Price Guide:
single from £98
double/twin from £125
four poster from £157

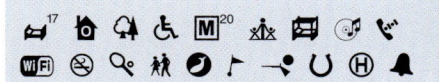

Awards/Recognition: 2 AA Rosettes 2007-2008

Location: on the A448; M42 jct 1, 8 miles; M5 jct 4, 12 miles; Birmingham International Airport, 28 miles

Attractions: Severn Valley Railway; Worcester Cathedral & Porcelain Museum; Ironbridge Gorge; Warwick Castle

In an unspoilt corner of English countryside, the Brockencote estate reaches back over three centuries, and its gatehouse, lake, half-timbered dovecote, European and North American trees and elegant conservatory give you a flavour of the changes in fashion and taste over the years. This multi award winning hotel including 3 AA Red Stars is matched by the Hall's friendly staff. Owners Alison and Joseph Petitjean provide excellent service. In true country house style each bedroom is different, and interiors combine classical architecture with creature comforts and elaborate décor. The Hall specialises in traditional French cuisine with occasional regional and seasonal dishes.. Just to the south of Birmingham, you'll find it conveniently situated whether travelling for business or pleasure, and a fine base for touring historic Worcestershire.

WORCESTERSHIRE - EVESHAM

THE EVESHAM HOTEL

COOPER'S LANE, OFF WATERSIDE, EVESHAM, WORCESTERSHIRE WR11 1DA
Tel: 0845 365 2487 **International:** +44 (0)1386 765566 **US toll free:** Reservations: 0800 716969 **Fax:** 01386 765443
Web: www.johansens.com/evesham **E-mail:** reception@eveshamhotel.com

Our inspector loved: *The huge range of drinks and the compendium which is the wine list - use both hands to pick it up.*

Price Guide:
single £77–£87
double/twin £123
family suite £166

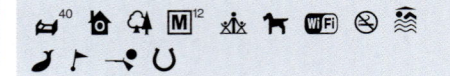

Awards/Recognition: 1 AA Rosette 2007-2008

Location: Just off B4035; A44/A46, 1 mile; M5 jct 9, 11 miles; Birmingham Airport, 34 miles

Attractions: The Cotswolds; Warwick; Stratford-upon-Avon; Severn Valley

It's the appealingly unconventional atmosphere at the Evesham Hotel that sticks in your mind! Combining a refreshing, award-winning welcome to families with style and efficiency, it has been very successfully run by the Jenkinsons for over 30 years. All bedrooms come complete with a teddy bear and toy duck for the bath, and the restaurant menus are imaginative and versatile. And somewhat unique is the "Euro-sceptic" wine list - everything but French and German! However, the full drinks selection is dazzling. An indoor pool has a seaside theme, while the peace of the 2.5 acre garden belies the hotel's proximity to the town - a 5-minute walk away. In the gardens are six 300-year-old mulberry trees and a magnificent cedar of Lebanon, planted in 1809. Closed at Christmas.

WORCESTERSHIRE - MALVERN WELLS

The Cottage in the Wood

HOLYWELL ROAD, MALVERN WELLS, WORCESTERSHIRE WR14 4LG
Tel: 0845 365 2431 **International:** +44 (0)1684 588860 **Fax:** 01684 560662
Web: www.johansens.com/cottageinthewood **E-mail:** reception@cottageinthewood.co.uk

Our inspector loved: *The gentle stroll down to the delightful Beech Cottage rooms after enjoying some of the many different gins.*

Price Guide:
single £79-£112
double/twin £99-£185

Awards/Recognition: Condé Nast Johansens Taittinger Wine List Award, Best English Wine List 2008; 2 AA Rosettes 2006-2007

Location: A449, 0.25 mile; M5 jct 7/8, 15 miles; Birmingham Airport, 48 miles

Attractions: Hereford Cathedral; Three Counties Showground; The Cotswolds; Various Historic Castles & Gardens

The Malvern Hills - once home and inspiration for England's great composer, Sir Edward Elgar - provide a 30 mile Severn Valley outlook from The Cottage in the Wood. Accommodation is both in the main house, originally the Dower House to the Blackmore Park Estate, in Beech Cottage - an old scrumpy house - and the magnificent "The Pinnacles", whose rooms with patios or balconies boast spectacular views. Owned and run by 2 generations of the Pattin family for 21 years, the hotel's atmosphere is genuinely warm and relaxing, and a regularly changing modern English menu is complemented by an almost obsessional wine list of 600 bins. If you are a little over-indulgent then take a walk to the tops of the Malvern Hills direct from the hotel grounds.

NORTH YORKSHIRE - BOLTON ABBEY (SKIPTON)

The Devonshire Arms Country House Hotel & Spa

BOLTON ABBEY, SKIPTON, NORTH YORKSHIRE BD23 6AJ
Tel: 0845 365 2461 **International:** +44 (0)1756 718111 **Fax:** 01756 710564
Web: www.johansens.com/devonshirearms **E-mail:** res@devonshirehotels.co.uk

Our inspector loved: *The exemplary service from beginning to end. The sumptuous cocktail lounge with open log fire, squishy sofas and beautiful paintings.*

Price Guide:
single £180–£370
double/twin £225–£370
suite £410

Reflecting its idyllic Yorkshire Dales setting, The Devonshire offers you a peaceful, welcome and relaxing escape, amidst 30,000 acres of rolling parkland, far from the bustling crowds. Owned by the Duke and Duchess of Devonshire the hotel features paintings from the Devonshire Collection at Chatsworth. You will be very easily enticed by the fine dishes created by Executive Head Chef Steve Smith in the elegant Burlington Restaurant - allow time to peruse the wine list of over 2,500 labels - or soak up the lively décor and contemporary art of the informal Brasserie and Bar. Make the most of a full range of leisure, health and beauty therapy facilities in the Spa, housed in a converted 17th-century barn. All this on the doorstep of the Bolton Abbey Estate with its 80 miles of footpaths, nature walks and hiking trails, church and ruins of the 12th century Augustinian Priory and picturesque village.

Awards/Recognition: Condé Nast Johansens / Taittinger Wine List Award 2005; 4 AA Rosettes 2007-2008

Location: On the B6160; A59, 400yds; Skipton, 6 miles; Leeds Bradford Airport, 12 miles

Attractions: Bolton Abbey Estate & Priory; Fountains Abbey; Fly Fishing on the River Wharfe; Harrogate for shopping and antiques.

NORTH YORKSHIRE - HAWES (UPPER WENSLEYDALE)

SIMONSTONE HALL

HAWES, NORTH YORKSHIRE DL8 3LY
Tel: 0845 365 2348 **International:** +44 (0)1969 667255 **Fax:** 01969 667741
Web: www.johansens.com/simonstonehall **E-mail:** email@simonstonehall.demon.co.uk

Our inspector loved: Location, location, location. The perfect setting for a romantic dinner, a special occasion or a wedding reception.

Price Guide:
single £75–£120
double/twin £110–£190

Location: A684, 1.5 miles; Hawes, 1.5 miles

Attractions: Hardraw Force; Wensleydale Creamery Cheese Factory; Yorkshire Dales; Bolton Castle

This former 18th-century hunting lodge has been lovingly restored and furnished with antiques, to create an idyllic and memorable retreat. The hall stands in a beautiful setting adjacent to 4,000 acres of grouse moors and upland grazing. Many period features have been retained such as the panelled dining room, mahogany staircase with ancestral stained glass windows and a lounge with ornamental ceilings. The bedrooms are of a high standard, 5 which offer four-poster and 2 with sleigh beds. In the restaurant, you can enjoy the freshest local produce presented most imaginatively, whilst absorbing stunning views across Upper Wensleydale. Excellent wines are available to complement any dish. Traditional country cuisine is served in the Game Tavern and The Orangery which provide a particularly warm and informal atmosphere.

NORTH YORKSHIRE - HELMSLEY

BLACK SWAN HOTEL

MARKET PLACE, HELMSLEY YO62 5BJ
Tel: 0845 365 3792 **International:** +44 (0)1439 770466 **Fax:** 01439 770174
Web: www.johansens.com/blackswan **E-mail:** enquiries@blackswan-helmsley.co.uk

Our inspector loved: Choosing from the sumptuous menus, which use the finest and freshest locally sourced produce.

Price Guide:
double/twin (single occupancy) from £100
double/twin from £140

As much a landmark as a hotel, the Black Swan has been in existence since the 15th century and today, as you step into its 6 warm and inviting lounges you can still enjoy a heady mix of Elizabethan, Georgian and Tudor architecture. Some bedrooms, including feature rooms and a junior suite, overlook the pretty market square and all are individually named after local dales, so you can walk from Bransdale to Glaisdale in under one minute! Take a swim before supper at the sister hotel, The Feversham Arms, and return to take full advantage of the passionate Head Chef Andrew Burton's locally sourced dinner menus. The Tearoom & Patisserie, whose artisan pastries and handmade chocolates are irresistible! Makes an indulgent destination after exploring this beautiful area of North Yorkshire.

Location: On the A170; Thirsk, 14 miles; York, 22 miles

Attractions: Rievaulx Abbey; Castle Howard; North York Moors; North York railways

NORTH YORKSHIRE - HELMSLEY (HAROME)

The Pheasant

HAROME, HELMSLEY, NORTH YORKSHIRE YO62 5JG
Tel: 0845 365 2641 **International:** +44 (0)1439 771241 **Fax:** 01439 771744
Web: www.johansens.com/pheasanthelmsley **E-mail:** reservations@thepheasanthotel.com

Our inspector loved: *The setting is stunning and the oak-beamed bar is charming. This country hotel has paid attention to detail and you will enjoy every comfort during your stay.*

Price Guide: (including 5-course dinner)
single £82–£98
double/twin £164–£178

Location: A170, 2 miles; Helmsley, 3 miles; York, 25 miles

Attractions: Rievaulx Abbeys; Castle Howard; Duncombe Park; North York Moors National Park

The Pheasant, rich in oak beams and open log fires, offers 2 types of accommodation, some in the hotel and some in a charming, 16th-century thatched cottage. The Binks family, who built the hotel have created a friendly atmosphere which is an essential part of the warm Yorkshire welcome that awaits you. The bedrooms and suites are brightly decorated in an attractive cottage style. Traditional English cooking is the speciality of the restaurant and many of the dishes are prepared using local fresh fruit and vegetables. During summer, guests may relax on the terrace overlooking the pond. An indoor heated swimming pool is an added attraction and dogs are most welcome if prior notice is given. Closed Christmas, January and February.

NORTH YORKSHIRE - MALTON

BURYTHORPE HOUSE

BURYTHORPE, MALTON, NORTH YORKSHIRE YO17 9LB
Tel: 0845 365 3709 **International:** +44 (0)1653 658 200 **Fax:** 01653 658204
Web: www.johansens.com/burythorpehouse **E-mail:** reception@burythorpehouse.co.uk

Our inspector loved: *The lavishly and individually furnished bedrooms.*

Price Guide:
petite £105-£130
superior £140-£165
luxury £165-£190

Location: A64, 3 miles; A1(M) jct 47, 21 miles; York, 18 miles

Attractions: York Racecourse; Castle Howard; Yorkshire Coast; Stamford Bridge

You will be welcomed like an old friend visiting a delightful home at Burythorpe House, a boutique country house hotel surrounded by idyllic countryside in the heart of Yorkshire's horse racing world. There is a relaxing quality to the hotel's interior and you can see the care that has been taken. From the individually decorated bedrooms to the oak-panelled restaurant where creatively prepared dishes are inspired by the seasons and local produce. Certainly worth considering for a wedding or party venue as the large lawn makes an ideal setting for a marquee. Discover the Minster city of York and its famed racecourse or experience the magnificent Yorkshire Coast, especially the cliffs around Bempton and Flamborough, but do leave time to enjoy the indoor pool or a game of tennis.

NORTH YORKSHIRE - YARM (KIRKLEVINGTON)

JUDGES COUNTRY HOUSE HOTEL

KIRKLEVINGTON HALL, KIRKLEVINGTON, YARM, NORTH YORKSHIRE TS15 9LW
Tel: 0845 365 1928 **International:** +44 (0)1642 789000 **Fax:** 01642 782878
Web: www.johansens.com/judges **E-mail:** enquiries@judgeshotel.co.uk

Our inspector loved: *The Dom Perignon room and dining in the conservatory restaurant.*

Price Guide:
double (single occupancy) £142–£197
double/twin £175–£194
suite/four poster £265

Awards/Recognition: 3 AA Rosettes 2007-2008

Location: A67, 0.1 miles; A19, 1.5 miles; Yarm, 1.5 miles

Attractions: Historic city of Durham; Croft Motor racing circuit; Cleveland Hills; North Yorkshire Moors

Located within 31 acres of idyllic landscaped gardens and woodlands, this charming country house hotel is an oasis of peace. The luxurious interior design makes it easy to relax and unwind from the stresses of daily life. Public rooms are elegantly decorated with fine fabrics, and you are surrounded by books, paintings and antiques. The bedrooms are very comfortable and each includes a foot spa, an iPod docking station and a pet goldfish ! Some rooms have Jacuzzi baths and all have an evening turndown service. Menus feature a 6-course meal which is served in the Conservatory Restaurant, accompanied by the finest of wines. Private dining is available, perfect for parties or the family. The hotel's location makes it ideal for exploring a host of attractions in the North East.

NORTH YORKSHIRE - YORK

The Grange Hotel

1 CLIFTON, YORK, NORTH YORKSHIRE YO30 6AA
Tel: 0845 365 2507 **International:** +44 (0)1904 644744 **Fax:** 01904 612453
Web: www.johansens.com/grangeyork **E-mail:** info@grangehotel.co.uk

Our inspector loved: *The richly decorated rooms, the warm welcome, the modern art in the Ivy Brasserie and the stone-flagged floors in the imposing front hall.*

Price Guide:
single £120–£190
double/twin £135–£230
suite £275

Awards/Recognition: 2 AA Rosettes 2007-2008

Location: York City Centre, ½ mile; A1237, 1.5 miles; A1M, 12 miles

Attractions: York Minster; Castle Howard; Yorkshire Dales and Moors; Leeds

Take a short walk from the world-famous Minster to find this sophisticated Regency town house, where beautiful stone-flagged floors lead to classic, richly decorated receptions rooms. The flower-filled Morning Room swallows you up with deep sofas and blazing fire in winter months, while antiques and English chintz reflect the proprietor's careful attention to detail in the bedrooms. A stunning six bedroom extension has recently opened, each one air conditioned and features 17" LCD televisions at the foot of each double end bath. Double doors between the panelled library and drawing room can be thrown open, creating a perfect venue for social and business events. The Ivy Brasserie has an excellent reputation for food, and the Cellar Bar welcomes you for lunch Monday to Saturday and dinner at weekends. Perfectly positioned to enjoy the endless list of attractions including National Railway Museum and the medieval Shambles.

NORTH YORKSHIRE - YORK

Middlethorpe Hall Hotel, Restaurant & Spa

BISHOPTHORPE ROAD, YORK, NORTH YORKSHIRE YO23 2GB
Tel: 0845 365 2061 **International:** +44 (0)1904 641241 **Fax:** 01904 620176
Web: www.johansens.com/middlethorpehall **E-mail:** info@middlethorpe.com

Our inspector loved: *Sipping champagne in the elegance of the drawing room - a showcase of fine art and antiques.*

Price Guide:
single £130–£185
double/twin £190–£260
suite from £270–£450

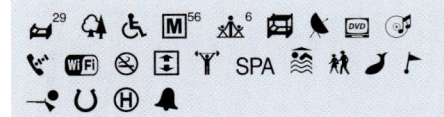

Awards/Recognition: 2 AA Rosettes 2007-2008

Location: A1036, 1.7 miles; A64, 3 miles; A1(M), 12.6 miles; Leeds, 23.3 miles

Attractions: York; York Racecourse; Castle Howard; Fountains and Rievaulx Abbey

This imposing William III house stands in 20 acres of gardens and parkland overlooking York Racecourse. Originally built in 1699 for Thomas Barlow, a wealthy merchant, Middlethorpe Hall was for a time the home of Lady Mary Wortley Montagu, the 18th-century diarist. It is now an immaculately restored example of its period renovated by Historic House Hotels. Each room is filled with period furniture and paintings, and the beautifully decorated bedrooms and suites are located in the main house and 18th-century courtyard. There is also a private cottage comprising 2 suites. The panelled dining rooms look out to the gardens and offer the best in contemporary English cooking that is rapidly gaining well-deserved recognition for its imaginative cuisine that maintains traditional brilliance. Treat yourself with a trip to the health and fitness spa with inviting pool and treatment rooms.

N Ireland & Ireland

N. Ireland & Ireland

For further information on Ireland, please contact:

The Irish Tourist Board
(Bord Fáilte Éireann)
Baggot Street Bridge
Dublin 2
Tel: +353 (0)1 602 4000
Internet: www.ireland.ie

Tourism Ireland
Tourism Centre
Suffolk Street
Dublin 2
Tel: 0800 039 7000
Internet: www.discoverireland.com

Northern Ireland Tourist Information
Belfast Welcome Centre
47 Donegall Place
Belfast, BT1 5AD
Tel: +44 (0)28 9024 6609
Internet: www.gotobelfast.com

or see **pages 270-273** for details of local historic houses, castles and gardens to visit during your stay.

For additional places to stay in Ireland, turn to **pages 268-269** where a listing of our Recommended Small Hotels, Inns & Restaurant Guide can be found.

CONDÉ NAST JOHANSENS
GREAT BRITAIN & IRELAND

RECOMMENDED SMALL HOTELS INNS & RESTAURANTS 2009

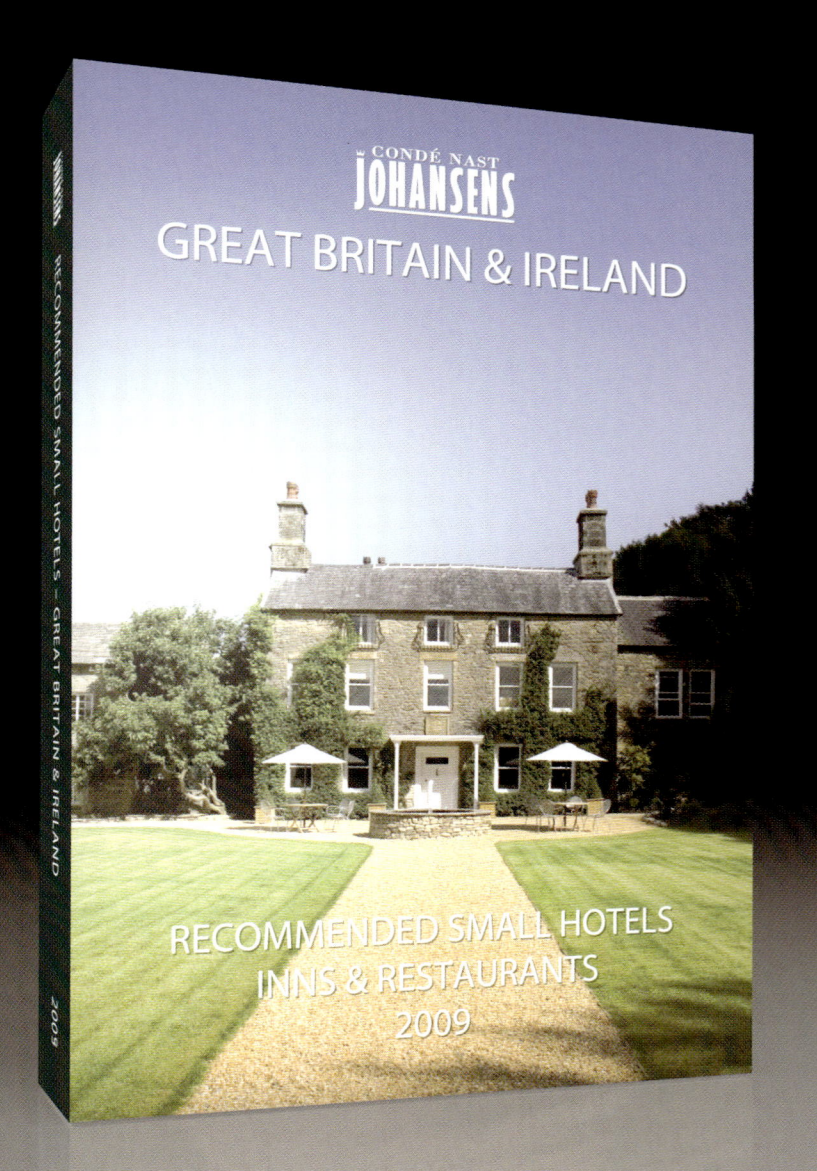

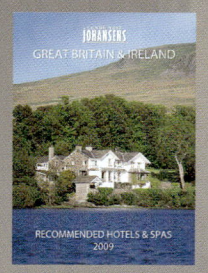

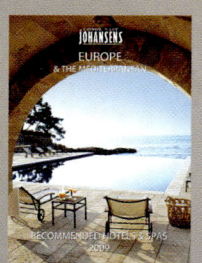

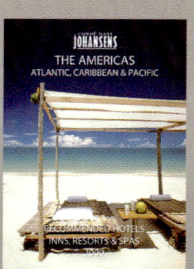

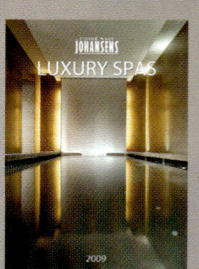

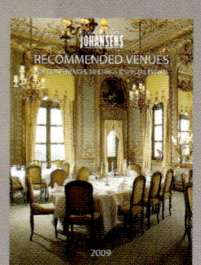

Hotels & Spas, Great Britain & Ireland 2009 • Hotels & Spas, Europe & The Mediterranean 2009
Hotels, Inns, Resorts & Spas, The Americas, Atlantic, Caribbean & Pacific 2009 • Luxury Spas Worldwide 2009
International Venues for Meetings & Special Events 2009

New Guides • New Destinations • New Experiences

Available at all good bookshops or by calling freephone 0800 269 397

Order online at www.johansens.com

ANTRIM - BELFAST (NORTHERN IRELAND)

Ten Square

10 DONEGALL SQUARE SOUTH, BELFAST BT1 5JD
Tel: 0845 365 4032 **International:** +44 (0)28 90 241 001 **Fax:** 028 90 243 210
Web: www.johansens.com/tensquare **E-mail:** reservations@tensquare.co.uk

Our inspector loved: *Enjoying the majestic views and striking architecture of Belfast City Hall from the rolltop bath in room 209.*

Price Guide:
single from £165
double from £165
suite from £265

Location: Belfast City Airport, 3 miles; Belfast International Airport, 17 miles; M1 / M2, 0.5 miles; Belfast Car Ferry Port, 0.5 mile

Attractions: Titanic Quarter; Giants Causeway; Mourne Mountains; Victoria Square

Refreshing and innovative from the moment you step through the door. The opulent and openly decadent reception area, with a magnificent spiral staircase and ornate stained-glass window leads you into a lavish interior influenced by 1920s Shanghai. This fine detail and elegance is reflected in the boutique-style guest rooms featuring oversized beds, custom-made furniture and beautiful fabrics. The Grill Room and Bar, has an eclectic menu and is deservedly popular with locals and guests alike. For intimate weddings and for those needing to entertain there's an impressive event room, the Porcelain Suite up on the first floor. The rejuvenated vibrancy of Belfast has made this a hot destination and Ten Square just adds to its attraction.

CARLOW - TULLOW

MOUNT WOLSELEY HOTEL, SPA & COUNTRY CLUB

TULLOW, CO CARLOW, IRELAND
Tel: 00 353 599 180100 **Fax:** 00 353 599 12123
Web: www.johansens.com/mountwolseley **E-mail:** info@mountwolseley.ie

Our inspector loved: The superb quality and array of facilities available.

Price Guide: (euro)
single from €115
double from €170
suite €205-€265

Tranquil, stylish and luxurious are all words we would use to describe this beautifully situated County Carlow hotel, just one hour from Dublin. Even the most jaded golf fanatic will melt at the sight of Mount Wolseley's 18-hole golf course - one of Ireland's finest. Yet golf widow/ers needn't fret, as there is the gorgeous Erre Esse Boutique or Sanctuary Spa as alternative ways to pass the time. As you would expect, the hotel's elegant, chic interior is matched by ultra-modern amenities and impeccable service, as well as excellent dining in Frederick's Restaurant. Alongside stunning countryside and cultural attractions nearby, the rivers Barrow and Slaney offer great fishing and County Carlow provides the perfect backdrop for walking, horse riding and canoeing.

Location: N9, 7 miles; Dublin, 50 miles; Dublin Airport, 55 miles

Attractions: Kilkenny Castle; Altamount Gardens; Arboretum Lifestyle & Garden Centre; Delta Garden Centre & Sensory Gardens

CORK - MALLOW

LONGUEVILLE HOUSE & PRESIDENTS' RESTAURANT

MALLOW, CO CORK, IRELAND
Tel: 00 353 22 47156 **Fax:** 00 353 22 47459
Web: www.johansens.com/longuevillehouse **E-mail:** info@longuevillehouse.ie

Our inspector loved: *The warm family welcome into this ancestral home.*

Price Guide: (euro)
single from €110
double/twin from €235

Location: Mallow N72, 3 miles; Cork Airport, 22 miles; Dublin, 2-hours train

Attractions: Mallow; Cork Racecourse; Anne's Grove Gardens

This superb listed Georgian manor will offer you a piece of early 18th century Ireland. Virtually self-sufficient - a tradition that has remained largely unaltered for almost 300 years - the hotel uses fresh produce from the estate's farm, gardens and river; including garden honey and preserves and house smoked salmon. Needless to say the daily menus under the direction of talented chef patron William O'Callaghan are a delight to the taste buds. Staying here you feel more like you are a house guest, a feeling that is aided by the attentive service and the personal touches such as O'Callaghan family photos and heirlooms. The conservatory is a master piece of ironwork completed by Richard Turner, 1866 who previous works had included the Botanical Gardens at Kew and in Belfast. Fishing & shooting is available on the estate and it would make an ideal venue for exclusive weddings, corporate events and house takeovers.

DONEGAL - DONEGAL TOWN (LOUGH ESKE)

Harvey's Point

LOUGH ESKE, DONEGAL TOWN, CO DONEGAL, IRELAND
Tel: 00 353 74 972 2208 **Fax:** 00 353 74 972 2352
Web: www.johansens.com/harveyspoint **E-mail:** info@harveyspoint.com

Our inspector loved: The quality of the food and the setting of the restaurant overlooking the Lough Eske

Price Guide: (euro)
single €240
double/twin €290-€360
suite from €580

Awards/Recognition: Condé Nast Johansens Most Excellent Service Award 2008

Location: Donegal Town, 3 miles; Donegal Airport, 50 miles; Sligo Airport, 50 miles

Attractions: Top Championship Golf Courses; Donegal Town; Glenvagh National Park and Castle

Against a backdrop of the beautiful Blue Stack Mountains, Harvey's Point Nestles on the edge of Lough Eske and has all the ingredients of a haven to which you would wish to retreat, unwind and rejuvenate. Bedrooms are spacious and all have large bathrooms with sunken baths large enough for two. Though if you really want to indulge, a penthouse suite has a lofty living-room, dressing room, bar, bath jet pool and mini-plasma in the bathroom. The restaurant delights with innovative modern celtic dishes as well as international fare worked around the seasons. Entertainment is important here and on top of the resident pianist, throughout the year on Wednesday and Friday diverse performers from amongst Irelands most sought after perform.

DUBLIN - KILLINEY

Fitzpatrick Castle Hotel

KILLINEY, CO DUBLIN
Tel: 00 353 1 230 5400 **Fax:** 00 353 1 230 5430
Web: www.johansens.com/fitzpatrickcastle **E-mail:** info@fitzpatricks.com

Our inspector loved: The new stylish Dungeon Bar & Grill located in the oldest part of this magnificent castle.

Price Guide: (Euros)
single from €120
double/twin from €160
suite from €250

Awards/Recognition: 1 AA Rosette 2008-2009

Location: M50, 2 miles; Dun Laoghaire Ferry Port, 3 miles; Dublin City Centre, 9 miles; Dublin Airport, 25 miles

Attractions: Dalkey Heritage Centre; Powerscourt House and Gardens; Dun Laoghaire Harbour and James Joyce Tower; Leopardstown Race Course

Perched on the brow of Killiney Hill overlooking Dublin bay this 18th Century castle is the epitome of elegance and Irish hospitality. Standing impressively in its own grounds, this luxury hotel is now in the expert hands of Eithne Fitzpatrick Scott-Lennon, daughter of the original owners who took over in 1971. Choose between rooms and suites of old world charm or luxury rooms overlooking Dublin bay. For fine dining the highly-acclaimed PJ's restaurant is popular with both locals and residents and menus focus on local seasonal produce. In the oldest part of the Castle the recently refurbished Dungeon Bar & Grill shows a contemporary and relaxed sophistication that understandably is a destination in its own right for drinks and succulent grills. Plenty of other facilities including a 20-metre swimming pool, gym, hair and beauty salon and creche. With Dublin only 14 miles away this is a great alternative to staying in the city centre.

GALWAY - CLIFDEN (CONNEMARA)

Abbeyglen Castle

SKY ROAD, CLIFDEN, CO GALWAY, IRELAND
Tel: 00 353 95 21201 **Fax:** 00 353 95 21797
Web: www.johansens.com/abbeyglen **E-mail:** info@abbeyglen.ie

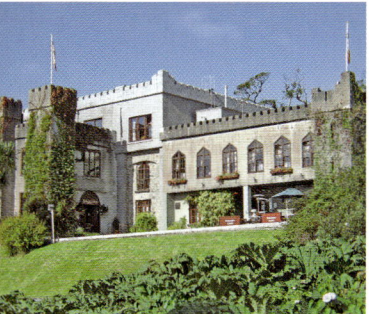

Perched just off the famous Sky Road near Clifden, the "capital" of Connemara, this 205-year-old castle is nestled amongst sheltered parkland and intriguing gardens. Facing Clifden Bay and with its back to the glorious rolling hills more fondly known as the Twelve Bens. Inside, large open fires and traditional furnishings provide a warm and welcoming atmosphere. For those who enjoy fishing, this hotel is ideally situated for shore angling and guests can have their catch cooked for them in the restaurant. Other activities include snooker, tennis and pony trekking which can be arranged locally. In the evening you can curl up with a glass of fine wine in the charming Resident's lounge that often hosts spontaneous music evenings. Abbeyglen now has a new Beauty & Relaxation Centre.

Our inspector loved: The truly open and genuine warmth of the proprietor's Paul and Brian.

Price Guide: (euro)
single from €130
standard double from €198
superior from €340

Awards/Recognition: 2 AA Rosettes 2008-2009

Location: Sky Road (Clifden), 0.5 miles; Galway (N59), 50 miles; Galway Airport, 55 miles

Attractions: Connemara National Park; Kylemore Abbey & Gardens; Connemara Golf Club, the Sky Road, great walking

GALWAY - CONNEMARA

Cashel House

CASHEL, CONNEMARA, CO GALWAY, IRELAND
Tel: 00 353 95 31001 **Fax:** 00 353 95 31077
Web: www.johansens.com/cashelhouse **E-mail:** res@cashel-house-hotel.com

Our inspector loved: *The serenity and timelessness of this beautiful country house hotel.*

Price Guide: (euro)
single €105–€270
double/twin €210–€350
suite €300–€395

Awards/Recognition: 2 AA Rosettes 2008-2009

Location: N59, 6km; Galway, 65km; Galway Airport, 70km

Attractions: Connemara National Park; Stud Farm; Delightful Gardens and Garden School; Private Beach

Surrounded by exotic flowering gardens and woodland walks at the head of Cashel Bay, this pretty hotel exudes tranquillity. Built by the owners' great, great grandfather for Captain Thomas Hazel, an English landowner, you will be welcomed today by proprietors the McEvilly family for whom nothing is too much trouble. Turf and log fires glow in public areas where the furnishings and décor reflect good taste. Bedrooms and suites are comfortable and overlook the hill or garden. In the dining room, Ray Doorley oversees the preparation of imaginative dishes from the constantly changing menu. The emphasis is on local seafood, lamb, beef, game and home-grown vegetables, complemented by a carefully chosen wine list. Swimming from the private beach is just one of a variety of pursuits.

GALWAY - RECESS

BALLYNAHINCH CASTLE HOTEL

RECESS, CONNEMARA, GALWAY, IRELAND
Tel: 00 353 953 1006 **Fax:** 00 353 953 1085
Web: www.johansens.com/ballynahinch **E-mail:** bhinch@iol.ie

Our inspector loved: *The setting that is simply breathtaking.*

Price Guide: (euro)
double from €260
suite from €390

Awards/Recognition: AA 2 Rosettes 2008-2009

Location: Recess Village, 3 miles; Clifden, 12 miles; Galway, 40 miles; Galway Airport, 45 miles

Attractions: Connemara National Park & The Twelve Bens Mountains; Kylemore Abbey & Victorian Walled Gardens; Connemara Championship Golf Links; Aran Islands

This beautiful old castle, perched on the banks of the Ballynahinch River, offers a warm and inviting ambience. Set in the heart of the Connemara Hills, this wonderful retreat is steeped in history and boasts beautifully appointed bedrooms some with four-poster beds but all decorated with great care and attention to detail. The stately rooms are decorated in soft pastels to create a harmonious atmosphere for those looking to unwind. The estate spans out across 450 acres, where guests can try their hand at fishing, shooting, horse-riding and sailing. For a more leisurely day, simply take a ramble through the walled garden with its labyrinth or head to the lakes and woodlands, where wildlife such as mallards, foxes and kestrels reside. Fine dining is available at the Owenmore Restaurant where Head Chef Xin Sun creates gourmet dishes including chilled Atlantic oysters with shallot and red wine vinegar, oven roasted Connemara lamb with rosemary and seared Cleggan scallops.

KERRY - KENMARE

Park Hotel Kenmare & Sámas

KENMARE, CO. KERRY, IRELAND
Tel: 00 353 64 41200 **Fax:** 00 353 64 41402
Web: www.johansens.com/parkkenmare **E-mail:** info@parkkenmare.com

Our inspector loved: *The spectacular setting of this outstanding hotel.*

Price Guide: (euro)
single €226–€280
double €452–€606
suite €696–€846

Awards/Recognition: 3 AA Rosettes 2006-2007; Top 10 Spas in Europe - Conde Nast Traveller Spa Awards 2007; Condé Nast Traveler (USA) Gold List 2007

Location: R569; Kenmare, 0.1 mile; Kerry Airport, 28 miles

Attractions: The Ring of Kerry; Bantry Bay; Dingle; The Killarney National park

SÁMAS, a Deluxe Destination Spa has been added to the much applauded Park Hotel Kenmare, and the mystical magic of Ireland can certainly be found in this enchanting corner of County Kerry. Samas offers over 60 Holistic treatments combined with heat experiences and relaxation to rejuvenate body, mind and spirit. Male and female areas are on hand to spare any blushes! Park Hotel Kenmare itself is elegant with glorious country views, and holds numerous awards. Bedrooms are deeply comfortable with traditional furnishings and the hallways are filled with wonderful antiques and treasures. The restaurant over looks the terraced garden and serves acclaimed seasonal menus that lean towards local seafood. There is also a 12-seat cinema, tennis, croquet and golf next door.

KERRY - KILLARNEY

THE BREHON

MUCKROSS ROAD, KILLARNEY, CO. KERRY, IRELAND
Tel: 00 353 64 30700 **Fax:** 00 353 64 30701
Web: www.johansens.com/thebrehon **E-mail:** info@thebrehon.com

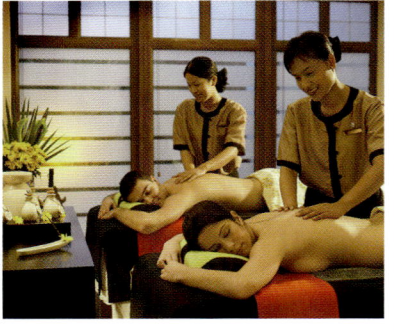

Our inspector loved: *The care and attentiveness of all the staff.*

Price Guide: (euro)
single €125-€175
double €150-€290
suite €250-€480

Awards/Recognition: 1 AA Rosette 2008-2009

Location: Town Centre, 0.5 miles; Kerry Airport, 14 miles; Cork Airport, 54 miles

Attractions: Killarney National Park; Killarney Golf and Fishing Club; The Ring of Kerry; The Dingle Peninsula

A majestic hotel in "the Garden of the Blest", 25,000 acres of woodlands and mountains in the Killarney National Park. The contemporary rooms are creatively decorated in calm natural tones with bold, colourful touches. Elegant ensuite bathrooms feature an aromatic natural amenities range. All rooms enjoy far-reaching views of the national park, while Superior Deluxe rooms boast balconies or bay windows from which to savour them. Award-winning chefs create extensive and enticing Irish and international cuisine, to be enjoyed in the contemporary Brehon restaurant. The impressive afternoon teas, served on the sun-drenched Mezzanine are not to be missed. Active guests will revel in the wealth of leisure opportunities available at the Brehon, while those seeking relaxation will visit the beautiful Angsana Spa.

KERRY - KILLARNEY

CAHERNANE HOUSE HOTEL

MUCKROSS ROAD, KILLARNEY, CO KERRY, IRELAND
Tel: 00 353 64 31895 **Fax:** 00 353 64 34340
Web: www.johansens.com/cahernane **E-mail:** info@cahernane.com

Our inspector loved: *The history seeping from every pore of this very comfortable home.*

Price Guide: (euro)
single from €180
double from €200
suite from €320

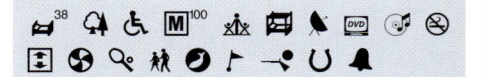

Awards/Recognition: 2 AA Rosette 2007-2008

Location: Killarney, 1 mile; Kerry Airport, 14 miles

Attractions: Ring of Kerry; Muckross House; Killarney Golf club; Killarney National Park

A shady tunnel of greenery frames the ¼ mile long drive to this welcoming 17th-century house, where time seems to move at a wonderfully sedate pace. The former home to the Earls of Pembroke it stands in gorgeous parklands on the edge of Killarney's National Park. You'll find the Browne family pride themselves on their hospitality and will be keen to ensure you make the most of your stay. Bedrooms have plenty of individual personality and the suites are enhanced with beautiful antiques. Recipient of numerous awards, Herbert Room restaurant offers menus by chef Pat Karney, or you can eat more informally in the Cellar Bar, home to an impressive stock of wines. There's tennis and croquet or simply enjoy garden walks and views of the National Parks untamed beauty.

KERRY - KILLARNEY

The Europe Hotel & Resort

KILLARNEY, CO KERRY, IRELAND
Tel: 00 353 64 71300 **Fax:** 00 353 64 37900
Web: www.johansens.com/europekerry **E-mail:** reservations@theeurope.com

Our inspector loved: *The constant attention to detail.*

Price Guide: (euro)
single €170-€310
double €210-€360
suite €400-€1750

Location: Killarney, 3 miles; Cork Airport, 53 miles

Attractions: Ring of Kerry; Gap of Dunloe; Dingle Peninsula

The panoramic views through the vast windows of The Europe Hotel & Resort lobby are priceless, however, the €50 million investment to this fabulous property is evident in every thoughtful and refined detail. Our Inspector described the hotel as "luxury personified," and it's easy to see why. Most bedrooms have spacious balconies with views over Killarney's lakes or countryside but if you're feeling particularly generous why not entertain up to 40 friends on the balcony of the Presidential Suite! Having enjoyed Irish and International cuisine in the Panorama Restaurant, you should find a space to relax and meet your mood – whether you are feeling studious in the Library, peaceful in the Lounge or chilled with a glass of champagne in the Brasserie Bar.

KERRY - KILLARNEY

Hotel Dunloe Castle

BEAUFORT, KILLARNEY, CO KERRY, IRELAND
Tel: 00 353 64 44111 **Fax:** 00 353 64 44583
Web: www.johansens.com/dunloecastle **E-mail:** hotelsales@liebherr.com

Our inspector loved: *This piece of heaven placed in an awe-inspiring landscape.*

Price Guide: (euro, closed late October 2008 to early April 2009)
single €170-€250
double €210-€290

Location: Beaufort, 1 miles; Killarney, 6 miles; Kerry Airport, 10 miles

Attractions: Ring of Kerry; Gap of Dunloe; Killarney National Park; Dingle Peninsula

This modern hotel is situated in 64 acres of picturesque rolling parkland, with pastures of Halfinger Ponies and views towards the breathtaking Gap of Dunloe. Take a stroll through the grounds to the original 12th-century Dunloe Castle ruins in whose shadow lies a historically important garden flaunting a myriad of plants including the Killarney strawberry tree and the rare Chinese swamp cypress. Inside, the elegant interior oozes tranquillity and features natural materials alongside antique paintings and carefully selected furnishings. Bedrooms benefit from floor to ceiling windows and most have balconies. Fine cuisine and great views are complemented by an extensive menu of wines in the Oak Room Restaurant, while lighter dishes are served in the Garden Café. Enjoy the 25m pool, complimentary gentle morning pony rides and fishing on the River Laune with equipment supplied by the hotel for free; the catch from which can be cooked by the kitchen.

MAYO - BALLINA

Mount Falcon Country House Hotel & Spa

FOXFORD ROAD, BALLINA, CO MAYO, IRELAND
Tel: 00 353 967 4472 **Fax:** 00 353 967 4473
Web: www.johansens.com/mountfalcon **E-mail:** info@mountfalcon.com

Our inspector loved: *The harmonious mix of the old with the new, and the wonderfully spacious grounds.*

Price Guide: (euro, There is a discretionary service charge of 10%)
single from €165
deluxe from €270
suite from €450

It is easy to see why Mount Falcon's new owners fell in love with the estate when they first visited this beautiful corner of Co Mayo. An impressive amount of time and money has been spent on a refurbishment and development programme that has successfully managed to capture the hotel's original charm and in many ways enhanced the experience. This is a luxurious venue offering golf, angling and spa breaks throughout the year with bedrooms oozing quality. The lovingly restored suites truly spoil with 15-foot ceilings, marble fireplaces, antique furniture and cast-iron baths. Award-winning Head Chef , Philippe Farineau, takes inspiration from seasonal and local organic produce ; Key dishes include wild game, trout, salmon, wild Halibut and lemon sole.

Awards/Recognition: 1 AA Rosette 2008–2009

Location: N26; Ballina, 3 miles; Ireland West Airport Knock, 20 miles; Sligo, 58 miles

Attractions: Exclusive wild Atlantic salmon fishing on The Moy; 12 Golf courses in a 30 mile radius including 3 championship links courses : Enniscrone, Carne - Belmullet and Rosses; The Ceide fileds; The Foxford Wollen Mills

MAYO - CONG

Ashford Castle

CONG, CO MAYO, IRELAND
Tel: 00 353 94 95 46003 **Fax:** 00 353 94 95 46260
Web: www.johansens.com/ashfordcastle E-mail: ashford@ashford.ie

Our inspector loved: *The unadulterated opulence of this majestic hotel.*

Price Guide: (euro, room only)
single/twin/double €244–€590
stateroom/suite €522–€1187

Location: N84, 9km; Galway City, 42km; Galway Airport, 44km

Attractions: Connemara Loop; Connemara National Park; Westport: Ceidhe Fields; Leenane

Set amidst stunning surroundings and formerly the home of Lord Ardilaun and the Guinness family, this 13th-century castle became a luxury hotel in 1939. A choice of restaurants include: the award-winning George "V" dining room offering modern and traditional dishes and the elegant Connaught Room which is open from May to September, Thursday to Sunday and where menus feature the very best Irish produce. The Drawing Room serves lunch, afternoon tea and more relaxed evening dining. Take a short stroll across the River Cong to Cullen's at the Cottage, where you can enjoy a bistro-style menu and choose a lobster from the tank! Don't miss the nightly entertainment in the Dungeon Bar. Activities include; falconry, fishing, clay pigeon shooting, tennis, a 9-hole golf course, health centre and treatment rooms. Boat trips can be arranged on Lough Corrib.

MAYO - CASTLEBAR

The Harlequin

LANNAGH ROAD, CASTLEBAR, CO MAYO, IRELAND
Tel: 00 353 949 286 200 **Fax:** 00 353 949 286 201
Web: www.johansens.com/harlequin **E-mail:** reservations@harlequin.ie

Our inspector loved: *The modern, crisp and sleek comfortable bedrooms.*

Price Guide: (euro)
single €69-€179
double/twin €79-€199
suite €119-€259

Location: N5, ½ mile; Ireland West International Airport (Knock), 28 miles; Westport, 10 miles; Galway City, 48 miles

Attractions: Royal Theatre, Castlebar; National Museum of Ireland, Turlough; Croagh Patrick; Kylemore Abbeyw

This chic and very contemporary 4-star boutique-style hotel is located in the heart of Castlebar, directly adjacent to The Royal Theatre, the largest entertainment venue outside Dublin, and just a few steps from the major shopping districts. Its fresh and open atmosphere embraces you as soon as you walk into the bright reception area, which is adorned with attractive modern furniture. All 90 guest rooms and mini-suites are designed in a refreshing, unfussy style, and offer all creature comforts, including complimentary Internet broadband. The Harlequin Restaurant is creatively laid out and cleverly switches menus throughout the day. A sumptuous buffet breakfast, light bites and evening menus of freshly prepared Irish and international cuisine.

MAYO - WESTPORT

Knockranny House Hotel & Spa

WESTPORT, CO MAYO, IRELAND
Tel: 00 353 98 28600 **Fax:** 00 353 98 28611
Web: www.johansens.com/knockranny **E-mail:** info@khh.ie

Our inspector loved: *All the excellent well-trained and attentive staff.*

Price Guide: (euro)
single from €105
double/twin from €140
suite from €210

Awards/Recognition: 1 AA Rosette 2007-2008

Location: Just off the N5; Town Centre 10-min walk; Train & Bus Station 15-min walk; Knock Airport, 45-mins drive

Attractions: Westport House Estate & Country Gardens; Clew Bay & Islands; Croagh patrick Mountain; Blue Flag Beaches

Rising into view against Croagh Patrick Mountain this Victorian hotel and spa evokes an image of a bygone era. Knockranny has a reputation as one of Ireland's finest hotels since 1997. You have a wide choice of bedrooms with courtyard or mountain views including Grand De Luxe - De Luxe - Master Suites and Executive Suites. The new rooms are very spacious and feature king-size beds, 32" LCD TVs, surround-sound systems, free broadband Internet access, oversized bathrooms with spa bath as standard. Antique furniture features throughout the hotel and the conservatory and library look out onto magnificent scenery. You can enjoy contemporary Irish cuisine and fish dishes in the restaurant. Spa Salveo features a vitality pool, a serail mud chamber and 12 treatment rooms.

MONAGHAN - CARRICKMACROSS

Nuremore Hotel and Country Club

CARRICKMACROSS, CO MONAGHAN, IRELAND
Tel: 00 353 42 9661438 **Fax:** 00 353 42 9661853
Web: www.johansens.com/nuremore **E-mail:** info@nuremore.com

Nuremore is set amidst 200 acres of rolling countryside with beautifully landscaped gardens. Its facilities include a swimming pool, treatment rooms and a health club featuring a gymnasium, spa bath, sauna and steam room. The hotel's renowned 18-hole championship golf course makes superb use of the surrounding lakes and landscape. Resident professional, Maurice Cassidy, is on hand to offer advice and tuition. All 72 bedrooms and suites are well appointed to ensure a generous sense of personal space and you can sample classic European cuisine, with Irish and French influences, prepared by award-winning Chef Raymond McArdle. The restaurant features in the Bridgestone Guide to Ireland's best 100 restaurants. Ideal for weddings and meetings, the impressive conference centre constantly evolves to ensure cutting edge facilities.

Our inspector loved: The sweeping entrance, immaculate grounds and genuine warmth of hospitality.

Price Guide: (Euro)
single €150–€200
double/twin €220–€280
suite from €250–€300

Awards/Recognition: 3 AA Rosettes 2007-2008

Location: N2, 1 mile; Dublin, 45-min drive; Belfast, 75-min drive

Attractions: Knockabbey Castle & Grounds; Monaghan County Museum; Carrickmacross Lace Gallery; Patrick Kavanagh Centre

TIPPERARY - THURLES

The Horse and Jockey Hotel

THURLES, CO TIPPERARY, IRELAND
Tel: 00 353 504 44192 **Fax:** 00 353 504 44747
Web: www.johansens.com/horseandjockey **E-mail:** info@horseandjockeyhotel.com

Our inspector loved: *The sumptuous bedrooms and the wonderful spa.*

Price Guide: (euro)
single from €80
double from €130
suite from €200

Location: N8, on the doorstep; Dublin Airport, 95 miles; Cork Airport, 80 miles

Attractions: Rock of Cashel; Cahir Castle; Kilkenny City; Holy Cross Abbey

Set literally 75 minutes from all of Ireland's major cities, The Horse and Jockey is the perfect hub for business and conference events, and once your work for the day is done kick back and relax in its atmosphere of comfort and ease. Public rooms are bright, airy and spacious and bedrooms are pleasingly well designed and contemporary in style. Indulge yourself at the Elemis Spa and leisure centre where there are no less than seven treatment rooms, a relaxation area, hydrotherapy area and exercise studio. And treat your tastebuds with a visit to Silks Restaurant where the best of County Tipperary's local produce is served. Bar and à la carte menus are also available at The Enclosure Bar. Nearby attractions of the Midlands region include Cahir and Kilkenny Castles, the Rock of Cashel and Kilkenny City.

WEXFORD - ARTHURSTOWN (NEAR WATERFORD)

Dunbrody Country House & Cookery School

ARTHURSTOWN, CO WEXFORD, IRELAND
Tel: 00 353 51 389 600 **Fax:** 00 353 51 389 601
Web: www.johansens.com/dunbrody **E-mail:** info@dunbrodyhouse.com

Our inspector loved: The unique combination of period house, cookery school and intimate Spa, make this a 'must visit' hotel.

Price Guide: (euro)
single €145-€360
double/twin €240-€360
suite €395-€450

Location: Arthurstown, 0.5km; Passage East Car Ferry, 2km; Waterford, 12km; Wexford N11, 30km

Attractions: The Hook Peninsula; Viking towns of Waterford and Wexford; Dunbrody Abbey; Waterford Crystal

Contemporary canvases hang next to portrait oils and gives you some clue as to the ingenuity of the owners of this former home of the Marquess of Donegall. Kevin and Catherine Dundon have created a seriously good small luxury hotel. As a renowned chef Kevin oversees the cooking school and restaurant whilst Catherine is a meticulous and welcoming host. Bedrooms are spacious and delightful and many look over the garden and lawns. A lovely alternative to the excellent restaurant is the new champagne and seafood bar with impressive glass chandeliers, high wide counter, comfy stools and a menu full of local fish from the Hook Peninsula. On a short break you could fit in a cookery class, be pampered in the chic and intimate spa and tour this beautiful part of Ireland - wonderful.

WEXFORD - GOREY

Marlfield House

COURTOWN ROAD R742, GOREY, CO WEXFORD, IRELAND
Tel: 00 353 53 94 21124 **Fax:** 00 353 53 94 21572
Web: www.johansens.com/marlfieldhouse **E-mail:** info@marlfieldhouse.ie

Our inspector loved: *The wonderful ambience upon arrival accompanied by the care and attention of such gracious hosts.*

Price Guide: (euro)
single from €140
double/twin from €250
state rooms from €405
(closed mid-December - 1st February)

Awards/Recognition: Relais & Châteaux

Location: N11, 0.5 miles; Gorey, 0.5 miles; Dublin Airport, 60 miles

Attractions: Many golf courses including Druids Glen and The European; The 12th Century city of Kilkenny with its castle & cathedral; Waterford Crystal; County Wicklow "The Garden of Ireland" home of the mediaval site Glendalough

Staying at the award-winning Marlfield House is a truly memorable experience, as this former residence of the Earl of Courtown presents Regency lifestyle in all its glory. Recognised as one of the finest country houses in Ireland, its welcoming hosts Raymond and Mary Bowe, and daughters Margaret and Laura, maintain it brilliantly. Interiors abound with original antiques and period detail such as classical decoupage prints and garlands. Bedrooms are the epitome of comfort and elegance and many have views over the extensive gardens and lake. The entrance hall is certainly imposing. However it is a house with a truly warm atmosphere and endless architectural delights including the Richard Turner conservatory. Ingredients from the kitchen garden influences the daily menus and enhance the succulent flavours of local seafood and meats.

WEXFORD - ROSSLARE

Kelly's Resort Hotel & Spa

ROSSLARE, CO WEXFORD, IRELAND
Tel: 00 353 53 91 32114 **Fax:** 00 353 53 32222
Web: www.johansens.com/kellysresort **E-mail:** info@kellys.ie

Our inspector loved: *The stunning beach location and wonderful recreational amenities of this family focused resort and spa.*

Price Guide: (euro, all inclusive, except some spa facilities and hire equipment, includes 10% s.c.)
2 night break from €285 per person sharing
5 night break from €693 per person sharing
Bed & Breakfast midweek from €88 per person sharing

Location: N25, 7 miles; N11/ Wexford, 17 miles; Waterford airport, 45 miles; Dublin, 94 miles

Attractions: Hook Lighthouse; National Heritage Park; Johnstown Castle Garden; Waterford

The long sandy beach of Rosslare fronts Kelly's in an area regarded as having the best weather in Ireland. There's a very light and fresh feel to this award-winning hotel. Walls are lined with an exceptional collection of contemporary art, many of which you can admire as you enjoy the delicious food of Beaches Restaurant. There is also the informal and buzzy atmosphere of the La Marine Bistro & Bar. Whilst you would enjoy a relaxing break here alone, Kelly's is great for families looking to have fun together yet when needed relaxing time apart. Kids have their own high-tea, crèche, entertainment and mini-activities whilst for adults, amongst other things, in & outdoor tennis, golf, aqua club and indulging at SeaSpa whose clever design using light and texture stimulates a feeling of calm.

WICKLOW - ENNISKERRY

THE RITZ-CARLTON, POWERSCOURT

POWERSCOURT ESTATE, ENNISKERRY, CO WICKLOW
Tel: 00 353 1 274 8888 **Fax:** 00 353 1 274 9999
Web: www.johansens.com/ritzcarlton **E-mail:** powerscourtreservations@ritzcarlton.com

Our inspector loved: *The oversized guest rooms accompanied by fantastic service from every member of staff.*

Price Guide: (euro)
deluxe from €255
garden suite from €295
mountain suite from €335

Location: Dublin Airport, 45-min drive; Dublin City Centre, 30-min drive; Glendalough, 40-min drive; Dun Laoghaire Ferry Port, 25-min drive

Attractions: Powerscourt House & Gardens; Glendalough; Dublin City Centre; Trinity College

Surrounded by the serene woodlands, gentle green hills and sparkling lakes of Powerscourt Estate, with glorious views of the Wicklow countryside, this sumptuous hotel beckons with an irresistible blend of luxurious country living and impeccable service, and yet cosmopolitan Dublin is only half an hour away. The bedrooms and suites are generously sized and decorated in a casually elegant style; many offer floor-to-ceiling windows, panoramic views and terraces. Dining is a delight: choose between Gordon Ramsay at Powerscourt, where the professional team creates culinary delights and the more casual Sugar Loaf Lounge, which also houses a welcoming bar. For ultimate relaxation, the peaceful ESPA treats guests to absolute luxury with 22 treatment rooms, a 20-metre Swarovski crystal-lit pool, fitness suite and state-of-the-art thermal suite. The stunning 36-hole Powerscourt championship golf complex is located only a few steps from the hotel.

Scotland

Scotland

For further information on Scotland, please contact:

Visit Scotland
Ocean Point 1,
94 Ocean Drive, Leith
Edinburgh EH6 6JH
Tel: +44 (0)131 472 2222 or +44 (0)1463 716 996
Internet: www.visitscotland.com

Greater Glasgow & Clyde Valley Tourist Board
110 George Square
Glasgow G2 1DY
Tel: +44 (0)141 204 4400
Internet: www.seeglasgow.com

Edinburgh & Lothians Tourist Board
Tel: +44 (0)845 2255 121
Internet: www.edinburgh.org

The Scottish Borders Tourist Board
Tel: 0870 608 0404
Internet: www.scot-borders.co.uk

or see **pages 270-273** for details of local historic houses, castles and gardens to visit during your stay.

For additional places to stay in Scotland, turn to **pages 268-269** where a listing of our Recommended Small Hotels, Inns & Restaurant Guide can be found.

ABERDEENSHIRE - CRAIGELLACHIE (BANFFSHIRE)

CRAIGELLACHIE HOTEL OF SPEYSIDE

CRAIGELLACHIE, ABERLOUR, BANFFSHIRE AB38 9SR
Tel: 0845 365 3874 **International:** +44 (0)1340 881204 **Fax:** 01340 881253
Web: www.johansens.com/craigellachie **E-mail:** reservations@ohiml.com

You can be sure of a warm Highland welcome at Craigellachie, a grand country hotel within spectacular surroundings. Located where the Fiddich and Spey Rivers meet, this an ideal spot for angling enthusiasts to land some of the world's best salmon due to its fast flowing current. Uninterrupted views over this breathtaking countryside are simply awe-inspiring, and for those of you in search of active pursuits, there are many to choose from. At the end of the day, there will be a inviting lounge complete with roaring log fire waiting for you or in the bar an impressive stock of over 700 whiskies can be discussed with the hotels own specialist. Fine Scottish cuisine with an emphasis on seasonal and local produce is served in the Ben Aigan Restaurant.

Our inspector loved: *The cosy library with welcoming fire and stunning view over River Spey.*

Price Guide: (room only)
single from £60
double/twin from £80
four poster from £125

Awards/Recognition: 2 AA Rosettes 2007–2008

Location: Just off the A95; A9, 38 miles; Inverness Airport, 43 miles; Elgin Train Station, 10 miles

Attractions: Whiskey Trail; Fishing on River Spey; Beaches at Lossiemouth

ARGYLL & BUTE - KILCHRENAN BY OBAN

Ardanaiseig

KILCHRENAN BY TAYNUILT, ARGYLL PA35 1HE
Tel: 0845 365 3614 **International:** +44 (0)1866 833333 **Fax:** 01866 833222
Web: www.johansens.com/ardanaiseig **E-mail:** ardanaiseig@clara.net

Our inspector loved: *A delightful place to totally unwind in a most stunning location by the loch.*

Price Guide:
double/twin £116–£326
suite £240-£386

Awards/Recognition: 2 AA Rosettes 2007-2008

Location: A85, 10 miles; Oban, 18 miles; Glasgow Airport, 2-hour frive

Attractions: The Ardanaiseig Open Air Theatre; Kilchurn Castle; Boating, Scenery

The surreal feeling you get when you approach Ardanaiseig is of being suspended in time. Built in 1834 and standing in an achingly beautiful spot at the foot of Ben Cruachan, overlooking Loch Awe you get a sense of the true history and romance of the Highlands. Roaring log fires in the drawing room, bowls of fresh flowers, antiques and paintings are complemented by dreamy views of the loch and faraway mountains. Peaceful bedrooms suit the house's style, but real Scottish hospitality comes to the fore in the restaurant, where award-winning chef, Gary Goldie works miracles using largely local produce. Outside, the gardens and estate are a riot of colour, and you can enjoy fishing, tennis and exhilarating hill or lochside walks.

ARGYLL & BUTE - TARBERT

Stonefield Castle

TARBERT, LOCH FYNE, ARGYLL PA29 6YJ
Tel: 0845 365 4605 **International:** +44 (0)1880 820836 **Fax:** 01880 820929
Web: www.johansens.com/stonefield **E-mail:** reservations.stonefieldcastle@ohiml.com

Our inspector loved: *The woodland gardens by the seashore hosting the finest collection of rhododendrons and azaleas.*

Price Guide: (including dinner)
double/twin from £180
suite from £250

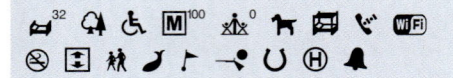

Location: Glasgow Airport, 2-hour drive; Lochgilphead, 11 miles

Attractions: Inverary Castle; Islands of Gigha and Islay

Garden lovers will adore the 60-acre grounds that surround Stonefield Castle where the woodlands rich in azaleas and rhododrendons look out over the beautiful Loch Fyne. Situated near the pretty village of Tarbert on the Mull of Kintyre, the scenery in the area is quite breathtaking, and this stunning Baronial castle is a classic example of elegant Victorian architecture. Vast fireplaces, richly decorated ceilings and beautiful wood panelling have been carefully restored and now provide a stunning setting that is complemented by a warm and welcoming atmosphere that greets each guest. The dining room has some simply staggering views that look right out to sea and is the ideal setting to enjoy some of the fantastic selection of locally sourced produce that is found within the estate.

DUMFRIES & GALLOWAY - MOFFAT (NEAR DUMFRIES)

Auchen Castle

BEATTOCK, NEAR MOFFAT, DUMFRIESSHIRE DG10 9SH
Tel: 0845 365 4015 **International:** +44 (0)1683 300407 **Fax:** 01683 300727
Web: www.johansens.com/auchencastle **E-mail:** reception@auchencastle.com

Our inspector loved: *The unrivalled position in the Borders offering excellent service and facilities.*

Price Guide:
single from £115
double from £164
suite from £235

Awards/Recognition: Eat Scotland - Bronze status

Location: A701, 2 miles; M74, 2 miles; M6, 55 miles; Glasgow Airport, 60 miles

Attractions: Drumlanrig Castle; Moffat Woollen Mill; Solway Coast Rockcliffe

Auchen Castle is a romantic sanctuary set amidst 40 acres of beautiful gardens and woodlands. Feature bedrooms in the main Castle are magnificent and some come with champagne stocked fridges and four-poster beds, including a replica of the one used by Anne Boleyn. There are also ten spacious rooms to be found at the lodge. Impressive menus are created by the hotel's master chef and served against a backdrop of the restaurants panoramic views of the Upper Annandale Mountains. After dinner sit back and enjoy the castles own 12 year old Single Malt. Firm favourite activities including hill walking, cycling and golf though for those wanting to go at a more leisurely pace a simple stroll around the private loch or a visit to the hotel's very own Golden Eagle at their falconry centre will all be a magical experience. A wonderful place for an exclusive takeover.

DUMFRIES & GALLOWAY - NEWTON STEWART

KIRROUGHTREE HOUSE

NEWTON STEWART, WIGTOWNSHIRE DG8 6AN
Tel: 0845 365 1962 **International:** +44 (0)1671 402141 **Fax:** 01671 402425
Web: www.johansens.com/kirroughtreehouse **E-mail:** info@kirroughtreehouse.co.uk

Our inspector loved: *The classic elegance, exceptional service and the wonderful gardens.*

Price Guide:
single £95–£120
double/twin £170–£210
suite £220

Awards/Recognition: 2 AA Rosettes 2007-2008

Location: off the B7079; A75, 0.8 miles; Prestwick Airport, 58 miles

Attractions: Wigtown; Castle Kennedy Gardens; Whithorn Priory and Dig; Gem Rock Musuem

Kirroughtree House was built by the Heron family in 1719 in the foothills of the Cairnsmore of Fleet, on the edge of Galloway Forest Park. You can linger over the spectacular views from 8 acres of landscaped gardens. The original staircase in the Oak panelled lounge is where Robert Burns often recited his poems. The bedrooms are comfortable and the deluxe rooms have spectacular views over the surrounding countryside. Kirroughtree's award winning culinary reputation, ensures that only the finest produce is used to create meals of originality and finesse. This is an ideal venue for small meetings, family parties and weddings; exclusive use of the hotel can be arranged. Pitch and putt and croquet can be enjoyed in the grounds and walking expeditions are recommended.

FIFE - ST ANDREWS

Old Course Hotel Golf Resort & Spa

ST ANDREWS, FIFE, SCOTLAND KY16 9SP
Tel: 0845 365 4018 **International:** +44 (0)1334 474371 **Fax:** 01334 477668
Web: www.johansens.com/oldcourse **E-mail:** reservations@oldcoursehotel.co.uk

Our inspector loved: *The magnificient views over the Old Course from the only 5-star hotel in St Andrews.*

Price Guide:
single from £360
double from £390
suite from £680

Awards/Recognition: 3 AA Rosettes 2008–2009

Location: A91, 50yds; M90, 20 miles; Dundee Airport, 20-min drive; Leuchars Rail Station, 10-min drive

Attractions: St Andrews Town; East Neuk of Fife; Edinburgh City

The Old Course Hotel is an impressive place to stay and a golfer's paradise. From many of the luxury rooms and suites you can admire the impeccably manicured lawns of the famous golf course and hotel's namesake. For those preferring more rugged but equally spectacular sights there are rooms looking out over the sea and rolling hillsides of Fife. Dining here is always a pleasure. You will be spoilt for choice with the many different styles of restaurant to choose from, ranging from informal Mediterranean cuisine to award-winning fine dining. All are excellent, with top-class service and stunning views. The Kohler Waters Spa with its unique cascading waterfall and extensive thermal suite focuses on replenishing and revitalising the body. Totally refreshing.

GLASGOW
Mar Hall Hotel & Spa

MAR HALL DRIVE, EARL OF MAR ESTATE, BISHOPTON, NEAR GLASGOW PA7 5NW
Tel: 0845 365 2054 **International:** +44 (0)141 812 9999 **Fax:** 0141 812 9997
Web: www.johansens.com/marhall **E-mail:** reservations@marhall.com

Our inspector loved: *The individually designed suites with the breathtaking views over the Kilpatrick Hills.*

Price Guide: (room only)
double (single occupancy) £135–£190
double/twin £175–£230
suite £250–£495

Hard to believe just 20 minutes from Glasgow's thriving city centre is the Earl of Mar Estate where the impressive Mar Hall Hotel is situated. Over the years the lush surroundings and crisp air have drawn guests including Mary Queen of Scots and Robert the Bruce. Now one of Scotland's premier 5-star hotels, its lavish rooms and suites have strong individuality, a striking blend of antiquity and the contemporary. Shades of gold and cream set the tone for a relaxing dining experience in The Cristal restaurant with huge windows allowing views across the formal gardens. The menu is inspirational under the direction of award-winning Chef Jim Kerr. Lighter meals & tea can be taken down at the Spa or in the Grand Hall under its beautiful fanned ceiling. Mar Hall is a great place to spend time relaxing on your own or with friends.

Location: M8 jct 30, 2 miles; Glasgow, 14 miles; Glasgow Airport, 6.2 miles

Attractions: Glasgow City Centre; Glasgow School of Art; Glasgow Cathedral; Kelvingrove Art Gallery

HIGHLAND - DINGWALL

TULLOCH CASTLE HOTEL

TULLOCH CASTLE DRIVE, DINGWALL, ROSSHIRE IV15 9ND
Tel: 0845 365 4021 **International:** +44 (0)1349 861325 **Fax:** 01349 863993
Web: www.johansens.com/tullochcastle **E-mail:** info@tullochcastle.co.uk

Our inspector loved: *The Grand Hall with its wood panelling and simply magnificent stone fireplace that creates a great atmosphere for any function.*

Price Guide:
single from £120
double from £155
suite from £195

Location: Dingwall, 15-min walk; Inverness, 15 miles; Inverness Airport, 20 miles

Attractions: Culloden Battlefield; Loch Ness; Dolphin Watching in Moray Firth; Whiskey Trail

It's all about atmosphere at this 12th-century castle, which at first seems a touch imposing, but soon bewitches you with its mix of painstakingly restored fireplaces, opulent wallpapers and magnificent wood panelling. You'll find the crisp bright days of winter just as enchanting as the warm summer months at Tulloch and staff will go the extra mile to ensure you have plenty of ideas to fill your hours. Dine on the best local Highland produce in the Turrets Restaurant and then retreat with a fine Scottish malt next to the roaring fire in the reception lounge. Each bedroom is well furnished with individual character and charm. You can imagine this would be a magical setting for a wedding or indeed any gathering of friends, family or business clients. Golfers will be pleased to find plenty of choice nearby.

HIGHLAND - FORT WILLIAM

INVERLOCHY CASTLE

TORLUNDY, FORT WILLIAM PH33 6SN
Tel: 0845 365 1926 **International:** +44 (0)1397 702177 **Fax:** 01397 702953
Web: www.johansens.com/inverlochy **E-mail:** info@inverlochy.co.uk

Our inspector loved: *Being made to feel very special in this fairy tale setting.*

Price Guide:
single £250-£350
double £390-£490
suite £450-£650

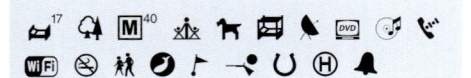

Awards/Recognition: Condé Nast Johansens Most Excellent Hotel Award 2008; 1 Star Michelin 2008; 3 AA Rosettes 2007-2008; Relais & Châteaux

Location: On A82; Fort William Railway Station, 4 miles; Inverness Airport, 69 miles; Glasgow Airport, 105 miles

Attractions: Ben Nevis; Glencoe; Glenfinnan; Loch Ness

Queen Victoria's words from 1873, "I never saw a lovelier or more romantic spot", describe Inverlochy perfectly, and the first Lord Abinger who built the castle in 1863 certainly knew how to pick a gorgeous location in the foothills of Ben Nevis. Today the castle makes a splendid hotel managed by Calum Milne and first impressions of the massive reception room featuring Venetian crystal chandeliers, a Michaelangelo-style ceiling and a handsome staircase leading to 3 elaborately decorated dining rooms, carry a real 'wow' factor. Bedrooms are spacious, individually furnished and offer every comfort. Michelin-starred chef Matt Gray, creates modern British cuisine using local game, hand picked wild mushrooms and scallops from the Isle of Skye. Various outdoor activities await you and stunning historical landscapes are nearby.

HIGHLAND - INVERNESS

BUNCHREW HOUSE HOTEL

INVERNESS IV3 8TA

Tel: 0845 365 3214 **International:** +44 (0)1463 234917 **Fax:** 01463 710620
Web: www.johansens.com/bunchrewhouse **E-mail:** welcome@bunchrew-inverness.co.uk

Our inspector loved: *The comfortable and cosy atmosphere situated in lovely grounds right on edge of this attractive sea-loch.*

Price Guide:
single £120–£180
double/twin £150–£260

Awards/Recognition: 2 AA Rosettes 2007-2008

Location: Inverness, 2 miles; A9, 3 miles; Inverness Airport, 13 miles

Attractions: Loch Ness & Castle Urquhart; Culloden Battle Field; 25 Golf Courses Wthin 90 minutes Drive; Dolphin Watching Cruise

This 17th-century Scottish mansion, the "Hotel on the Shore" sits amidst 20 acres of landscaped gardens and woodlands, catching the sound of the sea lapping at its garden walls and gazes at Ben Wyvis and the Black Isle. Careful restoration has preserved it's heritage, whilst providing you with the utmost in comfort and convenience; bedrooms are furnished to enhance their natural features, and the panelled drawing room's log fires in winter lend it added appeal. Savour the candle-lit restaurant where traditional cuisine includes prime Scottish beef, fresh lobster and langoustines, locally caught game and venison and freshly grown vegetables. Local places of interest include Cawdor Castle and Loch Ness, or if you fancy brushing off your skis head to nearby Aviemore.

HIGHLAND - INVERNESS

Rocpool Reserve

CULDUTHEL ROAD, INVERNESS, IV2 4AG
Tel: 0845 365 2304 **International:** +44 (0)1463 240089 **Fax:** 01463 248431
Web: www.johansens.com/rocpool **E-mail:** info@rocpool.com

You cannot help but be bowled over by Rocpool Reserve a boutique hotel overlooking Inverness's riverside – elegant and contemporary with bits of the classical blended in. The attention to detail is phenomenal and throughout the recurring colour scheme of red, black and white, bedrooms are fitted with plasma TVs, DVD players and iPod docking stations. Egyptian linens, king-size beds, and Italian ceramics in bathrooms, while one room even has a hot tub on the terrace! Cocktail hour amidst the bar's white leather seats and sparkling chandeliers will relax you before an indulgent dinner in the exceptional Reserve Restaurant, where a balcony overlooks the river. All this and wonderful staff. Definitely the place to stay in Europe's fastest growing city!

Our inspector loved: *Elegant boutique hotel with quite the most stunning bathrooms.*

Price Guide:
single £140–£160
double from £170
suite from £250

Awards/Recognition: Condé Nast Johansens Most Excellent Town/City Award 2008

Location: City Centre, 5-min walk; Inverness Airport, 10 miles

Attractions: Eden Court Theatre; Championship Golf Courses; Loch Ness; Culloden Battlefield

HIGHLAND - INVERNESS

Royal Highland Hotel

STATION SQUARE, 18 ACADEMY STREET, INVERNESS IV1 1LG
Tel: 0845 365 4621 **International:** +44 (0)1463 231926 **Fax:** 01463 710705
Web: www.johansens.com/royalhighland **E-mail:** info@royalhighlandhotel.co.uk

Our inspector loved: *The classic ambience of the "Station Hotel" that also has modern appeal.*

Price Guide:
single from £119
double from £149
suite £299

Location: Inverness Airport, 10 miles; Inverness Station, 50 metres

Attractions: Loch Ness; Dolphin Watching in Moray Firth; World Famous Golf Courses; Highland Scenery

Set in the heart of the city, by the historic Inverness railway station, the Royal Highland Hotel underwent a painstaking restoration in 2000 to maintain the vestiges of its grande dame past. The result is an opulent getaway that boasts the ambience from a bygone age. Historic touches include the grand staircase in the foyer, which was the inspiration for the impressive staircase in The Titanic. Venture up the stairs and enjoy the rich vibrant décor of the bedrooms, all of which feature antique-style furnishings. The à la carte restaurant, ASH, provides a contemporary backdrop for a pre-dinner drink or informal meal, while The Gallery has a more traditional environment. The area of the Scottish highlands is a haven for outdoor enthusiasts with canoeing, tennis, hiking and fishing.

HIGHLAND - ISLE OF SKYE (PORTREE)

CUILLIN HILLS HOTEL

PORTREE, ISLE OF SKYE IV51 9QU
Tel: 0845 365 3255 **International:** +44 (0)1478 612003 **Fax:** 01478 613092
Web: www.johansens.com/cuillinhills **E-mail:** info@cuillinhills-hotel-skye.co.uk

Our inspector loved: *Dining here with the views over Portree Bay with the sun on the hills beyond is an unforgettable experience.*

Price Guide:
single £70–£90
double/twin £120–£240
four poster £300–£400

What more could you ask for, stunning views of the majestic Cuillin Mountains and Portree Bay. Originally built in the 1870s as a hunting lodge, Cuillin Hills benefits from 15 acres of private mature grounds, which create a secluded setting and peaceful atmosphere. The bedrooms are spacious. The restaurant overlooks the bay and dishes include highland game, lobster, scallops and homemade desserts. Interesting more informal meals are served in the bar. After dinner select your favourite malt whisky and head for the lounge, on cooler evenings relax in front of the log fire. Discover the Isle of Skye's rich history through its castles, museums and visitor centres and the abundance of unspoilt coastal paths and woodland walks nearby. Portree town itself is a mere 10 minutes' walk.

Awards/Recognition: 2 AA Rosettes 2007–2008

Location: A855, 500yds; Skye Bridge, 33 miles; Portree, 10-min walk

Attractions: Exploring Skye, Sea Trips, Excellent views from the hotel

HIGHLAND - TORRIDON

The Torridon

TORRIDON, BY ACHNASHEEN, WESTER ROSS IV22 2EY
Tel: 0845 365 2037 **International:** +44 (0)1445 791242 **Fax:** 01445 712253
Web: www.johansens.com/thetorridon **E-mail:** info@thetorridon.com

Our inspector loved: *Peace and tranquility with their superb food is such a contrast to this dramatic wild location.*

Price Guide: (including dinner)
single £140–£170
double/twin £220–£475
suite £385–£475

Awards/Recognition: 2 AA Rosettes 2008-2009

Location: On the A896; Kinlochewe, 10 miles; Inverness Airport, 68 miles

Attractions: Torridon Activity Centre; Isle of Skye; Inverewe Gardens (NT); Eilean Donan Castle

Obviously a man with an eye for a view, the first Earl of Lovelace built this country house as a shooting lodge in 1887, and today Rohaise and Daniel Rose-Bristow continue its tradition of Highland hospitality. Some bedrooms are frankly indulgent; all are comfortable with delectable toiletries, crisp white linens and fresh fruit. The Victorian kitchen garden provides chef, Kevin Broome, with a plethora of produce to include in his world-class cuisine and serve in the beautiful dining room. The estate boasts a little sister property, The Torridon Inn, which provides a more informal alternative. Stroll out in the grounds amidst resident Highland cattle or be more adventurous and enjoy the many activities offered by Torridon Activities the hotels outdoor activity department, kayaking, climbing, guided low and high level walks, abseiling, mountain biking. A fabulous experience'

MIDLOTHIAN - EDINBURGH (BONNYRIGG)

Dalhousie Castle and Spa

BONNYRIGG, NEAR EDINBURGH EH19 3JB
Tel: 0845 365 3260 **International:** +44 (0)1875 820153 **Fax:** 01875 821936
Web: www.johansens.com/dalhousiecastle **E-mail:** info@dalhousiecastle.co.uk

Our inspector loved: *The rich tapestry of arts and culture. The decor creates a richly warm and luxurious feel.*

Price Guide:
single from £110
double from £230
suite from £385

An impressive castle with plenty of reminders of its rich and turbulent 800 year history. A mews containing the castle falconry, a vaulted dungeon restaurant serving classical French and Scottish cuisine whilst 18 of the bedrooms are historically themed and include Mary Queen of Scots, Robert the Bruce and William Wallace. The "de Ramseia" suite houses the 500-year-old "Well". Several rooms are found in the 100-year-old Lodge and The Orangery Restaurant, overlooks the South Esk River. If you are looking for an exceptional venue to gather friends or impress clients Dalhousie should be on your list – high standards, warm hospitality and a lot of fun. Edinburgh is just 7 miles away so after a day exploring retire to the Aqueous Spa, with its hydro pool, Laconium, Rasul mud room and treatment rooms. A von Essen hotel.

Awards/Recognition: 2 AA Rosettes 2008-2009; Eat Scotland Silver Award (The Dungeon Restaurant)

Location: Off the B704; Edinburgh, 7 miles; Edinburgh Airport, 16.4 miles; Glasgow, 55 miles

Attractions: Mining Museum at Newtongrange; Scottish Parliament; Edinburgh Castle; Roslyn Chapel

STIRLING - BANKNOCK (NEAR STIRLING)

GLENSKIRLIE HOUSE & CASTLE

KILSYTH ROAD, BANKNOCK, STIRLINGSHIRE FK4 1UF
Tel: 0845 365 4017 **International:** +44 (0)1324 840201 **Fax:** 01324 841054
Web: www.johansens.com/glenskirliehouse **E-mail:** macaloneys@glenskirliehouse.com

Our inspector loved: *The warm welcome at this exciting new boutique style castle.*

Price Guide:
double from £205
suite from £255

Location: A803, 100yds; M80, 1 mile; Glasgow Airport, 25 miles; Edinburgh Airport, 20 miles

Attractions: Falkirk Wheel; Stirling Castle; Wallace Monument; The Trossachs

This spectacular property in the village of Banknock is the first castle hotel to be built in Scotland in the 21st century. The lush, wonderfully manicured gardens create a tranquil environment within this peaceful location. Owned and run by the Macaloney family, the combination of traditional architectural design and modern luxury is a winning formula. Inside there is an eclectic mix of contemporary and classical furnishings. Each of the 15 indivdually themed bedrooms is named after a rose and details include those extra touches, such as flat screen TVs and sleep gifts that make your stay extra luxurious. The new grill restaurant, with its bespoke designed stained-glass windows and doors, and the more formal award-winning Glenskirlie House restaurant, reflect the hotel's passion for food, delivering beautifully presented dishes using fresh local produce.

Wales

Wales

For further information on Wales, please contact:

Wales Tourist Board
PO Box 113, Bangor, LL54 4WW
Tel: 08708 300 306
Web: www.visitwales.com

North Wales Tourism
77 Conway Road, Colwyn Bay, Conway LL29 7LN
Tel: +44 (0)1492 531731
Web: www.nwt.co.uk

Mid Wales Tourism
The Station, Machynlleth, Powys SY20 8TG
Tel: (Freephone) 0800 273747
Web: www.visitmidwales.co.uk

South West Wales Tourism Partnership
The Coach House, Aberglasney Gardens, Llangathen, Carmarthenshire SA32 8QH
Tel: +44 (0)1558 669091
Web: www.swwtp.co.uk

or see **pages 270-273** for details of local historic houses, castles and gardens to visit during your stay.

For additional places to stay in Wales, turn to **pages 268-269** where a listing of our Recommended Small Hotels, Inns & Restaurant Guide can be found.

CARDIFF - MISKIN

MISKIN MANOR COUNTRY HOUSE HOTEL

MISKIN, NR CARDIFF CF72 8ND
Tel: 0845 365 2069 **International:** +44 (0)1443 224204 **Fax:** 01443 237606
Web: www.johansens.com/miskinmanor **E-mail:** reservations@miskin-manor.co.uk

Our inspector loved: *The Oak Room, perfect for a small private dinner party.*

Price Guide:
single from £105
double/twin/four poster from £130
suite from £240

Awards/Recognition: 2 AA Rosette 2007-2008

Location: Off the A4119; M4 Jct 34, 1.73 miles; Cardiff, 12 miles; Cardiff Airport, 14 miles

Attractions: Cardiff Bay; Swansea; Brecon Beacons; Gower Peninsula

It may be just 10 minutes' drive from Cardiff Bay but it's 22 acres of undisturbed parkland criss-crossed with streams promise seclusion. Dating back to the 11th century it exudes a sense of history and indeed amongst those who have enjoyed its charms was the Prince of Wales, later King Edward VIII in the 1920s. Unusually large reception rooms have fireplaces, panelled walls and elaborate plasterwork ceilings whilst bedrooms are rich in colour and texture. In the restaurant the chef delights in taking inspiration from local Welsh produce and is deservedly a popular local destination. Building up an appetite can be achieved at the popular health club, which includes a glass-backed squash court and badminton.

CEREDIGION - LAMPETER

FALCONDALE MANSION HOTEL

LAMPETER, CEREDIGION SA48 7RX
Tel: 0845 365 3287 **International:** +44 (0)1570 422910 **Fax:** 01570 423559
Web: www.johansens.com/falcondale **E-mail:** info@falcondalehotel.com

Our inspector loved: *The glorious views from the terrace that will entice you to stop and enjoy. Tastefully decorated bedrooms are all fresh and bright.*

Price Guide:
single from £99
double/twin from £139

Awards/Recognition: 2 AA Rosettes 2008-2009

Location: A485, 1 mile; A40, 10 miles; Cardiff Airport, 95 miles; M4, 30 miles

Attractions: Llanerchaeron (NT); Dolaucothi Gold Mines (NT); University of Wales; National Botanic Garden of Wales

Only 10 miles from the Cardigan coast and the beautiful fishing village of Aberaeron, this elegant Victorian Italianate Mansion is rapidly gaining an excellent reputation and putting this charming area of Wales firmly on the map. Discover it before everyone else and stroll the grounds with their 14 acres of ornamental woods and sweeping lawns. The 19 guest rooms have luxurious bathrooms and new LCD televisions . You can book the entire hotel for exclusive use and tailor-made events. With a Welsh head chef, menus are proudly created from local produce using international flare. Seasonal options inspire excellent vegetarian dishes and for seafood lovers include lobster and local catches. There is an outstanding 5 course evening menu though you can equally enjoy more informal dining a la carte.

253

CEREDIGION - MACHYNLLETH

Ynyshir Hall

EGLWYSFACH, MACHYNLLETH, POWYS SY20 8TA
Tel: 0845 365 3426 **International:** +44 (0)1654 781209 **Fax:** 01654 781366
Web: www.johansens.com/ynyshirhall **E-mail:** info@ynyshirhall.co.uk

Our inspector loved: The unique atmosphere of creativity and excellence. A food and wine connoisseurs paradise.

Price Guide:
single from £215
superior double from £285
suite from £330

Awards/Recognition: Relais & Châteaux; 3 AA Rosettes 2008-2009

Location: A487, 1 mile; A470, 12 miles; Birmingham Airport, 88 miles; Cardif, 110 miles

Attractions: RSPB Ynys-hir Reserve; Glorious Beaches; Cambrian Mountains; Centre for Alternative Energy

Ynyshir Hall is so much more than just a country house nestled in the heart of idyllic Welsh countryside: it's a rich and cultured hospitality experience. Rebelliously non corporate in style and atmosphere, this Relais & Châteaux hotel was once owned by Queen Victoria. Creative flair is apparent throughout, particularly in the stylish décor, stunning paintings, and uniquely styled bedrooms. For example, the "Hogarth" room is dramatically styled in red silk and midnight blue and features a four-poster bed with sweeping views across the broad gardens. The pinnacle is the dining room, decorated in duck-egg blue, which is the perfect venue to grace the imaginative cuisine of Ynyshir Hall's 'true' artistic genius: head chef Shane Hughes. Dishes can include Welsh lamb and Welsh Black beef, farmhouse cheeses and locally sourced seafood, often enhanced with such wild ingredients as wood sorrel, samphire and wild garlic. The wine list is nothing short of a masterpiece. A von Essen hotel.

CONWY - LLANDUDNO

BODYSGALLEN HALL & SPA

LLANDUDNO, NORTH WALES LL30 1RS
Tel: 0845 365 3039 **International:** +44 (0)1492 584466 **Fax:** 01492 582519
Web: www.johansens.com/bodysgallenhall **E-mail:** info@bodysgallen.com

Our inspector loved: *The classic elegance of this magnificent stately home. The view of Conwy Castle across the herb garden is simply Wales at its finest.*

Price Guide:
single from £140
double/twin from £175
suite from £225

Awards/Recognition: Condé Nast Johansens Most Excellent Country Hotel 2007; 3 AA Rosettes 2008–2009

Location: A 470; A 55, 1 mile; Holyhead - Ireland Ferry Terminal, 45-min drive; Manchester Airport 75-mins drive; London, 3 hours-train

Attractions: Bodnant Gardens; Conwy and Caernarfon Castles; Welsh Highland Railway, The Island of Anglesey; Snowdonia National Park

Just a short drive from the historic towns of Conwy and Llandudno, Bodysgallen feels like a magical world of its own. You simply can't help but be inspired in this self-contained oasis of elegance. With spectacular views of Snowdonia and Conwy Castle, this Grade I listed country house has grown from a 13th-century fortified tower into one of the finest hotels in Wales. Breathtaking gardens set in over 200 acres include a 17th-century parterre of box hedges filled with scented herbs and a restored formal walled rose garden. Within the grounds is a cluster of 16 cottage suites, and the 15 bedrooms inside the house include four brand new Principal Suites. From the moment you enter the Hall you are enveloped in comfort. Impressive antique furniture, splendid oak paneling and open fireplaces set the tone and the staff is impeccably discreet. The spa is complete with beauty treatment rooms, relaxation room and indoor pool.

CONWY - LLANDUDNO

St Tudno Hotel & Restaurant

NORTH PROMENADE, LLANDUDNO, NORTH WALES LL30 2LP
Tel: 0845 365 2361 **International:** +44 (0)1492 874411 **Fax:** 01492 860407
Web: www.johansens.com/sttudno **E-mail:** sttudnohotel@btinternet.com

Our inspector loved: *The sea front location at the very heart of historic and picturesque Llandudno. As always a food and wine gem.*

Price Guide:
single from £75
double/twin £95–£230
suite from £260

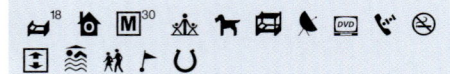

Undoubtedly one of the most delightful small hotels to be found on the coast of Britain, St Tudno now in its 37th year offers a very special experience. A former winner of the Johansen's Hotel of the Year Award for Excellence, the hotel which is elegantly and lovingly refurbished provides a particular warm welcome from Martin Bland and his staff. The individually designed bedrooms have many thoughtful extras and the Terrace Restaurant is regarded as one of Wales' leading places to eat. A little oasis of this town house is the indoor heated swimming pool and secret garden. This 3 AA Red Star Hotel has won a host of prestigious awards: Best Seaside Resort Hotel in Great Britain (Good Hotel Guide), Welsh Hotel of the Year, 2 major wine awards and even an accolade for having the Best Hotel Loos in Britain. St Tudno is ideally situated for visits to Snowdonia, Conwy and Caernarfon Castles, World Famous Bodnant Gardens, Anglesey and glorious walks on the Great Orme.

Awards/Recognition: 2 AA Rosettes 2006-2007;

Location: On the A470; A55, 4 miles; Chester, 45 miles; Manchester Airport, 65 miles

Attractions: Great Orme Copper Mines; Theatre at Llandudno; Bodnant Gardens; Dry Ski Slope and Tobaggan run on the Great Orme

GWYNEDD - BALA (LLANDDERFEL)

PALÉ HALL

PALÉ ESTATE, LLANDDERFEL, BALA, GWYNEDD LL23 7PS
Tel: 0845 365 2096 **International:** +44 (0)1678 530285 **Fax:** 01678 530220
Web: www.johansens.com/palehall **E-mail:** enquiries@palehall.co.uk

Our inspector loved: *The elegance of this country manor so rich in history. Bedrooms and bathrooms fit for royalty.*

Price Guide:
single £85–£150
double/twin £115–£200

Awards/Recognition: 1 AA Rosette 2007-2008

Location: A 494, 2 miles; A 5, 6 miles; Chester, 40 miles; Liverpool Airport, 65 miles

Attractions: Snowdonia National Park; Portmeirion; Lake Bala; Llechwedd Slate Mines at Blaenau Ffestiniog

Illustrious guests including Queen Victoria and Winston Churchill have stayed at Palé Hall, a beautifully preserved building with magnificent period details; galleried entrance hall, vaulted ceiling and the Boudoir with handpainted dome. Bedrooms all have their own character and many with delightful surprises. You could choose to sleep in the half tester bed enjoyed by Queen Victoria and relax in her original royal bath. Views towards the Snowdonia National Park are in abundance and there is a wonderful feeling of tranquillity. The restaurant menu has British and French dishes strongly influenced by the wealth of local produce. An inspired spot to take over for a house party of friends or colleagues.

GWYNEDD - DOLGELLAU (PENMAENPOOL)

Penmaenuchaf Hall

PENMAENPOOL, DOLGELLAU, GWYNEDD LL40 1YB
Tel: 0845 365 2104 **International:** +44 (0)1341 422129 **Fax:** 01341 422787
Web: www.johansens.com/penmaenuchafhall **E-mail:** relax@penhall.co.uk

Our inspector loved: *The special way a new restaurant and lounge have been created, still maintaining intimacy.*

Price Guide:
single £95–£145
double/twin £150–£220

Awards/Recognition: 2 AA Rosettes 2008-2009

Location: A493, 0.5 mile; A470, 1.5 miles; Shrewsbury, 60 miles; Chester, 64 miles

Attractions: Snowdonia National Park; Narrow Guage Railways; Bodnant Garden; Portmeirion

From the moment you've climbed Penmaenuchaf's long tree-lined driveway you'll begin to relax as you take in this glorious setting. Nestled within the Snowdonia National Park, this 3 AA Red starred hotel and winner of Visit Wales Gold Award 2008 offers views across Mawddach Estuary and the panoramic distant wooded mountain slopes. The 21-acre grounds blend lawns, a sunken rose garden, water garden and woodland. A handsome Victorian house, with oak and mahogany panelling, stained glass windows, polished slate floors and log fires in winter. Penmaenuchaf Hall is always discreetly evolving - including the recently opened garden room restaurant and new bedrooms with fabulous balconies. Dinners are imaginative and seasonal. You can fish along 10 miles of the Mawddach River or the soon to be completed lake within the hotel's grounds, mountain bike or enjoy nearby golf courses and sandy beaches.

NEWPORT

CELTIC MANOR RESORT

COLDRA WOODS, THE USK VALLEY, NEWPORT, NP18 1HQ
Tel: 0845 365 3297 **International:** +44 (0)1633 413000 **Fax:** 01633 412910
Web: www.johansens.com/celticmanor **E-mail:** postbox@celtic-manor.com

Our inspector loved: *Relaxing in the beautiful spa, amazing food in the Crown restaurant and the attentive friendly service from all the team.*

Price Guide:
single £165–£195
double £198–£228
suite £323–£1098

Location: Just off B4237; M4 Jct 24, 0.5 mile; A48, 0.5 mile; Newport, 3 miles

Attractions: Brecon Beacons; Roman Town of Caerleon; Chepstow Castle; Tintern Abbey

Rising majestically above the Usk Valley, Celtic Manor Resort, the host venue for the 2010 Ryder Cup has not only 3 championship courses and a world-class Golf Academy but plenty of other activities to keep the body and mind distracted. Two outstanding spa zones, tennis, shooting, mountain biking and walking trails and for young families there is a children's club and crèche, which should give plenty of quality time and space to both parents and the kids. Whilst the Resort Hotel is unashamedly modern in stature those seeking a little more tradition can stay in the Victorian Manor House hotel. Another great thing about this resort is the number of dining options from the formal to relaxed bistro and in summer The Rooftop Garden and Barbecue Terrace.

PEMBROKESHIRE - SAUNDERSFOOT

St Brides Spa Hotel

SAUNDERSFOOT, PEMBROKESHIRE SA69 9NH
Tel: 0845 365 3925 **International:** +44 (0)1834 812 304 **Fax:** + 44 (0)1834 811 766
Web: www.johansens.com/stbrides **E-mail:** reservations@stbridesspahotel.com

Our inspector loved: *The breathtaking infinity pool perched high above the bay. You can't help but be impressed.*

Price Guide:
double £150-£280

Awards/Recognition: Taste of Wales Silver Award 2008

Location: Off the B4316; Swansea, 50 miles; Cardiff, 90 miles; M4, 30 miles

Attractions: St David's Cathedral; National Botanic Gardens of Wales; Pembrokeshire Coast National Park; Pembroke Castle

Perched high above picturesque Saundersfoot harbour and beach, St Brides Spa Hotel personifies a new, contemporary British seaside experience combining a powerful sense of place with the highest quality in service and hospitality. The inviting décor is enhanced by a magnificent collection of contemporary Welsh art and sets off the breathtaking Pembrokeshire sea views. The bedrooms are imaginatively designed and superbly equipped, many enjoy balconies and great views. The marine spa has an impressive menu of therapies using oceanic minerals, algae and seaweed. Not to be missed is the spectacularly positioned infinity edge vitality pool. A myriad of locally caught fish is available on the menu in the 3 restaurants; 2 located just a short stroll away. This is a place to enjoy the height of relaxation and the revitalising properties of the ocean.

PEMBROKESHIRE - ST DAVID'S

WARPOOL COURT HOTEL

ST DAVID'S, PEMBROKESHIRE SA62 6BN
Tel: 0845 365 2786 **International:** +44 (0)1437 720300 **Fax:** 01437 720676
Web: www.johansens.com/warpoolcourt **E-mail:** info@warpoolcourthotel.com

Our inspector loved: *The breathtaking location. You'll have to travel a very, very long way to find a better view*

Price Guide:
single £125–£140
double/twin £180–£300

Awards/Recognition: 2 AA Rosettes 2008-2009

Location: A40, 16 miles; Severn Bridge, 135 miles; Cardiff, 100 miles

Attractions: Pembrokeshire Heritage Coastal Walk; St David's Cathedral and Bishops Palace; Pembroke Castle; Graham Sutherland Gallery

Warpool Court Hotel was originally built as the St David's Cathedral Choir School in the 1860s at this unparalleled setting over the spectacular coast and St Bride's Bay. With 25 comfortable bedrooms, many of which look out to the sea, the hotel has been offering a warm and friendly welcome for over 40 years. The restaurant, which is open to non-residents, serves imaginative menus that take advantage of the vast array of first-class, locally sourced ingredients. Stroll in the gardens, take a swim in the covered heated pool, open April-October, or head straight out onto the Pembrokeshire Coastal Path, with its rich variety of wildlife and scenery. Local boat trips to Skomer and Ramsey Island can be arranged to view the wide variety of bird and sea life. Closed in January.

PEMBROKESHIRE - TENBY (LAMPHEY)

LAMPHEY COURT HOTEL & SPA

LAMPHEY, NEAR TENBY, PEMBROKESHIRE SA71 5NT
Tel: 0845 365 1982 **International:** +44 (0)1646-672273 **Fax:** 01646-672480
Web: www.johansens.com/courtpembroke **E-mail:** info@LampheyCourt.co.uk

Our inspector loved: *The light, bright and airy dual-aspect main dining room and the fare on offer.*

Price Guide:
single £80–£100
double/twin £115–£160
2 nights dinner, bed & breakfast from £70 per person per night

Location: A477, 5-min drive; M4, 40-min drive; Pembroke, 10-min drive; Cardiff, 90 miles

Attractions: Tenby; St David's Cathedral; Ruins of Mediaeval Bishop's Palace; Carew Castle

Idyllically located for enjoying spectacular coastal walks and the pretty resorts of Tenby and Saundersfoot, Lamphey Court is a welcoming country house with excellent facilities. Bedrooms offer high standard of comfort and family suites, located in a former coach house, feature generously sized rooms and extra space. The formal candle-lit Georgian restaurant's dinner menu features fresh local produce including lobster caught at Freshwater Bay and Pembrokshire lamb, while the bright Conservatory Restaurant is a more informal alternative for lunch and lighter meals. Take advantage of the leisure spa with its large indoor pool overlooking the gardens and floodlit tennis courts, spa pool, saunas and gym. Skilled therapists are also on hand to provide a range of treatments. Alternatively, the adjacent mediaeval Bishop's Palace is well worth a visit.

POWYS - BRECON (LLYSWEN)

Llangoed Hall

LLYSWEN, BRECON, POWYS LD3 0YP
Tel: 0845 365 2034 **International:** +44 (0)1874 754525 **Fax:** 01874 754545
Web: www.johansens.com/llangoedhall **E-mail:** enquiries@llangoedhall.com

Our inspector loved: *A level of service and attention to detail that befits this grand and classic country manor set in handsome grounds.*

Price Guide:
single upon request
double/twin from £210
suite from £385

Awards/Recognition: Condé Nast Johansens Most Excellent Country House Award 2008; 2 AA Rosettes 2008-2009

Location: A470, 0.75 miles; Hay-on-Wye, 9 miles; Hereford, 35 miles; Cardiff Airport, 45 miles

Attractions: Hay-on-Wye Specialist Book Shops; Brecon Beacons National Park; Black Mountains; Powis Castle

With a spectacular location close to the Brecon Beacons, Llangoed Hall is a place where you will be treated like a king or queen. The building oozes tremendous charm and is fitted with glorious fabrics, log fires to enjoy and a fascinating collection of paintings. In the restaurant Sean Ballington and his team create sophisticated dishes with panache from local produce. A keen eye for detail ensures that each guest feels special and the staff are only too pleased to arrange any special activities at your request. The beautiful gardens, with a restored maze complement the breathtaking setting.

POWYS - LAKE VYRNWY

Lake Vyrnwy Hotel

LAKE VYRNWY, MONTGOMERYSHIRE SY10 0LY
Tel: 0845 365 1976 **International:** +44 (0)1691 870 692 **Fax:** 01691 870 259
Web: www.johansens.com/lakevyrnwy **E-mail:** info@lakevyrnwyhotel.co.uk

The location of Lake Vyrnwy Hotel is just magical: overlooking the stunning lake and surrounded by wild moorland, forest and the rugged Berwyn Mountains. This picturesque getaway is enveloped by walking trails and opportunities for many leisure pursuits. The wonderful setting can be admired through the windows of the warm and inviting drawing room from sumptuous sofas and balconies located off most of the bedrooms. As the sun goes down the Tower Bar's balcony is the perfect place to savour a glass of wine before enjoying dinner in the restaurant where the menus reflect a genuine enthusiasm for food and utilise as much local produce as possible. Why not pamper yourself and visit the new spa and thermal suite with its comprehensive range of therapies and treatments and array of facilities that include an Arabian rasul mud therapy chamber and Monsoon shower.

Our inspector loved: Sitting on the balcony watching the sun set - what a view!!! This is a truly memorable place.

Price Guide:
single £90–£185
double/twin £120–£210
suite £200–£220

Awards/Recognition: 1 AA Rosette 2007-2008

Location: A490, 8 miles; A495, 12 miles; Welshpool, 20 miles; Chester, 50 miles

Attractions: Powis Castle; Snowdonia National Park; Portmeirion; Centre for Alternative Technology

POWYS - LLANGAMMARCH WELLS

The Lake Country House and Spa

LLANGAMMARCH WELLS, POWYS LD4 4BS
Tel: 0845 365 2571 **International:** +44 (0)1591 620202 **Fax:** 01591 620457
Web: www.johansens.com/lakecountryhouse **E-mail:** info@lakecountryhouse.co.uk

Our inspector loved: *The fabulous lake side views from the hot tub. This hotel and spa simply oozes quality, charm and relaxation.*

Price Guide:
single from £115
superior from £220
suite from £250

Awards/Recognition: 2 AA Rosettes 2008-2009

Location: A 485, 3 miles; A 470, 8 miles; Hay on Wye, 21 miles; Cardiff Airport, 52 miles

Attractions: Brecon Beacons National Park; Aberglasney House and Gardens; Elan Valley; Raglan Castle

A trout leaping up from a serene lake, carpets of wild flowers bobbing in the breeze and badgers ambling by the woods nearby are all sights to be savoured at this glorious country house, surrounded by 50 acres of unspoilt grounds. This hidden gem is a haven for wildlife enthusiasts with over 100 bird-nesting boxes within the grounds and ample opportunities for fishing and horse riding. You can feast on traditional Welsh teas in the decadent lounges by roaring log fires in the winter or beneath the chestnut tree in the summer. The final 18 of the individually designed bedrooms are shortly due to be refurbished. Fresh produce and herbs from the garden are used in the Condé Nast Johansens award-winning restaurant whilst the superb wine list boasts over 300 choices. The lakeside spa is an inspired setting for when you totally want to unwind.

VALE OF GLAMORGAN - CARDIFF (PENARTH)

HOLM HOUSE

MARINE PARADE, PENARTH, VALE OF GLAMORGAN CF64 3BG
Tel: 0845 365 2869 **International:** +44 (0)2920 701572 **Fax:** 02920 709875
Web: www.johansens.com/holmhouse **E-mail:** info@holmhouse.co.uk

Our inspector loved: Wow! The inspector loved everything, and the sea view! A great place for a romantic retreat.

Price Guide: (including dinner)
single £160-£240
double £215-£325
suite £355-£405

Location: A4160, 0.5 miles; A4232, 2.2 miles; M4 jct 28, 10.5 miles; Cardiff, 5 miles

Attractions: Cardiff Castle; St Fagans - Museum of Welsh Life; Glamorgan Heritage Coastline; Castell Coch

Originally built in the 1920s, today, Holm House is cosy, quirky, eccentric, bohemian, opulent, decadent and sumptuous! Hip and funky, the brand new guest rooms, including 3 loft suites and an amazing white spa bedroom, are individually designed, beautifully decorated and warmly lit. Each is furnished to the highest standard and filled with delightful extras that will make you feel particularly spoilt and pampered. Frette bed linen, Jo Malone bathroom products, a Tassimo beverage machine and Bang & Olufsen hi-tech entertainment system are standard to each bedroom. The house is just a stone's throw from Penarth's seafront, with its smart yachts and cruisers, impressive pier and esplanade, and for those of you in need of retail therapy, Cardiff's bustling city centre is only about a 10 minutes' drive away.

Discover KOHLER. A world of innovative and inspiring bathroom design awaits.

KOHLER: As I See It, #5 in a series

ARTIST: Mark Holthusen

BATHROOM: Stillness® Collection, including basins, furniture, toilet, bidet and taps

Inspired by Mother Nature, without all of her storms and bluster.

+44 (0) 1242 221221
kohler.co.uk

THE BOLD LOOK OF **KOHLER**®

©2008 Kohler Co.

Small Hotels & Inns, Great Britain & Ireland

All the properties listed below can be found in our Recommended Small Hotels, Inns & Restaurants, Great Britain & Ireland 2009 Guide. More information on our portfolio of guides can be found on page 13.

Channel Islands

Château La Chaire ....Channel Islands 0845 365 2863

The Farmhouse ....**Channel Islands** **0845 365 4023**
La Sablonnerie...................................Channel Islands 0845 365 1972
The White House ....Channel Islands 0845 365 2735

England

Saco House, Bath ....B & NE Somerset 0845 365 3782
Cornfields Restaurant & Hotel ....Bedfordshire 0845 365 3246
Cantley House Hotel.........................Berkshire 0845 365 3223
The Christopher Hotel Bar & Grill ...Berkshire 0845 365 2418
The Inn on the Green ....Berkshire 0845 365 2547
The Olde Bell Coaching Inn ....Berkshire 0845 365 4038
Stirrups Country House Hotel........Berkshire 0845 365 2369
The Crown Hotel ....Buckinghamshire 0845 365 3270
Fox Country Inn ....Buckinghamshire 0845 365 4039
The Anchor Inn at Sutton Gault......Cambridgeshire..........0845 365 4029
The Tickell Arms, Restaurant..........Cambridgeshire..........0845 365 2710
The Cormorant Hotel and Restaurant...Cornwall 0845 365 2875
The Old Coastguard Hotel ....Cornwall 0845 365 2610
Rose-In-Vale Country House Hotel...Cornwall 0845 365 2306
The Rosevine ....Cornwall 0845 365 2678
Talland Bay Hotel ....Cornwall 0845 365 2386
Trevalsa Court Country House Hotel...Cornwall 0845 365 2765
Broadoaks Country House ....Cumbria 0845 365 3201
Crosby Lodge Country House Hotel ...Cumbria 0845 365 3253
Fayrer Garden House Hotel ....Cumbria 0845 365 3292
Hipping Hall ....Cumbria 0845 365 1859
The Pheasant ....Cumbria 0845 365 2643
West Vale Country House & Restaurant...Cumbria 0845 365 2795
The Wheatsheaf @ Brigsteer ....Cumbria 0845 365 2734
The Crown Inn ....Derbyshire 0845 365 3608
Dannah Farm Country House.........Derbyshire 0845 365 3262
Donington Manor Hotel ....Derbyshire 0845 365 3916
East Lodge Country House Hotel ...Derbyshire 0845 365 3278
The Plough Inn ....Derbyshire 0845 365 2647
The Edgemoor ....Devon 0845 365 3224
Kingston House ....Devon 0845 365 1937
Mill End..Devon 0845 365 2062

The Turtley Corn Mill ....Devon 0845 365 3921
The White House ....Devon 0845 365 4615
BridgeHouse Beaminster ....Dorset 0845 365 2408
The Grange at Oborne.....................Dorset 0845 365 2506
Channels Lodge ....Essex 0845 365 3918
Beaumont House...............................Gloucestershire 0845 365 3912
Bibury Court ....Gloucestershire 0845 365 3035
The Dial House ....Gloucestershire 0845 365 2463
Lower Brook House...........................Gloucestershire 0845 365 2045
Lypiatt House.....................................Gloucestershire 0845 365 2051
New Inn At Coln ....Gloucestershire 0845 365 3754
The Redesdale Arms ....Gloucestershire 0845 365 1873
Langrish House ....Hampshire 0845 365 1986
The Mill At Gordleton ....Hampshire 0845 365 2597
The Nurse's Cottage Restaurant with Rooms ..Hampshire ...0845 365 2609
The Old House Hotel ....Hampshire 0845 365 3951
Aylestone Court ....Herefordshire 0845 365 3022
The Chase Hotel ....Herefordshire 0845 365 3741
Glewstone Court ....Herefordshire 0845 365 1782
Moccas Court....................................Herefordshire 0845 365 2071
Wilton Court Hotel ....Herefordshire 0845 365 2809
Auberge du Lac ....Hertfordshire 0845 365 3756
Kick & Dicky ....Hertfordshire 0845 365 3907
The White House and
  Lion & Lamb Bar & Restaurant......Hertfordshire..............0845 365 2736
The Hambrough.................................Isle of Wight...............0845 365 2517
The Priory Bay Hotel ....Isle of Wight...............0845 365 2649
Rylstone Manor ....Isle of Wight...............0845 365 2318
Winterbourne Country House ....Isle of Wight...............0845 365 2813
Little Silver Country Hotel ....Kent 0845 365 2032
Romney Bay House Hotel................Kent 0845 365 2305
The Royal Harbour Hotel ....Kent 0845 365 4853
Wallett's Court Hotel & Spa ....Kent 0845 365 2784
The White Cliffs Hotel.....................Kent 0845 365 4026
Brooklands Country Retreat & Health Spa ..Lancashire 0845 365 4623
Ferrari's Restaurant & Hotel ....Lancashire 0845 365 3293
Number One South Beach ....Lancashire 0845 365 3759
The Crown Hotel ....Lincolnshire 0845 365 2451
Tree Tops Country House ....Merseyside..................0845 365 2759
Broad House.......................................Norfolk........................0845 365 4856
Felbrigg Lodge ....Norfolk........................0845 365 2853

The Kings Head Hotel................................**Norfolk** **0845 365 2567**
The Old Rectory ....Norfolk........................0845 365 2614
Titchwell Manor Hotel ....Norfolk........................0845 365 2861
Braunston Manor ....Northamptonshire 0845 365 3256

Small Hotels & Inns, Great Britain & Ireland

All the properties listed below can be found in our Recommended Small Hotels, Inns & Restaurants, Great Britain & Ireland 2009 Guide. More information on our portfolio of guides can be found on page 13.

The Orchard House	Northumberland	0845 365 3726
The Otterburn Tower	Northumberland	0845 365 3748
Waren House Hotel	Northumberland	0845 365 2785
Cockliffe Country House Hotel	Nottinghamshire	0845 365 3237
Greenwood Lodge	Nottinghamshire	0845 365 2891
Langar Hall	Nottinghamshire	0845 365 1983
Burford House	Oxfordshire	0845 365 3914
Burford Lodge Hotel & Restaurant	Oxfordshire	0845 365 3215
Duke Of Marlborough Country Inn	Oxfordshire	0845 365 3273
The Goose	Oxfordshire	0845 365 1938
The Lamb Inn	Oxfordshire	0845 365 2576
The Nut Tree Inn	Oxfordshire	0845 365 3789
Weston Manor	Oxfordshire	0845 365 2798
Barnsdale Lodge	Rutland	0845 365 3028
The Lake Isle Hotel & Restaurant	Rutland	0845 365 2573
Nick's Restaurant	Rutland	0845 365 3924
The Inn at Grinshill	Shropshire	0845 365 4634
Pen-Y-Dyffryn Country Hotel	Shropshire	0845 365 2106
Soulton Hall	Shropshire	0845 365 2356
Bellplot House Hotel	Somerset	0845 365 3033
Beryl	Somerset	0845 365 3034
Bindon Country House Hotel	Somerset	0845 365 3037
Binham Grange	Somerset	0845 365 1806
Compton House	Somerset	0845 365 3243
Farthings Country House Hotel	Somerset	0845 365 3290
Karslake Country House and Cottage	Somerset	0845 365 1935
Three Acres Country House	Somerset	0845 365 2751
Woodlands Country House Hotel	Somerset	0845 365 3242
Dunsley Hall Hotel	Staffordshire	0845 365 3908
The Manor at Hanchurch	Staffordshire	0845 365 4618
The Angel Hotel	Suffolk	0845 365 1802
Clarice House	Suffolk	0845 365 3235
The Cornwallis Country Hote	Suffolk	0845 365 4603
The Westleton Crown	Suffolk	0845 365 2731
The Crown Inn	Surrey	0845 365 3252
Pride of the Valley	Surrey	0845 365 3791
The Mill House Hotel	West Sussex	0845 365 2598
Episode Hotel	Warwickshire	0845 365 3764
The George Hotel	Warwickshire	0845 365 3762
Beechfield House	Wiltshire	0845 365 3031
The Castle Inn	Wiltshire	0845 365 2894
The Lamb at Hindon	Wiltshire	0845 365 2574
The Pear Tree Inn	Wiltshire	0845 365 1746
Stanton Manor Hotel	Wiltshire	0845 365 2364
Widbrook Grange	Wiltshire	0845 365 2805
The Old Rectory	Worcestershire	0845 365 2615
Riverside Hotel and Restaurant	Worcestershire	0845 365 3607
Royal Forester Country Inn	Worcestershire	0845 365 2865
The White L on Hotel	Worcestershire	0845 365 2738
Kilham Hall	E Riding of Yorkshire	0845 365 3285
The Austwick Traddock	North Yorkshire	0845 365 2396
The Devonshire Fell	North Yorkshire	0845 365 2462
Dunsley Hall	North Yorkshire	0845 365 3276
George and Dragon Inn	North Yorkshire	0845 365 4609
Marmadukes Hotel	North Yorkshire	0845 365 4852
The Worsley Arms Hotel	North Yorkshire	0845 365 2746
The Dusty Miller & Coiners Restaurant	West Yorkshire	0845 365 3781
Hey Green Country House Hotel	West Yorkshire	0845 365 1846
The Shibden Mill Inn	West Yorkshire	0845 365 4617

Ireland

Ard Na Sidhe	Kerry	00 353 66 976 9105

Scotland

Darroch Learg	Aberdeenshire	0845 365 3263
Balcary Bay Hotel	Dumfries & Galloway	0845 365 3026
Corsewall Lighthouse Hotel	Dumfries & Galloway	0845 365 2859
The Hudson Hotel	Edinburgh	0845 365 4627
Dunain Park Hotel & Restaurant	Highland	0845 365 3275
Forss House Hotel	Highland	0845 365 1749
Greshornish House	Highland	0845 365 1798
Loch Ness Lodge	**Highland**	**0845 365 4625**
Royal Marine Hotel, Restaurant & Spa	Highland	0845 365 2309
Ruddyglow Park	Highland	0845 365 2315
Skeabost Country House	Highland	0845 365 4016
The Steadings at The Grouse & Trout	Highland	0845 365 2698
Toravaig House	Highland	0845 365 2756
Knockomie Hotel	Moray	0845 365 1963
Castle Venlaw	Scottish Borders	0845 365 3226
Fauhope Country House	Scottish Borders	0845 365 4631
Culzean Castle – The Eisenhower Apartment	South Ayrshire	0845 365 3257

Wales

Ty Mawr Country Hotel	Carmarthenshire	0845 365 2781
Tan-Y-Foel Country House	Conwy	0845 365 2387
Pentre Mawr Country House	Denbighshire	0845 365 4051
Bae Abermaw	Gwynedd	0845 365 3023
Llwyndu Farmhouse	Gwynedd	0845 365 3721
Porth Tocyn Country House Hotel	Gwynedd	0845 365 2136
The Bell At Skenfrith	Monmouthshire	0845 365 2403
The Crown At Whitebrook	Monmouthshire	0845 365 2439
Penally Abbey	Pembrokeshire	0845 365 2103
Wolfscastle Country Hotel & Restaurant	Pembrokeshire	0845 365 2817
Egerton Grey	Vale of Glamorgan	0845 365 3281

Historic Houses, Castles & Gardens

We are pleased to feature over 150 places to visit during your stay at a Condé Nast Johansens Recommendation.
More information about these attractions, including opening times and entry fees, can be found on www.johansens.com

England

Bath & North East Somerset

Cothay Manor and Gardens – Greenham, Wellington, Bath & North East Somerset TA21 0JR. Tel: 01823 672283
Great House Farm – Wells Rd, Theale, Wedmore, Bath & North East Somerset BS28 4SJ. Tel: 01934 713133
Maunsel House – North Newton, Nr Bridgwater, Bath & North East Somerset TA7 0BU. Tel: 01278 661076
Orchard Wyndham – Williton, Taunton, Bath & North East Somerset TA4 4HH. Tel: 01984 632309

Bedfordshire

Woburn Abbey – Woburn, Bedfordshire MK17 9WA. Tel: 01525 290666
Moggerhanger Park – Park Road, Moggerhanger, Bedfordshire MK44 3RW. Tel: 01767 641007

Berkshire

Eton College – The Visits Office, Windsor, Berkshire SL4 6DW. Tel: 01753 671177

Buckinghamshire

Nether Winchendon House – Nr Aylesbury, Buckinghamshire HP18 0DY. Tel: 01844 290199

Waddesdon Manor – Waddesdon, Nr Aylesbury, Buckinghamshire HP18 0JH. Tel: 01296 653211

Cambridgeshire

Mannington Hall – King's Parade, Cambridge, Cambridgeshire CB2 1ST. Tel: 01223 331212
The Manor – Hemingford Grey, Huntingdon, Cambridgeshire PE28 9BN. Tel: 01480 463234

Cheshire

Dorfold Hall – Nantwich, Cheshire CW5 8LD. Tel: 01270 625245
Holmston Hall Barn – Little Budworth, Tarporley, Cheshire CW6 9AW. Tel: 01829 760366
Ness Botanic Gardens – Ness, Neston, South Wirral, Cheshire CH64 4AY. Tel: 0151 353 0123
Rode Hall and Gardens – Scholar Green, Cheshire ST7 3QP. Tel: 01270 882961

Cornwall

Mount Edgcumbe House & Country Park – Cremyll, Cornwall PL10 1HZ. Tel: 01752 822236

Cumbria

Holker Hall and Gardens – Cark-in-Cartmel, nr Grange-over-Sands, Cumbria LA11 7PL. Tel: 01539 558328
Isel Hall – Cockermouth, Cumbria CA13 0QG. Tel: 01900 821778

Derbyshire

Haddon Hall – Bakewell, Derbyshire DE45 1LA. Tel: 01629 812855
Melbourne Hall & Gardens – Melbourne, Derbyshire DE73 8EN. Tel: 01332 862502
Renishaw Hall Gardens – Nr Sheffield, Derbyshire S21 3WB. Tel: 01246 432310

Devon

Anderton House – Goodleigh, Devon EX32 7NR. Tel: 01628 825920
Bowringsleigh – Kingsbridge, Devon TQ7 3LL. Tel: 01548 852014
Downes – Crediton, Devon EX17 3PL. Tel: 01392 439046

Dorset

Clavell Tower – Kimmeridge, Nr Wareham, Dorset. Tel: 01628 825920
Lulworth Castle & Park – East Lulworth, Wareham, Dorset BH20 5QS. Tel: 0845 450 1054
Mapperton Gardens – Mapperton, Beaminster, Dorset DT8 3NR. Tel: 01308 862645
Minterne Gardens – Minterne Magna, Nr Dorchester, Dorset DT2 7AU. Tel: 01300 341370
Moignes Court – Owermoigne, Dorchester, Dorset DT2 8HY. Tel: 01305 853300
Sherborne Castle – New Road, Sherborne, Dorset DT9 5NR. Tel: 01935 813182

Durham

Raby Castle – Staindrop, Darlington, Durham DL2 3AH. Tel: 01833 660 202

Essex

Hedingham Castle – Bayley Street, Castle Hedingham, Nr Halstead, Essex CO9 3DJ. Tel: 01787 460261
Ingatestone – Hall Lane, Ingatestone, Essex CM4 9NR. Tel: 01277 353010

Gloucestershire

Cheltenham Art Gallery & Museum – Clarence Street, Cheltenham, Gloucestershire GL50 3JT. Tel: 01242 237431
Hardwicke court – Nr Gloucester, Gloucestershire GL2 4RS. Tel: 01452 720212
Old Campden House – Chipping Campden, Gloucestershire GL55 6LR. Tel: 01628 825920
Owlpen Manor – Owlpen, Nr Uley, Gloucestershire GL11 5BZ. Tel: 01453 860261
Sezincote House & Garden – Moreton-in-Marsh, Gloucestershire GL56 9AW. Tel: 01386 700444
Sudeley castle – Winchcombe, Gloucestershire GL54 SJP. Tel: 01242 602308

Hampshire

Beaulieu – Beaulieu Enterprises Ltd, John Montagu Bldg, Hampshire SO42 7ZN. Tel: 01590 612345
Buckler's Hard – Beaulieu, Brockenhurst, Hampshire SO42 7XB. Tel: 01590 614641

Historic Houses, Castles & Gardens

We are pleased to feature over 150 places to visit during your stay at a Condé Nast Johansens Recommendation.
More information about these attractions, including opening times and entry fees, can be found on www.johansens.com

Gilbert White's House & The Oates M – Selborne, Nr. Alton, Hampshire GU34 3JH. Tel: 01420 511275
Greywell Hill House – Greywell, Hook, Hampshire RG29 1DG

Hertfordshire

Ashridge – Berkhamsted, Hertfordshire HP4 1NS. Tel: 01442 841027
Hatfield House – Hatfield, Hertfordshire AL9 5NQ. Tel: 01707 287010
Knebworth House – Knebworth, Hertfordshire SG3 6PY. Tel: 01462 812661

Kent

Belmont House – Belmont Park, Throwley, Faversham, Kent ME13 0HH. Tel: 01795 890202
Bromley Museum – The Priory, Church Hill, Orpington, Kent BR6 0HH. Tel: 01689 873826
Finchcocks, Living Museum of Music – Goudhurst, Kent TN17 1HH. Tel: 01580 211702
The Grange – Ramsgate, Kent. Tel: 01628 825925
Groombridge Place Gardens & Enchanted Forest – Groombridge, Tunbridge Wells, Kent TN3 9QG. Tel: 01892 861444
Marle Place Gardens – Marle Place Road, Brenchley, Kent TN12 7HS. Tel: 01892 722304
Mount Ephraim Gardens – Hernhill, Nr Faversham, Kent ME13 9TX. Tel: 01227 751496
The New College of Cobham – Cobhambury Road, Cobham, Nr Gravesend, Kent DA12 3BG. Tel: 01474 812503
Rochester Castle – The Lodge, Rochester-upon-Medway, Medway, Kent ME1 1SX. Tel: 01634 402276
Upnor Castle – Upnor, Kent ME2 4XG. Tel: 01634 718742

Lancashire

Townhead House – Slaidburn, via Clitheroe, Lancashire BBY 3AG. Tel: 01772 421566

London

Burgh House – New End Square, Hampstead, London NW3 1LT. Tel: 020 7431 0144
Pitzhanger Manor House – Walpole Park, Mattock Lane, Ealing, London W5 5EQ. Tel: 020 8567 1227
Royal Institution Michael Faraday Museum – 21 Albemarle Street, London W1S 4BS. Tel: 020 7409 2992
Spencer House – 27 St. Jame's Place, London SW1A 1NR. Tel: 020 7514 1958
St Paul's Cathedral – The Chapter House, St Paul's Churchyard, London EC4M 8AD. Tel: 020 7246 8350
Syon park – Syon Park, Brentford, London TW8 8JF. Tel: 020 8560 0881

Norfolk

Mannington Estate – Mannington Hall, Norfolk NR11 7BB. Tel: 01263 584175
Mannington Hall – Saxthorpe, Norfolk NR11 7BB. Tel: 01263 584175
Stody Lodge Gardens – Melton Constable, Norfolk NR24 2EW. Tel: 01263 860572
Walsingham Abbey Grounds – Little Walsingham, Norfolk NR22 6BP. Tel: 01328 820259

Northamptonshire

Coton Manor Garden – Nr Guilsborough, Northamptonshire NN6 8RQ. Tel: 01604 740219
Haddonstone Show Gardens – The Forge House, Church Lane, East Haddon, Northamptonshire NN6 8DB. Tel: 01604 770711

Northumberland

Alnwick Castle – Alnwick, Northumberland NE66 1NQ. Tel: 01665 510777/ 511100
Chipchase Castle & Gardens – Wark on Tyne, Hexham, Northumberland NE48 3NT. Tel: 01434 230203

Oxfordshire

Kingston Bagpuize House – Abingdon, Oxfordshire OX13 5AX. Tel: 01865 820259
Mapledurham House – Nr Reading, Oxfordshire RG4 7TR. Tel: 01189 723350
Stonor Park – Nr Henley-on-Thames, Oxfordshire RG9 6HF. Tel: 01491 638587
Sulgrave Manor – Manor Road, Sulgrave, Banbury, Oxfordshire OX17 2SD. Tel: 01295 760205

Wallingford Castle Gardens – Castle Street, Wallingford, Oxfordshire OX10 0AL. Tel: 01491 835373

Shropshire

Hawkstone Park & Follies – Weston-under-Redcastle, Nr Shrewsbury, Shropshire SY4 5UY. Tel: 01939 200 611
Shrewsbury castle – Castle Street, Shrewsbury, Shropshire SY1 2AT. Tel: 01743 358516
Shrewsbury Museum & Art Gallery – Barker Street, Shrewsbury, Shropshire SY1 1QH. Tel: 01743 361196

Somerset

East Lambrook Manor Gardens – East Lambrook, South Petherton, Somerset TA13 5HH
Hestercombe Gardens – Cheddon Fitzpaine, Taunton, Somerset TA2 8LG. Tel: 01823 413923
Milton Lodge Gardens – Old Bristol Road, Wells, Somerset BA5 3AQ. Tel: 01749 672168
Robin Hood's Hut – Halswell, Goathurst, Somerset. Tel: 01628 825925

Staffordshire

Izaak Walton's Cottage – Worston Lane, Shallowford, Staffordshire ST15 0PA. Tel: 01785 760278
Stafford Castle & Visitor Centre – Newport Road, Stafford, Staffordshire ST16 1DJ. Tel: 01785 257698
The Ancient High House – Greengate Street, Stafford, Staffordshire ST16 2JA. Tel: 01785 619131
Whitmore Hall – Whitmore, Nr Newcastle-under-Lyme, Staffordshire ST5 5HW. Tel: 01782 680478

Historic Houses, Castles & Gardens

We are pleased to feature over 150 places to visit during your stay at a Condé Nast Johansens Recommendation. More information about these attractions, including opening times and entry fees, can be found on www.johansens.com

Suffolk

Freston Tower – Near Ipswich, Suffolk. Tel: 01628 825920
Kentwell Hall – Long Melford, Sudbury, Suffolk CO10 9BA. Tel: 01787 310207
Newbourne Hall – Newbourne, Nr Woodbridge, Suffolk IP12 4NP. Tel: 01473 736764
Otley Hall – Hall Lane, Otley, Nr Ipswich, Suffolk IP6 9PA. Tel: 01473 890264

Surrey

Claremont – Claremont Drive, Esher, Surrey KT10 9LY. Tel: 01372 473623
Guildford House Gallery – 155 High Street, Guildford, Surrey GU1 3AJ. Tel: 01483 444740
Loseley Park – Guildford, Surrey GU3 1HS. Tel: 01483 304 440

East Sussex

Anne of Cleves House and Museum – 52 Southover High Street, Lewes, East Sussex BN7 1JA. Tel: 01273 474610
Bentley Wildfowl & Motor Museum – Halland, Nr. Lewes, East Sussex BN8 5AF. Tel: 01825 840573
Charleston – Firle, Nr Lewes, East Sussex BN8 6LL. Tel: 01323 811626
Gardens and Grounds of Herstmonceux Castle – Hailsham, East Sussex BN27 1RN. Tel: 01323 833816
Michelham Priory – Upper Dicker, Hailsham, East Sussex BN27 3QS. Tel: 01323 844224
Pashley Manor Gardens – Ticehurst, East Sussex TN5 7HE. Tel: 01580 200888
Wilmington Priory – Wilmington, Nr Eastbourne, East Sussex BN26 5SW. Tel: 01628 825920

West Sussex

Borde Hill – Balcombe Road, Haywards Heath, West Sussex RH16 1XP. Tel: 01444 450326
Denmans Garden – Denmans Lane, Fontwell, West Sussex BN18 0SU. Tel: 01243 542808
Fishbourne Roman Palace – Salthill Road, Fishbourne, Chichester, West Sussex PO19 3QR. Tel: 01243 785859
High Beeches Gardens – Handcross, West Sussex RH17 6HQ. Tel: 01444 400589
Leonardslee Lakes and Gardens – Lower Beeding, West Sussex RH13 6PP. Tel: 01403 891212
Lewes Castle and Barbican House Museum – Barbican House, 169 High Street, Lewes, West Sussex BN7 1YE. Tel: 01273 486290
Marlipins Museum – High Street, Shoreham-by-Sea, West Sussex BN43 5DA. Tel: 01273 462994
Parham House & Gardens – Parham Park, Nr Pulborough, West Sussex RH20 4HS. Tel: 01903 742021
The Priest's House – North Lane, West Hoathly, West Sussex RH19 4PP. Tel: 01342 810479
West Dean Gardens – The Edward James Foundation, Estate Office West Dean, Chichester, West Sussex PO18 0QZ. Tel: 01243 818210
Worthing Museum & Art Gallery – Chapel Road, Worthing, West Sussex BN11 1HP. Tel: 01903 221448

Warwickshire

Arbury Hall – Nuneaton, Warwickshire CV10 7PT. Tel: 02476 382804
Shakespeare Houses – The Shakespeare Centre, Henley Street, Stratford-upon-Avon, Warwickshire CV37 6QW. Tel: 01789 204016

West Midlands

The Barber Institute of Fine Arts – University of Birmingham, Edgbaston, Birmingham, West Midlands B15 2TS. Tel: 0121 414 7333
The Birmingham Botanical Gardens & Glasshouses – Westbourne Road, Edgbaston, Birmingham, West Midlands B15 3TR. Tel: 0121 454 1860

Worcestershire

Harvington Hall – Harvington, Kidderminster, Worcestershire DY10 4LR. Tel: 01562 777846
Little Malvern Court – Nr Malvern, Worcestershire WR14 4JN. Tel: 01684 892988

North Yorkshire

Allerton castle – Allerton Castle, Allerton Park, North Yorkshire HG5 0SE. Tel: 01423 331123
Duncombe Park – Helmsley, Ryedale, York, North Yorkshire YO62 5EB. Tel: 01439 770213
Forbidden Corner – Tupgill Park Estate, Coverham, Nr Middleham, North Yorkshire DL8 4TJ. Tel: 01969 640638
Fountains Abbey and Studley Royal Water Garden – Ripon, Nr Harrogate, North Yorkshire HG4 3DY. Tel: 01765 608888
Newburgh Priory – Coxwold, York, North Yorkshire YO61 4AS. Tel: 01347 868 435
Skipton Castle – Skipton, North Yorkshire BD23 1AW. Tel: 01756 792442

West Yorkshire

Bramham Park – The Estate Office, Bramham Park, Wetherby, West Yorkshire LS23 6ND. Tel: 01937 846000
Ledston Hall – Hall Lane, Ledston, Castleford, West Yorkshire WF10 2BB. Tel: 01423 523 423

N Ireland

Down

North Down Museum – Town Hall, Bangor, Down BT20 4BTN. Tel: 02891 271200
Seaforde Gardens – Seaforde, Downpatrick, Down BT30 8PG. Tel: 02844 811225

Ireland

Cork

Blarney Castle, House and Garden – Blarney, Cork. Tel: 00 353 21 4385252

Offaly

Birr Castle Demesne – Birr Co.Offaly, Offaly. Tel: 00 353 5791 20336

Historic Houses, Castles & Gardens

We are pleased to feature over 150 places to visit during your stay at a Condé Nast Johansens Recommendation.
More information about these attractions, including opening times and entry fees, can be found on www.johansens.com

Wexford

Kilmokea Country Manor and Gardens – Great Island, Campile, Wexford. Tel: 00 353 51 388109

Wicklow

Mount Usher Gardens – Ashford, Wicklow. Tel: 00 353 40440205

Scotland

Ayrshire

Kelburn Castle and Country Centre – Kelburn, Fairlie (Nr Largs), Ayrshire KA29 0BE. Tel: 01475 568685

Borders

Floors Castle – Kelso, Borders TD5 7SF. Tel: 01573 223333

Dumfries & Galloway

Ardwell Gardens – Ardwell House, Ardwell, Stranraer, Dumfries & Galloway DG9 9LY. Tel: 01776 860227
Castle Kennedy Gardens – The Estates Office, Rephad, Stranraer, Dumfries & Galloway DG9 8BX. Tel: 01776 702024
Drumlanrig Castle, Gardens & Country Park – Thornhill, Dumfriesshire, Dumfries & Galloway DG3 4AQ. Tel: 01848 331555
Gilnockie Tower – 7 Riverside Park, , Canonbie , Dumfriesshire, Dumfries & Galloway DG14 0UG. Tel: 01387 371876
Glenmalloch Lodge – Newton Stewart, Dumfries & Galloway. Tel: 01628 825920

Highland

Armadale Castle Gardens & Museum of the Isles – Armadale, Sleat, Isle of Skye, Highland IV45 8RS. Tel: 01471 844305
Inveraray castle – Cherry Park, Inveraray, Highland PA32 8XF. Tel: 01499 302203
Mount Stuart – Mount Stuart, Isle of Bute, Highland PA20 9LR. Tel: 01700 503877
Scone Palace – Scone, Perth, Perthshire, Highland PH2 6BD. Tel: 01738 552300

North Ayrshire

Auchinleck House – Ochiltree, North Ayrshire. Tel: 01628 825920

Scottish Borders

Bowhill House & Country Park – Bowhill, Selkirk, Scottish Borders TD7 5ET. Tel: 01750 22204
Manderston – Duns, Berwickshire, Scottish Borders TD11 3PP. Tel: 01361 883 450
Paxton House & Country Park – Paxton, Nr Berwick upon Tweed, Scottish Borders TD15 1SZ. Tel: 01289 386291
Traquair House – Innerleithen, Peebles, Scottish Borders EH44 6PW. Tel: 01896 830 323

West Lothian

Newliston – South Queensferry, West Lothian, West Lothian EH30 9SL. Tel: 0131 333 3231
Hopetoun House – South Queensferry, West Lothian, West Lothian EH30 9SL. Tel: 0131 331 2451

Wales

Conwy

Bodnant Garden – Tal Y Cafn, Conwy LL28 5RE. Tel: 01492 650460

Denbighshire

Dolbelydr – Trefnant, Denbighshire. Tel: 01628 825920

Flintshire

Golden Grove – Llanasa, Nr Holywell, Flintshire CH8 9NA. Tel: 01745 854452

Gwynedd

Oriel Plas Glyn-Y-Weddw Art Gallery – Llanbedrog, Pwllheli, Gwynedd LL53 7TT. Tel: 01758 740 763
Plas Brondanw Gardens – Llanfrothen, Nr Penrhyndeudraeth, Gwynedd LL48 6ET. Tel: 01743 241181
Portmeirion Village & Gardens – Portmeirion Village, Portmeirion, Gwynedd LL48 6ET. Tel: (01766) 770228

Monmouthshire

Llanvihangel Court – Nr Abergavenny, Monmouthshire NP7 8DH. **Tel: 01873 890 217**
Usk Castle – Castle House, Monmouth Rd, Usk, Monmouthshire NP15 1SD. Tel: 01291 672563

Pembrokeshire

St David's Cathedral – The Deanery, The Close, St Davids, Pembrokeshire SA62 6RH. Tel: 01437 720 199

France

Loire Valley

Château de Chenonceau – 37150 Chenonceaux, Loire Valley 37150. Tel: 00 33 2 47 23 90 07

Pays-de-Loire

Château de Goulaine – 44115 Haute-Goulaine, Pays-de-Loire Loire-Atlantique. Tel: 00 33 2 40 54 91 42

The Netherlands

Het Loo Palace National Museum – Koninklijk Park 1, NL–7315 JA Apeldoorn,. Tel: 00 31 55 577 2400

Sleepeezee

BY APPOINTMENT TO
H.M. THE QUEEN
BEDDING MANUFACTURERS
SLEEPEEZEE LIMITED, ROCHESTER

BY APPOINTMENT TO
H.R.H. THE PRINCE OF WALES
BEDDING MANUFACTURERS
SLEEPEEZEE LIMITED, ROCHESTER

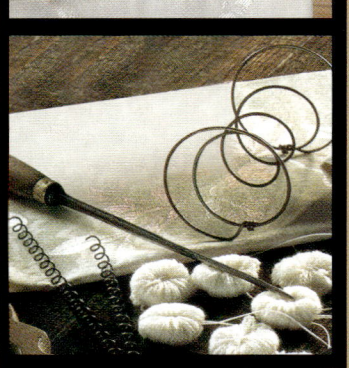

the perfect end to every day.

Makers of world-class, quality pocket sprung beds for over 80 years, Sleepeezee has become one of the leading and most respected bed manufacturers in the UK.

Recognised and highly regarded for craftsmanship, design and innovation, we have remained dedicated to the creation of luxurious beds and mattresses which provide supreme comfort and support, night after night.

Preferred bed supplier to Condé Nast Johansens.

Sleepeezee Contract Beds enquiries:
Tel: +44 (0) 1384 455515 • email: contractservices@sleepeezee.co.uk • online: www.sleepeezee.co.uk

Hotels, Europe & The Mediterranean

All the properties listed below can be found in our Recommended Hotels & Spas, Europe & The Mediterranean 2009 Guide. More information on our portfolio of guides can be found on page 13.

Andorra

Hotel Grau Roig	Grau Roig	+376 75 55 56
Sport Hotel Hermitage & Spa	Soldeu	+376 87 06 70

Austria

Palais Coburg Residenz	Vienna	+43 1 518 180

Belgium

Grand Hotel Damier	Kortrijk	+32 56 22 15 47
Hostellerie Trôs~Marets	Malmédy	+32 80 33 79 17
Hostellerie Ter Driezen	Turnhout	+32 14 41 87 57

Czech Republic

Aria Hotel Prague	Prague	+420 225 334 111
Bellagio Hotel Prague	Prague	+420 221 778 999
Golden Well Hotel	Prague	+420 257 011 213
MaMaison Pachtuv Palace	Prague	+420 234 705 111
MaMaison Riverside Hotel	Prague	+420 225 994 611
Hotel Nautilus	Tábor	+420 380 900 900

Estonia

Ammende Villa	Pärnu	+372 44 73 888

France

Domaine de la Grange de Condé	Alsace~Lorraine	+33 3 87 79 30 50
Hostellerie les Bas Rupts Le Chalet Fleuri	Alsace~Lorraine	+33 3 29 63 09 25
Hôtel à la Cour d'Alsace	Alsace~Lorraine	+33 3 88 95 07 00
Hôtel Les Têtes	Alsace~Lorraine	+33 3 89 24 43 43
Romantik Hôtel le Maréchal	Alsace~Lorraine	+33 3 89 41 60 32
Château de Bonaban	Brittany	+33 2 99 58 24 50
Domaine de Rochevilaine	Brittany	+33 2 97 41 61 61
Hôtel l'Agapa & Spa	Brittany	+33 2 96 49 01 10
Ti al Lannec	Brittany	+33 2 96 15 01 01
Château Hôtel André Ziltener	Burgundy - Franche~Comte	+33 3 80 62 41 62
Abbaye de la Bussière	Burgundy - Franche~Comté	+33 3 80 49 02 29
Château de Vault de Lugny	Burgundy - Franche~Comté	+33 3 86 34 07 86
Hostellerie des Monts de Vaux	Burgundy - Franche~Comté	+33 3 84 37 12 50
Château d'Etoges	Champagne~Ardennes	+33 3 26 59 30 08
Château de Fère	Champagne~Ardennes	+33 3 23 82 21 13
Domaine du Château de Barive	Champagne~Ardennes	+33 3 23 22 15 15
Château Eza	Côte d'Azur	+33 4 93 41 12 24
Hôtel La Pérouse	Côte d'Azur	+ 33 4 93 62 34 63
La Ferme d'Augustin	Côte d'Azur	+33 4 94 55 97 00
La Villa Mauresque	Côte d'Azur	+33 494 83 02 42
Le Bailli de Suffren	Côte d'Azur	+33 4 98 04 47 00
Le Moulin de Mougins	Côte d'Azur	+33 4 93 75 78 24
Château de la Barre	Loire Valley	+33 2 43 35 00 17
Château de Pray	Loire Valley	+33 247 57 23 67
Château de Verrières	Loire Valley	+33 2 41 38 05 15
Château des Briottières	Loire Valley	+33 2 41 42 00 02
Hostellerie des Hauts de Sainte~Maure	Loire Valley	+33 2 47 65 50 65
Le Manoir les Minimes	Loire Valley	+33 2 47 30 40 40
Le Manoir Saint Thomas	Loire Valley	+33 2 47 23 21 82
Château de Floure	Midi~Pyrénées	+33 4 68 79 11 29
Hôtel Lous Grits	Midi~Pyrénées	+33 5 62 28 37 10
Château la Chenevière	Normandy	+33 2 31 51 25 25
Château les Bruyères	Normandy	+33 2 31 32 22 45
Manoir de la Poterie, Spa "Les Thermes"	Normandy	+33 2 31 88 10 40
Manoir de Mathan	Normandy	+33 2 31 22 21 73
Carlton Hôtel	North - Picardy	+33 3 20 13 33 13
Château de Cocove	North - Picardy	+33 3 21 82 68 29
Château de Courcelles	North - Picardy	+33 3 23 74 13 53
Hospes Lancaster	Paris	+33 1 40 76 40 76
Hôtel Balzac	Paris	+33 1 44 35 18 00
Hôtel de Sers	Paris	+33 1 53 23 75 75
Hôtel des Académies et des Arts	Paris	+33 1 43 26 66 44
Hôtel du Petit Moulin	Paris	+33 1 42 74 10 10
Hôtel Duc de Saint~Simon	Paris	+33 1 44 39 20 20
Hôtel Duret	Paris	+33 1 45 00 42 60
Hôtel le Tourville	Paris	+33 1 47 05 62 62
Hôtel San Régis	Paris	+33 1 44 95 16 16
La Trémoille	Paris	+33 1 56 52 14 00
Le Bellechasse	Paris	+33 1 45 50 22 31
Le Sainte~Beuve	Paris	+33 1 45 48 20 07
Château de l'Yeuse	Poitou~Charentes	+33 5 45 36 82 60
Hôtel "Résidence de France"	Poitou~Charentes	+33 5 46 28 06 00
Château de Massillan	Provence	+33 4 90 40 64 51
Château de Montcaud	Provence	+33 4 66 89 60 60
Domaine le Hameau des Baux	Provence	+33 4 90 54 10 30
L'Estelle en Camargue	Provence	+33 4 90 97 89 01
La Bastide Rose	Provence	+ 33 4 90 02 14 33
Le Mas de la Rose	Provence	+33 4 90 73 08 91
Le Spinaker	Provence	+33 4 66 53 36 37

Hotels, Europe & The Mediterranean

All the properties listed below can be found in our Recommended Hotels & Spas, Europe & The Mediterranean 2009 Guide. More information on our portfolio of guides can be found on page 13.

Manoir de la Roseraie	Provence	+33 4 75 46 58 15
Chalet Hôtel Kaya	Rhône~Alpes	+33 4 79 41 42 00
Chalet Hôtel La Marmotte	Rhône~Alpes	+33 4 50 75 80 33
Château de Bagnols	Rhône~Alpes	+33 4 74 71 40 00
Château de Coudrée	Rhône~Alpes	+33 4 50 72 62 33
Hôtel Helvie	Rhône~Alpes	+33 4 75 94 65 85
Le Beau Rivage	Rhône~Alpes	+33 4 74 56 82 82
Le Fer à Cheval	Rhône~Alpes	+33 4 50 21 30 39
Château de Sanse	South West	+33 5 57 56 41 10
Château les Merles	South West	+33 5 53 63 13 42
Hôtel du Palais	South West	+33 5 59 41 64 00
Le Relais du Château Franc Mayne	South West	+33 5 57 24 62 61

Great Britain

Ashdown Park Hotel	England	+44 1342 824 988
The French Horn	England	+44 1189 692 204
The Grand Hotel	England	+44 1323 412345
Jumeirah Carlton Tower	England	+44 20 7235 1234
Jumeirah Lowndes Hotel	England	+44 20 7823 1234
Luton Hoo Hotel, Golf & Spa	England	+44 1582 734437
The Mayflower Hotel	England	+44 20 7370 0991
The New Linden Hotel	England	+44 20 7221 4321
Twenty Nevern Square	England	+44 20 7565 9555
Tylney Hall	England	+44 1256 764881

Greece

O&B Athens Boutique Hotel	Athens	+30 21033 12940
Argentikon Luxury Suites	Chios	+30 22710 33111
OUT OF THE BLUE, Capsis Elite Resort	Crete	+30 21061 49563
Paradise Island Villas	Crete	+30 28970 22893
Pleiades Luxurious Villas	Crete	+30 28410 90450
St Nicolas Bay Resort Hotel & Villas	Crete	+30 28410 25041
Villas Hotel Domes of Elounda	Crete	+30 28410 41924
Pavezzo Country Retreat	Lefkada	+30 26450 71782
Apanema	Mykonos	+30 22890 28590
Mykonos Theoxenia Hotel	Mykonos	+30 22890 22230
Tharroe of Mykonos	Mykonos	+30 22890 27370
Petra Hotel	Patmos Island	+30 22470 34020
Canaves Oia	Santorini	+30 22860 71453
Ikies Traditional Houses	Santorini	+30 22860 71311

Hungary

Allegro Hotel - Tihany Centrum	Tihany - Lake Balaton	+36 87 448 456

Italy

Furore Inn Resort & Spa	Campania	+39 089 830 4711
Hotel Villa Maria	Campania	+39 089 857255
Hotel Posta (Historical Residence)	Emilia Romagna	+39 05 22 43 29 44
Hotel Villa Roncuzzi	Emilia Romagna	+39 0544 534776
Palazzo Dalla Rosa Prati	Emilia Romagna	+39 0521 386 429
Torre di San Martino - Historical Residence	Emilia Romagna	+39 0523 972002
Buonanotte Garibaldi	Lazio	+39 06 58 330 733
Casa Howard Guest Houses - Rome & Florence	Lazio	+39 06 69924555
Casa Montani - Luxury Town House	Lazio	+39 06 3260 0421
Hotel dei Borgognoni	Lazio	+39 06 6994 1505
Hotel dei Consoli	Lazio	+39 0668 892 972
Hotel Fenix	Lazio	+39 06 8540 741
La Posta Vecchia	Lazio	+39 0699 49501
Villa La Cerretana	Lazio	+39 0761 1762565
Villa Spalletti Trivelli	Lazio	+39 06 48907934
Abbadia San Giorgio - Historical Residence	Liguria	+39 0185 491119
Grand Hotel Diana Majestic	Liguria	+39 0183 402 727
Grand Hotel Miramare	Liguria	+39 0185 287013
Hotel Punta Est	Liguria	+39 019 600611
Hotel San Giorgio - Portofino House	Liguria	+39 0185 26991
Hotel Vis à Vis	Liguria	+39 0185 42661
Bagni di Bormio Spa Resort	Lombardy	+39 0342 910131
Grand Hotel Gardone Riviera	Lombardy	+39 0365 20261
Hotel Bellerive	Lombardy	+39 0365 520 410
Hotel de la Ville	Lombardy	+39 039 39421
Hotel Parco San Marco Beach Resort, Golf & SPA	Lombardy	+39 0344 629111
L'Albereta	Lombardy	+39 030 7760 550
Petit Palais Maison de Charme	Lombardy	+39 02 584 891
THE PLACE - Luxury serviced apartments	Lombardy	+39 02 76026633
Albergo L'Ostelliere	Piemonte	+39 0143 607 801
Cascina Langa	Piemonte	+39 0173 630289
Foresteria dei Poderi Einaudi	Piemonte	+39 0173 70414
Hotel Cristallo	Piemonte	+39 0163 922 822
Hotel Pironi	Piemonte	+39 0323 70624
Hotel Principi di Piemonte	Piemonte	+39 011 55151
Relais San Maurizio	Piemonte	+39 0141 841900
Villa dal Pozzo d'Annone	Piemonte	+39 0322 7255
Villa e Palazzo Aminta	Piemonte	+39 0323 933 818
Borgobianco Resort & SPA	Puglia	+39 080 8870001

Hotels, Europe & The Mediterranean

All the properties listed below can be found in our Recommended Hotels & Spas, Europe & The Mediterranean 2009 Guide. More information on our portfolio of guides can be found on page 13.

Country House Cefalicchio	Puglia	+39 0883 642123
Hotel Titano	San Marino Republic	+378 0549 991007
Grand Hotel in Porto Cervo	Sardinia	+39 0789 91533
Petra Segreta Resort & SPA	Sardinia	+39 0789 183 1365
Villa Las Tronas	Sardinia	+39 079 981 818
Baia Taormina Grand Palace Hotels & Spa	Sicily	+39 0942 756292
Grand Hotel Arciduca	Sicily	+39 090 9812136
Grand Hotel Atlantis Bay	Sicily	+39 0942 618011
Grand Hotel Mazzarò Sea Palace	Sicily	+39 0942 612111
Hotel Signum	Sicily	+39 090 9844222
Hotel Villa Carlotta	Sicily	+39 0942 626058
Hotel Villa Ducale	Sicily	+39 0942 28153
Locanda Don Serafino	Sicily	+39 0932 220065
Palazzo Failla Hotel	Sicily	+39 0932 941059
Poggio del Sole Resort	Sicily	+39 0932 666 452
Alpenpalace Deluxe Hotel & Spa Resort	Trentino - Alto Adige / Dolomites	+39 0474 670230
Castel Fragsburg	Trentino - Alto Adige / Dolomites	+39 0473 244071
Du Lac et Du Parc Grand Resort	Trentino - Alto Adige / Dolomites	+39 0464 566600
GranPanorama Hotel Miramonti	Trentino - Alto Adige / Dolomites	+39 0473 27 93 35
Hotel Gardena Grödnerhof	Trentino - Alto Adige / Dolomites	+39 0471 796 315
Romantik Hotel Cappella	Trentino - Alto Adige / Dolomites	+39 0471 836183
Romantik Hotel Post Cavallino Bianco	Trentino - Alto Adige / Dolomites	+39 0471 613113
Albergo Pietrasanta - Palazzo Barsanti Bonetti	Tuscany	+39 0584 793 727
Borgo La Bagnaia Resort, Spa and Events Venue	Tuscany	+39 0577 813000
Borgo San Felice	Tuscany	+39 0577 3964
Casa Howard Guest Houses - Rome and Florence	Tuscany	+39 066 992 4555
Castello Banfi - Il Borgo	Tuscany	+39 0577 877 700
Country House Casa Cornacchi	Tuscany	+39 055 998229
Hotel Byron	Tuscany	+39 0584 787 052
Hotel Plaza e de Russie	Tuscany	+39 0584 44449
Hotel Villa Ottone	Tuscany	+39 0565 933 042
Il Pellicano Hotel	Tuscany	+39 0564 858111
L'Andana	Tuscany	+39 0564 944 800
Lucignanello Bandini (Borgo Storico)	Tuscany	+39 0577 803 068
Marignolle Relais & Charme	Tuscany	+39 055 228 6910
Monsignor Della Casa Country Resort	Tuscany	+39 055 840 821
Palazzo Magnani Feroni - all-suites florence	Tuscany	+39 055 2399544
Petriolo Spa & Resort	Tuscany	+39 0564 9091
Relais la Suvera (Dimora Storica)	Tuscany	+39 0577 960 300
Relais Piazza Signoria	Tuscany	+39 055 3987239
Relais Poggio ai Santi	Tuscany	+39 0565 798032
Relais Santa Croce	Tuscany	+39 055 234 2230
Relais Villa Antea	Tuscany	+39 055 484106
Relais Villa Belpoggio (Historical House)	Tuscany	+39 055 9694411
Residenza del Moro	Tuscany	+39 055 290884
Tombolo Talasso Resort	Tuscany	+39 0565 74530
Villa le Piazzole	Tuscany	+39 055 223520
Villa Poggiano	Tuscany	+39 0578 758292
Abbazia San Faustino - Luxury Country House	Umbria	+39 339 720 1717
Castello di Petroia	**Umbria**	**+39 075 92 02 87**
I Casali di Monticchio	Umbria	+39 0763 62 83 65
L'Antico Forziere	Umbria	+39 075 972 4314
Le Torri di Bagnara (Mediaeval Historical Residences)	Umbria	+39 075 579 2001
Romantik Hotel le Silve di Armenzano	Umbria	+39 075 801 9000
Hotel Jolanda Sport	Valle d'Aosta	+39 0125 366 140
Mont Blanc Hotel Village	Valle d'Aosta	+39 0165 864 111
Albergo Quattro Fontane - Residenza d'Epoca	Veneto	+39 041 526 0227
Ca Maria Adele	Veneto	+39 041 52 03 078
Ca' Nigra Lagoon Resort	Veneto	+39 041 2750047
Ca' Sagredo Hotel	Veneto	+39 041 2413111
Charming House DD724	Veneto	+39 041 277 0262
Color Hotel	Veneto	+39 045 621 0857
Hotel Flora	Veneto	+39 041 52 05 844
Hotel Giorgione	Veneto	+39 041 522 5810
Hotel Sant' Elena Venezia	Veneto	+39 041 27 17 811
Locanda San Verolo	Veneto	+39 045 720 09 30
Locanda San Vigilio	Veneto	+39 045 725 66 88
Londra Palace	Veneto	+39 041 5200533
Methis Hotel	Veneto	+39 049 872 5555
Novecento Boutique Hotel	Veneto	+39 041 24 13 765
Park Hotel Brasilia	Veneto	+39 0421 380851
Relais Duca di Dolle	Veneto	+39 0438 975 809
Relais la Magioca	Veneto	+39 045 600 0167

Hotels, Europe & The Mediterranean

All the properties listed below can be found in our Recommended Hotels & Spas, Europe & The Mediterranean 2009 Guide. More information on our portfolio of guides can be found on page 13.

Latvia

TB Palace Hotel & Spa	Jūrmala	+371 6 7147094
Hotel Bergs	Riga	+371 6777 0900

Luxembourg

Hotel Saint~Nicolas & Spa	Remich	+35 226 663

The Netherlands

Ambassade Hotel	Amsterdam	+31 20 5550 222
Auberge de Campveerse Toren	Veere	+31 0118 501 291

Poland

MaMaison Le Régina Hotel	Warsaw	+48 22531 6000

Portugal

Convento de São Paulo	Alentejo	+351 266 989 160
Convento do Espinheiro, Heritage Hotel & Spa	Alentejo	+351 266 788 200
Quinta da Malhadinha Nova	Alentejo	+351 284 965 432
As Cascatas Hotel Apartamentos	Algarve	+351 289 304 900
Casa da Moura	Algarve	+351 282 770730
Hilton Vilamoura As Cascatas Golf Resort & Spa	Algarve	+351 289 304 000
Hotel Quinta do Lago	Algarve	+351 289 350 350
Quinta Jacintina - my secret garden hotel	Algarve	+351 289 350 090
Ria Park Hotel & Spa	Algarve	+351 289 359 800
Tivoli Marina Vilamoura	Algarve	+351 289 303 303
As Janelas Verdes	Lisbon & Tagus Valley	+351 21 39 68 143
Heritage Av Liberdade	Lisbon & Tagus Valley	+351 213 404 040
Hotel Albatroz	Lisbon & Tagus Valley	+351 21 484 73 80
Hotel Britania	Lisbon & Tagus Valley	+351 21 31 55 016
Hotel Cascais Mirage	Lisbon & Tagus Valley	+351 210 060 600
Lisboa Plaza Hotel	Lisbon & Tagus Valley	+351 213 218 218
Palacio Estoril, Hotel & Golf	Lisbon & Tagus Valley	+351 21 464 80 00
Solar do Castelo	Lisbon & Tagus Valley	+351 218 806 050
Tivoli Lisboa	Lisbon & Tagus Valley	+ 351 21 319 89 00
The Westin CampoReal Golf Resort & Spa	Lisbon & Tagus Valley	+351 261 960 900
CS Madeira Atlantic Resort & Sea Spa	Madeira	+351 291 717 600
Quinta da Bela Vista	Madeira	+351 291 706 400
Quinta das Vistas Palace Gardens	Madeira	+351 291 750 000
Quinta do Monte	Madeira	+351 291 780 100
CS Vintage House Hotel	Oporto & Northern Portugal	+351 254 730 230
Quinta de San José	Oporto & Northern Portugal	+351 254 422017

Russia

MaMaison Pokrovka Suite Hotel	Moscow	+7 495 229 5757

Slovenia

Hotel Golf Bled	Bled	+386 4579 1700

Spain

Barceló la Bobadilla	Andalucía	+34 958 32 18 61
Casa de los Bates	Andalucía	+34 958 349 495
Casa No 7	Andalucía	+34 954 221 581
Casa Romana Hotel Boutique	Andalucía	+34 954 915 170
Casa Viña de Alcantara	Andalucía	+34 956 393 010
El Ladrón de Agua	Andalucía	+34 958 21 50 40
El Molino de Santillán	Andalucía	+34 952 40 09 49
Fairplay Golf Hotel & Spa	Andalucía	+34 956 429100
Gran Hotel Elba Estepona & Thalasso Spa	Andalucía	+34 952 809 200
Hacienda Benazuza el Bulli Hotel	Andalucía	+34 955 70 33 44
Hacienda La Boticaria	Andalucía	+34 955 69 88 20
Hacienda La Colorá	Andalucía	+34 957 336077
Hospes las Casas del Rey de Baeza	Andalucía	+34 954 561 496
Hospes Palacio de los Patos	Andalucía	+34 958 535 790
Hospes Palacio del Bailío	Andalucía	+34 957 498 993
Hotel Casa Morisca	Andalucía	+34 958 221 100
Hotel Incosol	Andalucía	+34 952 860909
Hotel La Fuente del Sol	Andalucía	+34 951 70 07 70
Hotel Palacio de Los Granados	Andalucía	+34 955 905 344
Hotel Palacio de Santa Inés	Andalucía	+34 958 22 23 62
Mikasa Suites & Spa	Andalucía	+34 950 138 073
Palacio de los Navas	Andalucía	+34 958 21 57 60
Posada de Palacio	Andalucía	+34 956 36 4840
Santa Isabel la Real	Andalucía	+34 958 294 658
V...	Andalucía	+34 956 451 757

Hotels, Europe & The Mediterranean

All the properties listed below can be found in our Recommended Hotels & Spas, Europe & The Mediterranean 2009 Guide. More information on our portfolio of guides can be found on page 13.

Hotel La Cepada	Asturias	+34 985 84 94 45
Palacio de Cutre	Asturias	+34 985 70 80 72
Atzaró Agroturismo	Balearic Islands	+34 971 33 88 38
Blau Porto Petro Beach Resort & Spa	Balearic Islands	+34 971 648 282
Can Lluc	Balearic Islands	+34 971 198 673
Cas Gasi	Balearic Islands	+34 971 197 700
Hospes Maricel	Balearic Islands	+34 971 707 744
Hotel Aimia	Balearic Islands	+34 971 631 200
Hotel Cala Sant Vicenç	Balearic Islands	+34 971 53 02 50
Hotel La Moraleja	Balearic Islands	+34 971 534 010
Hotel Mirador de Dalt Vila	Balearic Islands	+34 971 30 30 45
Hotel Tres	Balearic Islands	+34 971 717 333
Palacio Ca Sa Galesa	Balearic Islands	+34 971 715 400
Read's Hotel & Vespasian Spa	Balearic Islands	+34 971 14 02 61
Son Brull Hotel & Spa	Balearic Islands	+34 971 53 53 53
Son Granot	Balearic Islands	+34 971 355 555
Valldemossa Hotel & Restaurant	Balearic Islands	+34 971 61 26 26
Abama	Canary Islands	+34 902 105 600
Gran Meliá Salinas	Canary Islands	+34 928 59 00 40
Princesa Yaiza Suite Hotel Resort	Canary Islands	+34 928 519 222
La Casona de Cosgaya	Cantabria	+34 942 733 077
Posada Los Nogales	Cantabria	+34 942 589 222
Hotel Rector	Castilla y León	+34 923 21 84 82
Posada de la Casa del Abad de Ampudia	Castilla y León	+34 979 768 008
Finca Canturias	Castilla~La Mancha	+34 925 59 41 08
Hotel Palacio de la Serna	Castilla~La Mancha	+34 926 84 2208
Valdepalacios Hotel	Castilla~La Mancha	+34 925 457 534
Abac Barcelona	Cataluña	+34 93 319 6600
Can Bonastre Wine Resort	Cataluña	+34 93 772 87 67
Dolce Sitges Hotel	Cataluña	+34 938 109 000
Hospes Villa Paulita	Cataluña	+34 972 884 662
Hotel Barcelona Catedral	Cataluña	+34 93 304 22 55
Hotel Casa Fuster	Cataluña	+34 93 255 30 00
Hotel Claris	Cataluña	+34 93 487 62 62
Hotel Cram	Cataluña	+34 93 216 77 00
Hotel Duquesa de Cardona	Cataluña	+34 93 268 90 90
Hotel Gran Derby	Cataluña	+34 93 445 2544
Hotel Granados 83	Cataluña	+34 93 492 96 70
Hotel Omm	Cataluña	+34 93 445 40 00
Hotel Rigat Park & Spa Beach Hotel	Cataluña	+34 972 36 52 00
Hotel Santa Marta	Cataluña	+34 972 364 904
Mas Passamaner	Cataluña	+34 977 766 333
Romantic Villa - Hotel Vistabella	Cataluña	+34 972 25 62 00
San Sebastian Playa Hotel	Cataluña	+34 93 894 86 76
Casa Palacio Conde de la Corte	Extremadura	+34 924 563 311
Gran Hotel Atlantis Bahía Real	Fuerteventura	+34 928 53 64 44
Augusta Spa Resort	Galicia	+34 986 72 78 78
AC Hotel Santo Mauro	Madrid	+34 91 319 69 00
Antiguo Convento	Madrid	+34 91 632 22 20
Gran Meliá Fénix	Madrid	+34 91 431 67 00
Hospes Madrid	Madrid	+34 914 322 911
Hotel Orfila	Madrid	+34 91 702 77 70
Hotel Urban	Madrid	+34 91 787 77 70
Hotel Villa Real	Madrid	+34 914 20 37 67
Hotel Etxegana	País Vasco	+34 946 338 448
Hotel Pampinot	País Vasco	+34 943 640 600
Hospes Américo	Valencia	+34 965 14 65 70
Hospes Palau de la Mar	Valencia	+34 96 316 2884
Hotel Ferrero	Valencia	+34 962 35 51 75
Hotel Mont Sant	Valencia	+34 962 27 50 81
Hotel Neptuno	Valencia	+34 963 567 777
Hotel Sidi Saler & Spa	Valencia	+34 961 61 04 11
Hotel Sidi San Juan & Spa	Valencia	+34 96 516 13 00
Hotel Termas Marinas el Palasiet	Valencia	+34 964 300 250
La Madrugada	Valencia	+34 965 733 156
Mas de Canicattí	Valencia	+34 96 165 05 34
Villa Marisol	Valencia	+34 96 587 57 00

Switzerland

Park Hotel Weggis	Weggis	+41 41 392 05 05
Hotel Caprice	Wengen	+41 33 856 06 06

Turkey

The Marmara Antalya	Antalya	+90 242 249 36 00
Tuvana Residence	Antalya	+90 242 247 60 15
Sungate Port Royal	Antalya - Kemer	+90 242 824 00 00
Ada Hotel	Bodrum	+90 252 377 59 15
Divan Bodrum Palmira	Bodrum	+90 252 377 5601
Kempinski Hotel Barbaros Bay	Bodrum	+90 252 311 0303
The Marmara Bodrum	Bodrum	+90 252 313 8130
Oyster Residence	Fethiye - Ölüdeniz	+90 252 617 0765
A'jia Hotel	Istanbul	+90 216 413 9300
Bosphorus Palace Hotel	Istanbul	+90 216 422 00 03
The Marmara Istanbul	Istanbul	+90 212 251 4696
The Marmara Pera	Istanbul	+90 212 251 4646
Sirkeci Konak	Istanbul	+90 212 528 4344
Sumahan On The Water	Istanbul	+90 216 422 8000
Villa Mahal	Kalkan	+90 242 844 32 68
Golden Key Bördübet	**Marmaris**	**+90 252 436 92 30**
Richmond Nua Wellness - Spa	Sapanca - Sakarya	+90 264 582 2100
Cappadocia Cave Resorts & Spa	Uchisar-Cappadocia	+90 384 219 3194
Sacred House	Ürgüp	+90 384 341 7102

Get your personalised red carpet experience with our **personal insurance approach**

Step this way for our Made-to-measure Personal Insurance Solutions

Very often personal insurance policies are not designed to your individual requirements; with JLT we are proud to be different.

As far as we're concerned, providing personal risk management and insurance solutions for some of the UK's most high profile, successful, affluent individuals demands a truly tailored service.

That's why we have a reputation for treating our clients like VIP's and why our highly personalised service is renowned for its 'red carpet' approach.

As one of our VIP Clients you could benefit from our highly personalised approach with all your insurance needs packaged into one policy: **Home, Car, Breakdown Travel, Boat, Property Let and Holiday Home.**

Take the first step towards a 'red carpet' service and a made-to-measure Personal Insurance Solution now.

To see how you could benefit from our service contact us today on:

0800 230 0833

if calling from outside the UK
Tel: +44(0)121 626 7855

Proud to be the recommended Personal Lines Insurance provider of Condé Nast Johansens

JARDINE LLOYD THOMPSON
Personal Risks

Jardine Lloyd Thompson Personal Risks. A division of Jardine Lloyd Thompson UK Limited. Lloyd's Broker. Authorised and Regulated by the Financial Services Authority. A member of the Jardine Lloyd Thompson Group. Registered Office: 6 Friars, London EC3N 2PH. Registered in England No 00338645. VAT No. 244 2321 59.

Hotels - The Americas

Properties listed below can be found in our Recommended Hotels, Inns, Resorts & Spas - The Americas, Atlantic, Caribbean & Pacific 2009 Guide. More information on our portfolio of guides can be found on page 13.

Recommendations in Canada

CANADA - BRITISH COLUMBIA (MALAHAT)
The Aerie Resort & Spa
P.O. Box 108, 600 Ebedora Lane, Malahat, Victoria, British Columbia V0R 2L0
Tel: +1 250 743 7115
Web: www.johansens.com/aeriebc

CANADA - BRITISH COLUMBIA (SALT SPRING ISLAND)
Hastings House Country Estate
160 Upper Ganges Road, Salt Spring Island, British Columbia V8K 2S2
Tel: +1 250 537 2362
Web: www.johansens.com/hastingshouse

CANADA - BRITISH COLUMBIA (SOOKE)
Sooke Harbour House
1528 Whiffen Spit Road, Sooke, British Columbia V9Z 0T4
Tel: +1 250 642 3421
Web: www.johansens.com/sookeharbour

CANADA - BRITISH COLUMBIA (TOFINO)
Clayoquot Wilderness Resort
Bedwell River Outpost, Box 130, Tofino, British Columbia V0R 2Z0
Tel: +1 250 726 8235
Web: www.johansens.com/clayoquot

CANADA - BRITISH COLUMBIA (TOFINO)
Wickaninnish Inn
Osprey Lane at Chesterman Beach, Tofino, British Columbia V0R 2Z0
Tel: +1 250 725 3100
Web: www.johansens.com/wickaninnish

CANADA - BRITISH COLUMBIA (VANCOUVER)
Pan Pacific Vancouver
300-999 Canada Place, Vancouver, British Columbia V6C 3B5
Tel: +1 604 662 8111
Web: www.johansens.com/panpacific

CANADA - BRITISH COLUMBIA (VANCOUVER)
The Sutton Place Hotel Vancouver
845 Burrard Street, Vancouver, British Columbia V6Z 2K6
Tel: +1 604 682 5511
Web: www.johansens.com/suttonplacebc

CANADA - BRITISH COLUMBIA (VANCOUVER)
Wedgewood Hotel & Spa
845 Hornby Street, Vancouver, British Columbia V6Z 1V1
Tel: +1 604 689 7777
Web: www.johansens.com/wedgewoodbc

CANADA - BRITISH COLUMBIA (VICTORIA)
Brentwood Bay Lodge & Spa
849 Verdier Avenue, Victoria, British Columbia V8M 1C5
Tel: +1 250 544 2079
Web: www.johansens.com/brentwood

CANADA - BRITISH COLUMBIA (VICTORIA)
Fairholme Manor
638 Rockland Place, Victoria, British Columbia V8S 3R2
Tel: +1 250 598 3240
Web: www.johansens.com/fairholme

CANADA - BRITISH COLUMBIA (VICTORIA)
Villa Marco Polo Inn
1524 Shasta Place, Victoria, British Columbia V8S 1X9
Tel: +1 250 370 1524
Web: www.johansens.com/villamarcopolo

CANADA - BRITISH COLUMBIA (WHISTLER)
Adara Hotel
4122 Village Green, Whistler, British Columbia V0N 1B4
Tel: +1 604 905 4009
Web: www.johansens.com/adara

CANADA - NOVA SCOTIA (EAST KEMPTVILLE)
Trout Point Lodge of Nova Scotia
189 Trout Point Road, Off the East Branch Road and Highway 203, East Kemptville, Nova Scotia B0W 1Y0
Tel: +1 902 761 2142
Web: www.johansens.com/troutpoint

CANADA - NOVA SCOTIA (WALLACE)
Fox Harb'r
1337 Fox Harbour Road, Wallace, Nova Scotia B0K 1Y0
Tel: +1 902 257 1801
Web: www.johansens.com/foxharbr

CANADA - ONTARIO (MCKELLAR)
Inn at Manitou
81 Inn Road, McKellar, Ontario P0G 1C0
Tel: +1 705 389 2171
Web: www.johansens.com/manitou

Hotels - The Americas

Properties listed below can be found in our Recommended Hotels, Inns, Resorts & Spas - The Americas, Atlantic, Caribbean & Pacific 2009 Guide. More information on our portfolio of guides can be found on page 13.

CANADA - ONTARIO (NIAGARA-ON-THE-LAKE)
The Charles Inn
209 Queen Street, Box 642, Niagara-on-the-Lake, Ontario L0S 1J0
Tel: +1 905 468 4588
Web: www.johansens.com/charlesinnca

CANADA - ONTARIO (NIAGARA-ON-THE-LAKE)
Harbour House
85 Melville Street, Box 760, Niagara-on-the-Lake, Ontario
Tel: +1 905 468 4683
Web: www.johansens.com/harbourhouseca

CANADA - ONTARIO (NIAGARA-ON-THE-LAKE)
Riverbend Inn & Vineyard
16104 Niagara River Parkway, Niagara-on-the-Lake, Ontario L0S 1J0
Tel: +1 905 468 8866
Web: www.johansens.com/riverbend

CANADA - ONTARIO (NIAGARA-ON-THE-LAKE)
Shaw Club Hotel & Spa
P.O. Box 642, 92 Picton Street, Niagara-on-the-Lake, Ontario L0S 1J0
Tel: +1 905 468 5711
Web: www.johansens.com/shawclub

CANADA - ONTARIO (TORONTO)
Windsor Arms
18 St. Thomas Street, Toronto, Ontario M5S 3E7
Tel: +1 416 971 9666
Web: www.johansens.com/windsorarms

CANADA - QUÉBEC (LA MALBAIE)
La Pinsonnière
124 Saint-Raphaël, Cap-à-l'Aigle, La Malbaie, Québec G5A 1X9
Tel: +1 418 665 4431
Web: www.johansens.com/lapinsonniere

CANADA - QUÉBEC (MONT-TREMBLANT)
Hôtel Quintessence
3004 chemin de la chapelle, Mont-Tremblant, Québec J8E 1E1
Tel: +1 819 425 3400
Web: www.johansens.com/quintessence

CANADA - QUÉBEC (MONTRÉAL)
Auberge du Vieux-Port
97 de la Commune Est, Montréal, Québec H2Y 1J1
Tel: +1 514 876 0081
Web: www.johansens.com/aubergeduvieuxport

CANADA - QUÉBEC (MONTRÉAL)
Hôtel Nelligan
106 rue Saint-Paul Ouest, Montréal, Québec H2Y 1Z3
Tel: +1 514 788 2040
Web: www.johansens.com/nelligan

CANADA - QUÉBEC (MONTRÉAL)
Le Place d'Armes Hôtel & Suites
55 rue Saint-Jacques Ouest, Montréal, Québec H2Y 3X2
Tel: +1 514 842 1887
Web: www.johansens.com/hotelplacedarmes

CANADA - QUÉBEC (NORTH HATLEY)
Manoir Hovey
575 Hovey Road, North Hatley, Québec J0B 2C0
Tel: +1 819 842 2421
Web: www.johansens.com/manoirhovey

Recommendations in Mexico

MEXICO - BAJA CALIFORNIA SUR (CABO SAN LUCAS)
Esperanza, an Auberge Resort
Km. 7 Carretera Transpeninsular, Punta Ballena, Cabo San Lucas, Baja California Sur 23410
Tel: +52 624 145 6400
Web: www.johansens.com/esperanza

MEXICO - BAJA CALIFORNIA SUR (LOS CABOS)
Marquis Los Cabos Beach Resort & Spa
Lote 74, Km. 21.5 Carretera Transpeninsular, Fraccionamiento Cabo Real, Los Cabos, Baja California Sur 23400
Tel: +52 624 144 2000
Web: www.johansens.com/marquisloscabos

MEXICO - BAJA CALIFORNIA SUR (SAN JOSÉ DEL CABO)
Casa del Mar Suites Golf & Spa Resort
KM 19.5 Carretera Transpeninsular, San José del Cabo, Baja California Sur 23400
Tel: +52 624 145 7700
Web: www.johansens.com/casadelmar

MEXICO - BAJA CALIFORNIA SUR (SAN JOSÉ DEL CABO)
Casa Natalia
Blvd. Mijares 4, San José Del Cabo, Baja California Sur 23400
Tel: +52 624 146 7100
Web: www.johansens.com/casanatalia

Hotels - The Americas

Properties listed below can be found in our Recommended Hotels, Inns, Resorts & Spas - The Americas, Atlantic, Caribbean & Pacific 2009 Guide. More information on our portfolio of guides can be found on page 13.

MEXICO - BAJA CALIFORNIA SUR (SAN JOSÉ DEL CABO)
Las Ventanas al Paraíso, A Rosewood Resort
KM 19.5 Carretera Transpeninsular, San José del Cabo, Baja California Sur 23400
Tel: +52 624 144 2800
Web: www.johansens.com/lasventanas

MEXICO - JALISCO (GUADALAJARA)
Clarum 101
Parque Juan Diego 101, Col. Chapalita, C.P. 45050, Guadalajara, Jalisco
Tel: +52 33 1201 7507
Web: www.johansens.com/clarum101

MEXICO - DISTRITO FEDERAL (MEXICO CITY)
Hotel Boutique Casa Vieja Mexico
Eugenio Sue 45 (Colonia Polanco), Mexico Distrito Federal 11560
Tel: +52 55 52 82 0067
Web: www.johansens.com/casavieja

MEXICO - JALISCO (PUERTO VALLARTA)
Casa Velas Hotel Boutique
Pelicanos 311, Fracc. Marina Vallarta, Puerto Vallarta, Jalisco 48354
Tel: +52 322 226 6688
Web: www.johansens.com/casavelas

MEXICO - GUANAJUATO (GUANAJUATO)
Quinta Las Acacias
Paseo de la Presa 168, Guanajuato, Guanajuato 36000
Tel: +52 473 731 1517
Web: www.johansens.com/acacias

MEXICO - MICHOACÁN (MORELIA)
Cantera Diez
Calle Benito Juárez 63, Centro, Morelia, Michoacán
Tel: +52 443 312 54 19
Web: www.johansens.com/canteradiez

MEXICO - GUERRERO (IXTAPA - ZIHUATANEJO)
Loma Del Mar
Fragatas Lote F17 Sec. Hotelera II, Ixtapa - Zihuatanejo, Guerrero 40884
Tel: +52 755 555 04 60
Web: www.johansens.com/lomadelmar

MEXICO - MICHOACÁN (MORELIA)
Hotel Virrey de Mendoza
Av. Madero Pte. 310, Centro Histórico, Morelia, Michoacán 58000
Tel: +52 44 33 12 06 33
Web: www.johansens.com/hvirrey

MEXICO - JALISCO (COSTALEGRE)
El Tamarindo Beach & Golf Resort
Km 7.5 Highway 200, Carretera Barra de Navidad - Puerto Vallarta, Cihuatlan, Jalisco 48970
Tel: +52 315 351 5031
Web: www.johansens.com/eltamarindo

MEXICO - MORELOS (CUERNAVACA)
Las Mañanitas
Ricardo Linares 107 Col Centro, Cuernavaca, Morelos 62000
Tel: +52 777 362 0023
Web: www.johansens.com/mananitas

MEXICO - JALISCO (COSTALEGRE - COSTA CAREYES)
El Careyes Beach Resort
Km 53.5, Carretera Barra de Navidad-Puerto Vallarta, Costa Careyes, Jalisco 48970
Tel: +52 315 351 0000
Web: www.johansens.com/elcareyes

MEXICO - MICHOACÁN (MORELIA)
Villa Montaña Hotel & Spa
Patzimba 201, Vista Bella, Morelia, Michoacán 58090
Tel: +52 443 314 02 31
Web: www.johansens.com/montana

MEXICO - JALISCO (COSTALEGRE - PUERTO VALLARTA)
Hotelito Desconocido
Playon de Mismaloya S/N, Municipio de Tomatlán, La Cruz de Loreto, Jalisco 48460
Tel: +52 322 281 4010
Web: www.johansens.com/hotelito

MEXICO - NAYARIT (NUEVO VALLARTA)
Grand Velas All Suites & Spa Resort
Av. Cocoteros 98 Sur, Nuevo Vallarta, Riviera Nayarit 63735
Tel: +52 322 226 8000
Web: www.johansens.com/grandvelas

MEXICO - JALISCO (COSTALEGRE - PUERTO VALLARTA)
Las Alamandas Resort
Carretera Barra de Navidad - Puerto Vallarta km 83.5, Col. Quemaro, Jalisco 48850
Tel: +52 322 285 5500
Web: www.johansens.com/alamandas

MEXICO - OAXACA (OAXACA)
Casa Cid de Leon
Av. Morelos 602, Centro, Oaxaca, Oaxaca 68000
Tel: +52 951 51 47013/60414
Web: www.johansens.com/leon

Hotels - The Americas

Properties listed below can be found in our Recommended Hotels, Inns, Resorts & Spas - The Americas, Atlantic, Caribbean & Pacific 2009 Guide. More information on our portfolio of guides can be found on page 13.

MEXICO - OAXACA (OAXACA)
Casa Oaxaca
Calle García Vigil 407, Centro, Oaxaca, Oaxaca 68000
Tel: +52 951 514 4173
Web: www.johansens.com/oaxaca

MEXICO - OAXACA (OAXACA)
La Casona de Tita
García Vigil 805, Centro, C.P. 68000 Oaxaca, Oaxaca
Tel: +52 951 5 16 1400
Web: www.johansens.com/lacasonadetita

MEXICO - QUINTANA ROO (PLAYA DEL CARMEN)
Grand Velas All Suites & Spa Resort, Riviera Maya
Carretera Cancún-Tulum Km. 62, Playa del Carmen, Municipio del Solidaridad, Quintana Roo 77710
Tel: +52 984 109 5600
Web: www.johansens.com/rivieramaya

MEXICO - QUINTANA ROO (PUERTO MORELOS)
Ceiba del Mar Spa Resort
Costera Norte Lte. 1, S.M. 10, MZ. 26, Puerto Morelos, Quintana Roo 77580
Tel: +52 998 872 8060
Web: www.johansens.com/ceibademar

MEXICO - QUINTANA ROO (TULUM)
Casa Nalum
Sian Ka'an Biosphere Reserve, Quintana Roo
Tel: +52 19991 639 510
Web: www.johansens.com/casanalum

MEXICO - YUCATÁN (MÉRIDA)
Hacienda Xcanatún - Casa de Piedra
Calle 20 S/N, Comisaría Xcanatún, Km. 12 Carretera Mérida - Progreso, Mérida, Yucatán 9730
Tel: +52 999 941 0273
Web: www.johansens.com/xcanatun

U.S.A. - ARIZONA (GREER)
Hidden Meadow Ranch
620 Country Road 1325, Greer, Arizona 85927
Tel: +1 928 333 1000
Web: www.johansens.com/hiddenmeadow

U.S.A. - ARIZONA (PARADISE VALLEY / SCOTTSDALE)
Sanctuary on Camelback Mountain
5700 East McDonald Drive, Scottsdale, Arizona 85253
Tel: +1 480 948 2100
Web: www.johansens.com/sanctuarycamelback

U.S.A. - ARIZONA (SEDONA)
Sedona Rouge Hotel & Spa
2250 West Highway 89A, Sedona, Arizona 86336
Tel: +1 928 203 4111
Web: www.johansens.com/sedonarouge

U.S.A. - ARIZONA (TUBAC)
Tubac Golf Resort & Spa
One Otero Road, Tubac, Arizona 85646
Tel: +1 520 398 2211
Web: www.johansens.com/tubac

U.S.A. - ARIZONA (TUCSON)
Arizona Inn
2200 East Elm Street, Tucson, Arizona 85719
Tel: +1 520 325 1541
Web: www.johansens.com/arizonainn

U.S.A. - ARIZONA (TUCSON)
Tanque Verde Ranch
14301 East Speedway Boulevard, Tucson, Arizona 85748
Tel: +1 520 296 6275
Web: www.johansens.com/tanqueverde

U.S.A. - ARIZONA (WICKENBURG)
Rancho de los Caballeros
1551 South Vulture Mine Road, Wickenburg, Arizona 85390
Tel: +1 928 684 5484
Web: www.johansens.com/caballeros

Recommendations in U.S.A

U.S.A. - ALABAMA (PISGAH)
Lodge on Gorham's Bluff
101 Gorham Drive, Pisgah, Alabama 35765
Tel: +1 256 451 8439
Web: www.johansens.com/gorhamsbluff

U.S.A. - CALIFORNIA (BIG SUR)
Post Ranch Inn
Highway 1, P.O. Box 219, Big Sur, California 93920
Tel: +1 831 667 2200
Web: www.johansens.com/postranchinn

Hotels - The Americas

Properties listed below can be found in our Recommended Hotels, Inns, Resorts & Spas - The Americas, Atlantic, Caribbean & Pacific 2009 Guide. More information on our portfolio of guides can be found on page 13.

U.S.A. - CALIFORNIA (BIG SUR)
Ventana Inn and Spa
Highway 1, Big Sur, California 93920
Tel: +1 831 667 2331
Web: www.johansens.com/ventanainn

U.S.A. - CALIFORNIA (HEALDSBURG)
Hotel Healdsburg
25 Matheson Street, Healdsburg, California 95448
Tel: +1 707 431 2800
Web: www.johansens.com/healdsburg

U.S.A. - CALIFORNIA (CALISTOGA)
Calistoga Ranch
580 Lommel Road, Calistoga, California 94515
Tel: +1 707 254 2800
Web: www.johansens.com/calistogaranch

U.S.A. - CALIFORNIA (HEALDSBURG)
Les Mars
27 North, Healdsburg, California 95448
Tel: +1 707 433 4211
Web: www.johansens.com/lesmarshotel

U.S.A. - CALIFORNIA (CALISTOGA)
Solage Calistoga
755 Silverado Trail, Calistoga, California 94515
Tel: +1 707 226 0800
Web: www.johansens.com/solagecalistoga

U.S.A. - CALIFORNIA (LA JOLLA)
Estancia La Jolla Hotel & Spa
9700 North Torrey Pines Road, La Jolla, California 92037
Tel: +1 858 550 1000
Web: www.johansens.com/estancialajolla

U.S.A. - CALIFORNIA (CARMEL VALLEY)
Bernardus Lodge
415 Carmel Valley Road, Carmel Valley, California 93924
Tel: +1 831 658 3400
Web: www.johansens.com/bernardus

U.S.A. - CALIFORNIA (LITTLE RIVER)
Stevenswood Spa Resort
8211 North Highway 1, Little River, California 95456
Tel: +1 707 937 2810
Web: www.johansens.com/stevenswood

U.S.A. - CALIFORNIA (CARMEL-BY-THE-SEA)
L'Auberge Carmel
Monte Verde at Seventh, Carmel-by-the-Sea, California 93921
Tel: +1 831 624 8578
Web: www.johansens.com/laubergecarmel

U.S.A. - CALIFORNIA (LOS ANGELES)
Hotel Bel-Air
701 Stone Canyon Road, Los Angeles, California 90077
Tel: +1 310 472 1211
Web: www.johansens.com/belair

U.S.A. - CALIFORNIA (CARMEL-BY-THE-SEA)
Tradewinds Carmel
Mission Street at Third Avenue, Carmel-by-the-Sea, California 93921
Tel: +1 831 624 2776
Web: www.johansens.com/tradewinds

U.S.A. - CALIFORNIA (MALIBU)
Malibu Beach Inn
22878 Pacific Highway, Malibu, California 90265
Tel: +1 310 456 6444
Web: www.johansens.com/malibubeach

U.S.A. - CALIFORNIA (EUREKA)
The Carter House Inns
301 L Street, Eureka, California 95501
Tel: +1 707 444 8062
Web: www.johansens.com/carterhouse

U.S.A. - CALIFORNIA (MENDOCINO)
The Stanford Inn By The Sea
Coast Highway One & Comptche-Ukiah Road, Mendocino, California 95460
Tel: +1 707 937 5615
Web: www.johansens.com/stanfordinn

U.S.A. - CALIFORNIA (HEALDSBURG)
The Grape Leaf Inn
539 Johnson Street, Healdsburg, California 95448
Tel: +1 707 433 8140
Web: www.johansens.com/grapeleaf

U.S.A. - CALIFORNIA (MILL VALLEY)
Mill Valley Inn
165 Throckmorton Avenue, Mill Valley, California 94941
Tel: +1 415 389 6608
Web: www.johansens.com/millvalleyinn

Hotels - The Americas

Properties listed below can be found in our Recommended Hotels, Inns, Resorts & Spas - The Americas, Atlantic, Caribbean & Pacific 2009 Guide. More information on our portfolio of guides can be found on page 13.

U.S.A. - CALIFORNIA (MONTEREY)
Old Monterey Inn
500 Martin Street, Monterey, California 93940
Tel: +1 831 375 8284
Web: www.johansens.com/oldmontereyinn

U.S.A. - CALIFORNIA (SANTA BARBARA)
Harbor View Inn
28 West Cabrillo Boulevard, Santa Barbara, California 93101
Tel: +1 805 963 0780
Web: www.johansens.com/harborview

U.S.A. - CALIFORNIA (NAPA)
1801 First Inn
1801 First Street, Napa, California 94559
Tel: +1 707 224 3739
Web: www.johansens.com/1801inn

U.S.A. - CALIFORNIA (SHELL BEACH)
Dolphin Bay Resort & Spa
2727 Shell Beach Road, Shell Beach, California 93449
Tel: +1 805 773 4300
Web: www.johansens.com/thedolphinbay

U.S.A. - CALIFORNIA (NAPA)
Milliken Creek Inn & Spa
1815 Silverado Trail, Napa, California 94558
Tel: +1 707 255 1197
Web: www.johansens.com/milliken

U.S.A. - CALIFORNIA (ST. HELENA)
The Inn at Southbridge
1020 Main Street, St. Helena, California 94574
Tel: +1 707 967 9400
Web: www.johansens.com/southbridge

U.S.A. - CALIFORNIA (NEWPORT BEACH)
Balboa Bay Club & Resort
1221 West Coast Highway, Newport Beach, California 92663
Tel: +1 949 645 5000
Web: www.johansens.com/balboabayclub

U.S.A. - CALIFORNIA (ST. HELENA)
Meadowood Napa Valley
900 Meadowood Lane, St. Helena, California 94574
Tel: +1 707 963 3646
Web: www.johansens.com/meadowood

U.S.A. - CALIFORNIA (OAKHURST)
Château du Sureau & Spa
48688 Victoria Lane, Oakhurst, California 93644
Tel: +1 559 683 6860
Web: www.johansens.com/chateausureau

U.S.A. - COLORADO (DENVER)
Castle Marne Bed & Breakfast Inn
1572 Race Street, Denver, Colorado 80206
Tel: +1 303 331 0621
Web: www.johansens.com/castlemarne

U.S.A. - CALIFORNIA (RANCHO SANTA FE)
The Inn at Rancho Santa Fe
5951 Linea del Cielo, Rancho Santa Fe, California 92067
Tel: +1 858 756 1131
Web: www.johansens.com/ranchosantafe

U.S.A. - COLORADO (DENVER)
Hotel Monaco
1717 Champa Street at 17th, Denver, Colorado 80202
Tel: +1 303 296 1717
Web: www.johansens.com/monaco

U.S.A. - CALIFORNIA (SAN DIEGO)
Tower23 Hotel
4551 Ocean Blvd., San Diego, California 92109
Tel: +1 858 270 2323
Web: www.johansens.com/tower23

U.S.A. - COLORADO (ESTES PARK)
Taharaa Mountain Lodge
3110 So. St. Vrain, Estes Park, Colorado 80517
Tel: +1 970 577 0098
Web: www.johansens.com/taharaa

U.S.A. - CALIFORNIA (SAN FRANCISCO BAY AREA)
Inn Above Tide
30 El Portal, Sausalito, California 94965
Tel: +1 415 332 9535
Web: www.johansens.com/innabovetide

U.S.A. - COLORADO (MANITOU SPRINGS)
The Cliff House at Pikes Peak
306 Cañon Avenue, Manitou Springs, Colorado 80829
Tel: +1 719 685 3000
Web: www.johansens.com/thecliffhouse

Hotels - The Americas

Properties listed below can be found in our Recommended Hotels, Inns, Resorts & Spas - The Americas, Atlantic, Caribbean & Pacific 2009 Guide. More information on our portfolio of guides can be found on page 13.

U.S.A. - COLORADO (MONTROSE)
Elk Mountain Resort
97 Elk Walk, Montrose, Colorado 81401
Tel: +1 970 252 4900
Web: www.johansens.com/elkmountain

U.S.A. - DELAWARE (REHOBOTH BEACH)
Boardwalk Plaza Hotel
Olive Avenue & The Boardwalk, Rehoboth Beach, Delaware 19971
Tel: +1 302 227 7169
Web: www.johansens.com/boardwalkplaza

U.S.A. - COLORADO (STEAMBOAT SPRINGS)
Vista Verde Guest Ranch
P.O. Box 770465, Steamboat Springs, Colorado 80477
Tel: +1 970 879 3858
Web: www.johansens.com/vistaverderanch

U.S.A. - DELAWARE (REHOBOTH BEACH)
Hotel Rehoboth
247 Rehoboth Avenue, Rehoboth Beach, Delaware 19971
Tel: +1 302 227 4300
Web: www.johansens.com/hotelrehoboth

U.S.A. - COLORADO (TELLURIDE)
Fairmont Heritage Place, Franz Klammer Lodge
567 Mountain Village Boulevard, Telluride, Colorado 81435
Tel: +1 970 728 4239
Web: www.johansens.com/fairmont

U.S.A. - DELAWARE (WILMINGTON)
Inn at Montchanin Village
Route 100 & Kirk Road, Montchanin, Wilmington, Delaware 19710
Tel: +1 302 888 2133
Web: www.johansens.com/montchanin

U.S.A. - COLORADO (TELLURIDE)
The Hotel Telluride
199 North Cornet Street, Telluride, Colorado 81435
Tel: +1 970 369 1188
Web: www.johansens.com/telluride

U.S.A. - DISTRICT OF COLUMBIA (WASHINGTON)
The Hay-Adams
Sixteenth & H. Streets N.W., Washington D.C., District of Columbia 20006
Tel: +1 202 638 6600
Web: www.johansens.com/hayadams

U.S.A. - COLORADO (VAIL)
Vail Mountain Lodge & Spa
352 East Meadow Drive, Vail, Colorado 81657
Tel: +1 970 476 0700
Web: www.johansens.com/vailmountain

U.S.A. - FLORIDA (FISHER ISLAND)
Fisher Island Hotel & Resort
One Fisher Island Drive, Fisher Island, Florida 33109
Tel: +1 305 535 6000
Web: www.johansens.com/fisherisland

U.S.A. - CONNECTICUT (GREENWICH)
Delamar Greenwich Harbor
500 Steamboat Road, Greenwich, Connecticut 06830
Tel: +1 203 661 9800
Web: www.johansens.com/delamar

U.S.A. - FLORIDA (FORT MYERS)
Sanibel Harbour Resort and Spa
17260 Harbor Pointe Drive, Fort Myers, Florida 33908
Tel: +1 239 466 4000
Web: www.johansens.com/sanibelresort

U.S.A. - CONNECTICUT (WESTPORT)
The Inn at National Hall
2 Post Road West, Westport, Connecticut 06880
Tel: +1 203 221 1351
Web: www.johansens.com/nationalhall

U.S.A. - FLORIDA (JUPITER BEACH)
Jupiter Beach Resort & Spa
5 North A1A, Jupiter, Florida 33477-5190
Tel: +1 561 746 2511
Web: www.johansens.com/jupiterbeachresort

U.S.A. - DELAWARE (REHOBOTH BEACH)
The Bellmoor
Six Christian Street, Rehoboth Beach, Delaware 19971
Tel: +1 302 227 5800
Web: www.johansens.com/thebellmoor

U.S.A. - FLORIDA (KEY WEST)
The Gardens Hotel
526 Angela Street, Key West, Florida 33040
Tel: +1 305 294 2661
Web: www.johansens.com/gardenshotel

Hotels - The Americas

Properties listed below can be found in our Recommended Hotels, Inns, Resorts & Spas - The Americas, Atlantic, Caribbean & Pacific 2009 Guide. More information on our portfolio of guides can be found on page 13.

U.S.A. - FLORIDA (KEY WEST)
Ocean Key Resort & Spa
Zero Duval Street, Key West, Florida 33040
Tel: +1 305 296 7701
Web: www.johansens.com/oceankey

U.S.A. - FLORIDA (SANTA ROSA BEACH)
WaterColor Inn & Resort
34 Goldenrod Circle, Santa Rosa Beach, Florida 32459
Tel: +1 850 534 5000
Web: www.johansens.com/watercolor

U.S.A. - FLORIDA (KEY WEST)
Sunset Key Guest Cottages
245 Front Street, Key West, Florida 33040
Tel: +1 305 292 5300
Web: www.johansens.com/sunsetkey

U.S.A. - FLORIDA (ST. PETE BEACH)
Don CeSar Beach Resort, A Loews Hotel
3400 Gulf Boulevard, St. Pete Beach, Florida 33706
Tel: +1 727 360 1881
Web: www.johansens.com/doncesar

U.S.A. - FLORIDA (MIAMI)
Grove Isle Hotel & Spa
Four Grove Isle Drive, Coconut Grove, Florida 33133
Tel: +1 305 858 8300
Web: www.johansens.com/groveisle

U.S.A. - GEORGIA (ADAIRSVILLE)
Barnsley Gardens Resort
597 Barnsley Gardens Road, Adairsville, Georgia 30103
Tel: +1 770 773 7480
Web: www.johansens.com/barnsleygardens

U.S.A. - FLORIDA (MIAMI BEACH)
Casa Tua
1700 James Avenue, Miami Beach, Florida 33139
Tel: +1 305 673 0973
Web: www.johansens.com/casatua

U.S.A. - GEORGIA (ATLANTA)
TWELVE Hotel Atlantic Station
361 17th Street, Atlanta, Georgia 30363
Tel: + 1 404 961 1212
Web: www.johansens.com/twelvehotelsas

U.S.A. - FLORIDA (MIAMI BEACH)
Hotel Victor
1144 Ocean Drive, Miami Beach, Florida 33139
Tel: +1 305 428 1234
Web: www.johansens.com/hotelvictor

U.S.A. - GEORGIA (ATLANTA)
TWELVE Hotel Centennial Park
817 West Peachtree Street, Atlanta, Georgia 30308
Tel: +1 404 418 1212
Web: www.johansens.com/twelvehotelscp

U.S.A. - FLORIDA (MIAMI BEACH)
The Setai Hotel & Resort
2001 Collins Avenue, Miami Beach, Florida 33139
Tel: +1 305 520 6000
Web: www.johansens.com/setai

U.S.A. - GEORGIA (CUMBERLAND ISLAND)
Greyfield Inn
Cumberland Island, Georgia
Tel: +1 904 261 6408
Web: www.johansens.com/greyfieldinn

U.S.A. - FLORIDA (NAPLES)
LaPlaya Beach & Golf Resort
9891 Gulf Shore Drive, Naples, Florida 34108
Tel: +1 239 597 3123
Web: www.johansens.com/laplaya

U.S.A. - GEORGIA (MADISON)
The James Madison Inn
260 West Washington Street, Madison, Georgia 30650
Tel: +1 706 342 7040
Web: www.johansens.com/jamesmadison

U.S.A. - FLORIDA (PALM BEACH)
The Brazilian Court
301 Australian Avenue, Palm Beach, Florida 33480
Tel: +1 561 655 7740
Web: www.johansens.com/braziliancourt

U.S.A. - GEORGIA (SAVANNAH)
The Presidents' Quarters Inn
225 East President Street, Savannah, Georgia 31401-3806
Tel: +1 912 233 1600
Web: www.johansens.com/presidentsquarters

Hotels - The Americas

Properties listed below can be found in our Recommended Hotels, Inns, Resorts & Spas - The Americas, Atlantic, Caribbean & Pacific 2009 Guide. More information on our portfolio of guides can be found on page 13.

U.S.A. - IDAHO (KETCHUM)

Knob Hill Inn

960 North Main Street, P.O. Box 800, Ketchum, Idaho 83340

Tel: +1 208 726 8010

Web: www.johansens.com/knobhillinn

U.S.A. - ILLINOIS (CHICAGO)

Hotel Sax Chicago

333 North Dearborn Street, Chicago, Illinois 60654

Tel: +1 312 245 0333

Web: www.johansens.com/hotelsax

U.S.A. - ILLINOIS (CHICAGO)

The Talbott Hotel

20 E. Delaware Place, Chicago, Illinois 60611

Tel: +1 312 944 4970

Web: www.johansens.com/talbotthotel

U.S.A. - KANSAS (LAWRENCE)

The Eldridge Hotel

701 Massachusetts, Lawrence, Kansas 66044

Tel: +1 785 749 5011

Web: www.johansens.com/eldridge

U.S.A. - LOUISIANA (NEW ORLEANS)

Soniat House

1133 Chartres Street, New Orleans, Louisiana 70116

Tel: +1 504 522 0570

Web: www.johansens.com/soniathouse

U.S.A. - MAINE (GREENVILLE)

The Lodge At Moosehead Lake

368 Lily Bay Road, P.O. Box 1167, Greenville, Maine 04441

Tel: +1 207 695 4400

Web: www.johansens.com/lodgeatmooseheadlake

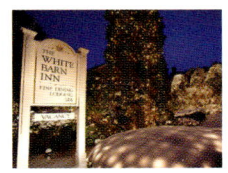

U.S.A. - MAINE (KENNEBUNKPORT)

The White Barn Inn

37 Beach Avenue, Kennebunkport, Maine 04043

Tel: +1 207 967 2321

Web: www.johansens.com/whitebarninn

U.S.A. - MAINE (PORTLAND)

Portland Harbor Hotel

468 Fore Street, Portland, Maine 04101

Tel: +1 207 775 9090

Web: www.johansens.com/portlandharbor

U.S.A. - MARYLAND (ANNAPOLIS)

The Annapolis Inn

144 Prince George Street, Annapolis, Maryland 21401-1723

Tel: +1 410 295 5200

Web: www.johansens.com/annapolisinn

U.S.A. - MARYLAND (FROSTBURG)

Savage River Lodge

1600 Mt. Aetna Road, Frostburg, Maryland 21532

Tel: +1 301 689 3200

Web: www.johansens.com/savageriver

U.S.A. - MASSACHUSETTS (BOSTON)

Boston Harbor Hotel

70 Rowes Wharf, Boston, Massachusetts 2110

Tel: +1 617 439 7000

Web: www.johansens.com/bhh

U.S.A. - MASSACHUSETTS (BOSTON)

Fifteen Beacon

15 Beacon Street, Boston, Massachusetts 2108

Tel: +1 617 670 1500

Web: www.johansens.com/xvbeacon

U.S.A. - MASSACHUSETTS (BOSTON)

The Liberty Hotel

215 Charles Street, Boston, Massachusetts 02114

Tel: +1 617 224 4000

Web: www.johansens.com/liberty

U.S.A. - MASSACHUSETTS (CAPE COD)

Wequassett Resort and Golf Club

On Pleasant Bay, Chatham, Massachusetts 02633

Tel: +1 508 432 5400

Web: www.johansens.com/wequassett

U.S.A. - MASSACHUSETTS (IPSWICH)

The Inn at Castle Hill

280 Argilla Road, Ipswich, Massachusetts 01938

Tel: +1 978 412 2555

Web: www.johansens.com/castlehill

U.S.A. - MASSACHUSETTS (LENOX)

Blantyre

16 Blantyre Road, P.O. Box 995, Lenox, Massachusetts 01240

Tel: +1 413 637 3556

Web: www.johansens.com/blantyre

Hotels - The Americas

Properties listed below can be found in our Recommended Hotels, Inns, Resorts & Spas - The Americas, Atlantic, Caribbean & Pacific 2009 Guide. More information on our portfolio of guides can be found on page 13.

U.S.A. - MASSACHUSETTS (LENOX)
Cranwell Resort, Spa & Golf Club
55 Lee Road, Route 20, Lenox, Massachusetts 01240
Tel: +1 413 637 1364
Web: www.johansens.com/cranwell

U.S.A. - NEW HAMPSHIRE (WHITEFIELD / WHITE MOUNTAINS)
Mountain View Grand Resort & Spa
101 Mountain View Road, Whitefield, New Hampshire 03598
Tel: +1 603 837 2100
Web: www.johansens.com/mountainview

U.S.A. - MASSACHUSETTS (MARTHA'S VINEYARD)
The Charlotte Inn
27 South Summer Street, Edgartown, Massachusetts 02539
Tel: +1 508 627 4151
Web: www.johansens.com/charlotte

U.S.A. - NEW MEXICO (ESPAÑOLA)
Rancho de San Juan
P.O. Box 4140, Highway 285, Española, New Mexico 87533
Tel: +1 505 753 6818
Web: www.johansens.com/ranchosanjuan

U.S.A. - MICHIGAN (ROCHESTER)
Royal Park Hotel
600 E. University Drive, Rochester, Michigan 48307
Tel: +1 248 652 2600
Web: www.johansens.com/royalparkmi

U.S.A. - NEW MEXICO (SANTA FE)
Encantado, an Auberge Resort
198 State Road 592, Santa Fe, New Mexico 87506
Tel: +1 505 988 9955
Web: www.johansens.com/encantado

U.S.A. - MISSISSIPPI (JACKSON)
Fairview Inn & Restaurant
734 Fairview Street, Jackson, Mississippi 39202
Tel: +1 601 948 3429
Web: www.johansens.com/fairviewinn

U.S.A. - NEW MEXICO (TAOS)
El Monte Sagrado Living Resort & Spa
317 Kit Carson Road, Taos, New Mexico 87571
Tel: +1 575 758 3502
Web: www.johansens.com/elmontesagrado

U.S.A. - MISSISSIPPI (NATCHEZ)
Monmouth Plantation
36 Melrose Avenue, Natchez, Mississippi 39120
Tel: +1 601 442 5852
Web: www.johansens.com/monmouthplantation

U.S.A. - NEW YORK (BUFFALO)
The Mansion on Delaware Avenue
414 Delaware Avenue, Buffalo, New York 14202
Tel: +1 716 886 3300
Web: www.johansens.com/mansionondelaware

U.S.A. - MISSISSIPPI (NESBIT)
Bonne Terre Country Inn
4715 Church Road West, Nesbit, Mississippi 38651
Tel: +1 662 781 5100
Web: www.johansens.com/bonneterre

U.S.A. - NEW YORK (HUNTINGTON)
OHEKA CASTLE Hotel & Estate
135 West Gate Drive, Huntington, New York 11743
Tel: +1 631 659 1400
Web: www.johansens.com/oheka

U.S.A. - MISSOURI (KANSAS CITY)
The Raphael Hotel
325 Ward Parkway, Kansas City, Missouri 64112
Tel: +1 816 756 3800
Web: www.johansens.com/raphael

U.S.A. - NEW YORK (LEWISTON)
Barton Hill Hotel & Spa
100 Center Street, Lewiston, New York 14092
Tel: +1 716 754 9070
Web: www.johansens.com/bartonhillhotel

U.S.A. - MONTANA (DARBY)
Triple Creek Ranch
5551 West Fork Road, Darby, Montana 59829
Tel: +1 406 821 4600
Web: www.johansens.com/triplecreek

U.S.A. - NEW YORK (NEW YORK CITY)
Hôtel Plaza Athénée
37 East 64th Street, New York City, New York 10065
Tel: +1 212 734 9100
Web: www.johansens.com/athenee

Hotels - The Americas

Properties listed below can be found in our Recommended Hotels, Inns, Resorts & Spas - The Americas, Atlantic, Caribbean & Pacific 2009 Guide. More information on our portfolio of guides can be found on page 13.

U.S.A. - NEW YORK (NEW YORK CITY)
The Inn at Irving Place
56 Irving Place, New York, New York City 10003
Tel: +1 212 533 4600
Web: www.johansens.com/irving

U.S.A. - NORTH CAROLINA (CHAPEL HILL)
The Franklin Hotel
311 West Franklin Street, Chapel Hill, North Carolina 27516
Tel: +1 919 442 9000
Web: www.johansens.com/franklinhotelnc

U.S.A. - NEW YORK (TARRYTOWN)
Castle On The Hudson
400 Benedict Avenue, Tarrytown, New York 10591
Tel: +1 914 631 1980
Web: www.johansens.com/hudson

U.S.A. - NORTH CAROLINA (CHARLOTTE)
Ballantyne Resort
10000 Ballantyne Commons Parkway, Charlotte, North Carolina 28277
Tel: +1 704 248 4000
Web: www.johansens.com/ballantyneresort

U.S.A. - NEW YORK (VERONA)
The Lodge at Turning Stone
5218 Patrick Road, Verona, New York 13478
Tel: +1 315 361 8525
Web: www.johansens.com/turningstone

U.S.A. - NORTH CAROLINA (CHIMNEY ROCK)
The Esmeralda
910 Main Street, Chimney Rock, North Carolina 28720
Tel: +1 828 625 2999
Web: www.johansens.com/esmeralda

U.S.A. - NEW YORK/LONG ISLAND (EAST HAMPTON)
The Baker House 1650
181 Main Street, East Hampton, New York 11937
Tel: +1 631 324 4081
Web: www.johansens.com/bakerhouse

U.S.A. - NORTH CAROLINA (DUCK)
The Sanderling Resort & Spa
1461 Duck Road, Duck, North Carolina 27949
Tel: +1 252 261 4111
Web: www.johansens.com/sanderling

U.S.A. - NEW YORK/LONG ISLAND (EAST HAMPTON)
The Mill House Inn
31 North Main Street, East Hampton, New York 11937
Tel: +1 631 324 9766
Web: www.johansens.com/millhouse

U.S.A. - NORTH CAROLINA (HIGHLANDS)
Inn at Half Mile Farm
P.O. Box 2769, 214 Half Mile Drive, Highlands, North Carolina 28741
Tel: +1 828 526 8170
Web: www.johansens.com/halfmilefarm

U.S.A. - NEW YORK/LONG ISLAND (SOUTHAMPTON)
1708 House
126 Main Street, Southampton, New York 11968
Tel: +1 631 287 1708
Web: www.johansens.com/1708house

U.S.A. - NORTH CAROLINA (HIGHLANDS)
Old Edwards Inn and Spa
445 Main Street, Highlands, North Carolina 28741
Tel: +1 828 526 8008
Web: www.johansens.com/oldedwards

U.S.A. - NORTH CAROLINA (ASHEVILLE)
Haywood Park Hotel
One Battery Park Avenue, Asheville, North Carolina 28801
Tel: +1 828 252 2522
Web: www.johansens.com/haywoodpark

U.S.A. - NORTH CAROLINA (SOUTHERN PINES)
The Jefferson Inn
150 West New Hampshire Avenue, Southern Pines, North Carolina 28387
Tel: +1 910 692 9911
Web: www.johansens.com/jeffersoninn

U.S.A. - NORTH CAROLINA (ASHEVILLE)
Inn on Biltmore Estate
One Antler Hill Road, Asheville, North Carolina 28803
Tel: +1 828 225 1600
Web: www.johansens.com/biltmore

U.S.A. - OKLAHOMA (OKLAHOMA CITY)
Colcord Hotel
15 North Robinson, Oklahoma City, Oklahoma 73102
Tel: +1 405 601 4300
Web: www.johansens.com/colcord

Hotels - The Americas

Properties listed below can be found in our Recommended Hotels, Inns, Resorts & Spas - The Americas, Atlantic, Caribbean & Pacific 2009 Guide. More information on our portfolio of guides can be found on page 13.

U.S.A. - OKLAHOMA (TULSA)
Hotel Ambassador
1324 South Main Street, Tulsa, Oklahoma 74119
Tel: +1 918 587 8200
Web: www.johansens.com/ambassador

U.S.A. - RHODE ISLAND (PROVIDENCE)
Hotel Providence
311 Westminster Street, Providence, Rhode Island 02903
Tel: +1 401 861 8000
Web: www.johansens.com/providence

U.S.A. - OREGON (ASHLAND)
The Winchester Inn & Restaurant
35 South Second Street, Ashland, Oregon 97520
Tel: +1 541 488 1113
Web: www.johansens.com/winchester

U.S.A. - SOUTH CAROLINA (BLUFFTON)
The Inn at Palmetto Bluff
476 Mount Pelia Road, Bluffton, South Carolina 29910
Tel: +1 843 706 6500
Web: www.johansens.com/palmettobluff

U.S.A. - OREGON (PORTLAND)
The Heathman Hotel
1001 S.W. Broadway, Portland, Oregon 97205
Tel: +1 503 241 4100
Web: www.johansens.com/heathman

U.S.A. - SOUTH CAROLINA (CHARLESTON)
The Boardwalk Inn at Wild Dunes Resort
5757 Palm Boulevard, Isle of Palms, South Carolina 29451
Tel: +1 843 886 6000
Web: www.johansens.com/boardwalk

U.S.A. - PENNSYLVANIA (NEW HOPE)
The Inn at Bowman's Hill
518 Lurgan Road, New Hope, Pennsylvania 18938
Tel: +1 215 862 8090
Web: www.johansens.com/bowmanshill

U.S.A. - SOUTH CAROLINA (CHARLESTON)
Charleston Harbor Resort & Marina
20 Patriots Point Road, Charleston, South Carolina 29464
Tel: +1 843 856 0028
Web: www.johansens.com/charlestonharbor

U.S.A. - PENNSYLVANIA (PHILADELPHIA)
Rittenhouse 1715, A Boutique Hotel
1715 Rittenhouse Square, Philadelphia, Pennsylvania 19103
Tel: +1 215 546 6500
Web: www.johansens.com/rittenhouse

U.S.A. - SOUTH CAROLINA (KIAWAH ISLAND)
The Sanctuary at Kiawah Island Golf Resort
One Sanctuary Beach Drive, Kiawah Island, South Carolina 29455
Tel: +1 843 768 6000
Web: www.johansens.com/sanctuary

U.S.A. - PENNSYLVANIA (SKYTOP)
Skytop Lodge
One Skytop, Skytop, Pennsylvania 18357
Tel: +1 570 595 7401
Web: www.johansens.com/skytop

U.S.A. - SOUTH CAROLINA (TRAVELERS REST)
La Bastide
10 Road Of Vines, Travelers Rest, South Carolina 29690
Tel: +1 864 836 8463
Web: www.johansens.com/labastide

U.S.A. - RHODE ISLAND (NEWPORT)
Chanler at Cliff Walk
117 Memorial Boulevard, Newport, Rhode Island 02840
Tel: +1 401 847 1300
Web: www.johansens.com/chanler

U.S.A. - TENNESSEE (MEMPHIS)
The River Inn of Harbor Town
50 Harbor Town Square, Memphis, Tennessee 38103
Tel: +1 901 260 3333
Web: www.johansens.com/riverinnmemphis

U.S.A. - RHODE ISLAND (NEWPORT)
La Farge Perry House
24 Kay Street, Newport, Rhode Island 02840
Tel: +1 401 847 2223
Web: www.johansens.com/lafargeperry

U.S.A. - TENNESSEE (NASHVILLE)
The Hermitage Hotel
231 Sixth Avenue North, Nashville, Tennessee 37219
Tel: +1 615 244 3121
Web: www.johansens.com/hermitagetn

Hotels - The Americas

Properties listed below can be found in our Recommended Hotels, Inns, Resorts & Spas - The Americas, Atlantic, Caribbean & Pacific 2009 Guide. More information on our portfolio of guides can be found on page 13.

U.S.A. - TEXAS (AUSTIN)
Mansion at Judges' Hill
1900 Rio Grande, Austin, Texas 78705
Tel: +1 512 495 1800
Web: www.johansens.com/judgeshill

U.S.A. - TEXAS (DALLAS)
The Joule
1530 Main Street, Dallas, Texas 75201
Tel: +1 214 748 1300
Web: www.johansens.com/thejoule

U.S.A. - TEXAS (GRANBURY)
The Inn on Lake Granbury
205 West Doyle Street, Granbury, Texas 76048
Tel: +1 817 573 0046
Web: www.johansens.com/lakegranbury

U.S.A. - TEXAS (HOUSTON)
Hotel Granduca
1080 Uptown Park Boulevard, Houston, Texas 77056
Tel: +1 713 418 1000
Web: www.johansens.com/granduca

U.S.A. - TEXAS (WASHINGTON)
Inn at Dos Brisas
10,000 Champions Drive, Washington, Texas 77880
Tel: +1 979 277 7750
Web: www.johansens.com/dosbrisas

U.S.A. - UTAH (MOAB)
Sorrel River Ranch Resort & Spa
Mile 17 Scenic Byway 128, H.C. 64 BOX 4002, Moab, Utah 84532
Tel: +1 435 259 4642
Web: www.johansens.com/sorrelriver

U.S.A. - UTAH (PARK CITY)
The Sky Lodge
201 Heber Avenue at Main Street, P.O. Box 683300, Park City, Utah 84068
Tel: +1 435 658 2500
Web: www.johansens.com/skylodge

U.S.A. - VERMONT (LUDLOW/OKEMO)
Castle Hill Resort & Spa
Jct. Routes 103 and 131, Cavendish, Vermont 05142
Tel: +1 802 226 7361
Web: www.johansens.com/castlehillvt

U.S.A. - VERMONT (MANCHESTER VILLAGE)
Equinox Resort & Spa
3567 Main Street, Manchester, Vermont 05254
Tel: +1 802 362 4700
Web: www.johansens.com/equinoxresort

U.S.A. - VERMONT (WARREN)
The Pitcher Inn
275 Main Street, P.O. Box 347, Warren, Vermont 05674
Tel: +1 802 496 6350
Web: www.johansens.com/pitcherinn

U.S.A. - VIRGINIA (GLOUCESTER)
The Inn at Warner Hall
4750 Warner Hall Road, Gloucester, Virginia 23061
Tel: +1 804 695 9565
Web: www.johansens.com/warnerhall

U.S.A. - VIRGINIA (IRVINGTON)
Hope and Glory Inn
65 Tavern Road, Irvington, Virginia 22480
Tel: +1 804 438 6053
Web: www.johansens.com/hopeandglory

U.S.A. - VIRGINIA (MIDDLEBURG)
The Goodstone Inn & Estate
36205 Snake Hill Road, Middleburg, Virginia 20117
Tel: +1 540 687 4645
Web: www.johansens.com/goodstoneinn

U.S.A. - VIRGINIA (RICHMOND)
The Jefferson
101 W. Franklin Street, Richmond, Virginia 23220
Tel: +1 804 788 8000
Web: www.johansens.com/jeffersonva

U.S.A. - VIRGINIA (STAUNTON)
Frederick House
28 North New Street, Staunton, Virginia 24401
Tel: +1 540 885 4220
Web: www.johansens.com/frederickhouse

U.S.A. - VIRGINIA (WILLIAMSBURG)
Wedmore Place
5810 Wessex Hundred, Williamsburg, Virginia 23185
Tel: +1 757 941 0310
Web: www.johansens.com/wedmoreplace

Hotels - The Americas

Properties listed below can be found in our Recommended Hotels, Inns, Resorts & Spas - The Americas, Atlantic, Caribbean & Pacific 2009 Guide. More information on our portfolio of guides can be found on page 13.

U.S.A. - WASHINGTON (BELLEVUE)
The Bellevue Club Hotel
11200 S.E. 6th Street, Bellevue, Washington 98004
Tel: +1 425 455 1616
Web: www.johansens.com/bellevue

U.S.A. - WISCONSIN (WAUKESHA)
The Clarke Hotel
314 West Main Street, Waukesha, Wisconsin 53186
Tel: +1 262 549 3800
Web: www.johansens.com/clarkehotel

U.S.A. - WASHINGTON (BELLINGHAM)
The Chrysalis Inn and Spa
804 10th Street, Bellingham, Washington 98225
Tel: +1 360 756 1005
Web: www.johansens.com/chrysalis

Recommendations in Central America

U.S.A. - WASHINGTON (KIRKLAND)
The Heathman Hotel
220 Kirkland Avenue, Kirkland, Washington 98033
Tel: +1 425 284 5800
Web: www.johansens.com/heathmanwa

BELIZE - AMBERGRIS CAYE
Matachica Beach Resort
5 miles North of San Pedro, Ambergris Caye
Tel: +501 220 5010/11
Web: www.johansens.com/matachica

U.S.A. - WASHINGTON (SEATTLE)
Hotel Ändra
2000 Fourth Avenue, Seattle, Washington 98121
Tel: +1 206 448 8600
Web: www.johansens.com/hotelandra

BELIZE - AMBERGRIS CAYE (SAN PEDRO)
Victoria House
P.O. Box 22, San Pedro, Ambergris Caye
Tel: +501 226 2067
Web: www.johansens.com/victoriahouse

U.S.A. - WASHINGTON (SEATTLE)
Inn at the Market
86 Pine Street, Seattle, Washington 98101
Tel: +1 206 443 3600
Web: www.johansens.com/innatthemarket

BELIZE - CAYO (SAN IGNACIO)
The Lodge at Chaa Creek
P.O. Box 53, San Ignacio, Cayo
Tel: +501 824 2037
Web: www.johansens.com/chaacreek

U.S.A. - WASHINGTON (SPOKANE)
The Davenport Hotel and Tower
10 South Post Street, Spokane, Washington 99201
Tel: +1 509 455 8888
Web: www.johansens.com/davenport

BELIZE - ORANGE WALK DISTRICT (GALLON JUG)
Chan Chich Lodge
Gallon Jug, Orange Walk District
Tel: +501 223 4419
Web: www.johansens.com/chanchich

U.S.A. - WASHINGTON (WINTHROP)
Sun Mountain Lodge
P.O. Box 1,000, Winthrop, Washington 98862
Tel: +1 509 996 2211
Web: www.johansens.com/sunmountain

COSTA RICA - ALAJUELA (BAJOS DEL TORO)
El Silencio Lodge & Spa
Bajos del Toro, Alajuela
Tel: +506 2291 3044
Web: www.johansens.com/elsilencio

U.S.A. - WASHINGTON (WOODINVILLE)
The Herbfarm
14590 North East 145th Street, Woodinville, Washington 98072
Tel: +1 425 485 5300
Web: www.johansens.com/herbfarm

COSTA RICA - ALAJUELA (LA FORTUNA DE SAN CARLOS)
Tabacón Grand Spa Thermal Resort
La Fortuna de San Carlos, Arenal
Tel: +506 2519 1999
Web: www.johansens.com/tabacon

Hotels - The Americas

Properties listed below can be found in our Recommended Hotels, Inns, Resorts & Spas - The Americas, Atlantic, Caribbean & Pacific 2009 Guide. More information on our portfolio of guides can be found on page 13.

COSTA RICA - GUANACASTE (ISLITA)
Hotel Punta Islita
Guanacaste
Tel: +506 2231 6122
Web: www.johansens.com/hotelpuntaislita

HONDURAS - ATLÁNTIDA (LA CEIBA)
The Lodge at Pico Bonito
A. P. 710, La Ceiba, Atlántida, C. P. 31101
Tel: +504 440 0388
Web: www.johansens.com/picobonito

COSTA RICA - GUANACASTE (PLAYA CONCHAL)
Paradisus Playa Conchal
Bahía Brasilito, Playa Conchal, Santa Cruz, Guanacaste
Tel: +506 2654 4123
Web: www.johansens.com/paradisusplayaconchal

HONDURAS - BAY ISLANDS (ROATAN)
Barefoot Cay
Roatan, Bay Islands
Tel: +504 455 6235
Web: www.johansens.com/barefootcay

COSTA RICA - OSA PENISULA (PUERTO JIMENEZ)
Lapa Rios Eco Lodge
Puerto Jimenez, Osa Penisula
Tel: +506 2735 5130
Web: www.johansens.com/laparios

HONDURAS - BAY ISLANDS (ROATAN)
Mayoka Lodge
Sandy Bay, Roatan, Bay Islands
Tel: +504 445 3043
Web: www.johansens.com/mayokalodge

COSTA RICA - PUNTARENAS (MANUEL ANTONIO)
Arenas del Mar
KM 3.7 Carretera Quepos, Manuel Antonio, Puntarenas
Tel: +506 2777 2777
Web: www.johansens.com/areanasdelmar

Recommendations in South America

COSTA RICA - PUNTARENAS (MANUEL ANTONIO)
Gaia Hotel & Reserve
Km 2.7 Carretera Quepos, Manuel Antonio, Puntarenas
Tel: +506 2777 9797
Web: www.johansens.com/gaiahr

ARGENTINA - BUENOS AIRES (CIUDAD DE BUENOS AIRES)
Home Buenos Aires
Honduras 5860, 1414 Ciudad de Buenos Aires, Buenos Aires
Tel: +54 11 4778 1008
Web: www.johansens.com/homebuenosaires

GUATEMALA - LA ANTIGUA GUATEMALA
El Convento Boutique Hotel Antigua Guatemala
2a Avenue Norte 11, La Antigua Guatemala, Antigua
Tel: +502 7720 7272
Web: www.johansens.com/elconventoantigua

ARGENTINA - BUENOS AIRES (CIUDAD DE BUENOS AIRES)
Krista Hotel Boutique
Bonpland 1665, CP1414 Ciudad de Buenos Aires, Buenos Aires
Tel: +54 11 4771 4697
Web: www.johansens.com/kristahotel

GUATEMALA - LA ANTIGUA GUATEMALA
Hotel Vista Real La Antigua
3a Calle Oriente 16, La Antigua Guatemala
Tel: +502 7832 9715/6
Web: www.johansens.com/vistareal

ARGENTINA - BUENOS AIRES (CIUDAD DE BUENOS AIRES)
Legado Mitico
Gurruchaga 1848, C1414DIL Ciudad de Buenos Aires, Buenos Aires
Tel: +54 11 4833 1300
Web: www.johansens.com/legadomitico

GUATEMALA - LA ANTIGUA GUATEMALA (SAN FELIPE)
Filadelfia Coffee Resort & Spa
150 meters North of the San Felipe Chapel, La Antigua Guatemala
Tel: +502 7728 0800
Web: www.johansens.com/filadelfia

ARGENTINA - BUENOS AIRES (CIUDAD DE BUENOS AIRES)
Mine Hotel Boutique
Gorriti 4770, Palermo Soho, C1414BJL Ciudad de Buenos Aires, Buenos Aires
Tel: +54 11 4832 1100
Web: www.johansens.com/minehotel

Hotels - The Americas

Properties listed below can be found in our Recommended Hotels, Inns, Resorts & Spas - The Americas, Atlantic, Caribbean & Pacific 2009 Guide. More information on our portfolio of guides can be found on page 13.

ARGENTINA - BUENOS AIRES (CIUDAD DE BUENOS AIRES)

Moreno Hotel Buenos Aires
Moreno 376, C1091AAH Ciudad de Buenos Aires, San Telmo, Buenos Aires
Tel: +54 11 6091 2000
Web: www.johansens.com/moreno

ARGENTINA - BUENOS AIRES (CIUDAD DE BUENOS AIRES)

Vain Boutique Hotel
Thames 2226/8, C1425FiF Ciudad de Buenos Aires, Buenos Aires
Tel: +54 11 4776 8246
Web: www.johansens.com/vainuniverse

ARGENTINA - CHUBUT (PATAGONIA - PUERTO MADRYN)

Territorio
Boulevard Alte. G. Brown 3251, U9120ACG Puerto Madryn, Patagonia - Chubut
Tel: +54 11 4114 6029
Web: www.johansens.com/hotelterritorio

ARGENTINA - NEUQUÉN (PATAGONIA - VILLA LA ANGOSTURA)

Correntoso Lake & River Hotel
Av. Siete Lagos 4505, Villa La Angostura, Patagonia
Tel: +54 11 4803 0030
Web: www.johansens.com/correntoso

ARGENTINA - NEUQUÉN (PATAGONIA - VILLA LA ANGOSTURA)

Hotel Las Balsas
Bahía Las Balsas s/n, 8407 Villa La Angostura, Neuquén
Tel: +54 2944 494308
Web: www.johansens.com/lasbalsas

ARGENTINA - RÍO NEGRO (PATAGONIA - SAN CARLOS BARILOCHE)

Isla Victoria Lodge
Isla Victoria, Parque Nacional Nahuel Huapi, C.C. 26 (R8401AKU)
Tel: +54 43 94 96 05
Web: www.johansens.com/islavictoria

BRAZIL - ALAGOAS (SÃO MIGUEL DOS MILAGRES)

Pousada do Toque
Rua Felisberto de Ataide, Povoado do Toque, São Miguel dos Milagres, 57940-000 Alagoas
Tel: +55 82 3295 1127
Web: www.johansens.com/pousadadotoque

BRAZIL - BAHIA (ARRAIAL D'ÁJUDA)

Maitei Hotel
Estrada do Mucugê 475, Arraial D'Ájuda, Porto Seguro, Bahia 45816-000
Tel: +55 73 3575 3877
Web: www.johansens.com/maitei

BRAZIL - BAHIA (CORUMBAU)

Fazenda São Francisco
Ponta do Corumbau s/n, Prado, Bahia
Tel: +55 11 3078 4411
Web: www.johansens.com/fazenda

BRAZIL - BAHIA (CORUMBAU)

Vila Naiá - Paralelo 17°
Ponta do Corumbau, Bahia
Tel: +55 11 3061 1872
Web: www.johansens.com/vilanaia

BRAZIL - BAHIA (ITACARÉ)

Txai Resort
Rod. Ilhéus-Itacaré km 48, Itacaré, Bahia 45530-000
Tel: +55 73 2101 5000
Web: www.johansens.com/txairesort

BRAZIL - BAHIA (PENINSULA OF MARAÚ - MARAÚ)

Kiaroa Eco-Luxury Resort
Loteamento da Costa, área SD6, Distrito de barra grande, Municipio de Maraú, Bahia, CEp 45 520-000
Tel: +55 71 3272 1320
Web: www.johansens.com/kiaroa

BRAZIL - BAHIA (PRAIA DO FORTE)

Tivoli Ecoresort Praia do Forte
Avenida do Farol, Praia do Forte - Mata de São João, Bahia
Tel: +55 71 36 76 40 00
Web: www.johansens.com/praiadoforte

BRAZIL - BAHIA (TRANCOSO)

Etnia Pousada and Boutique
Trancoso, Bahia 45818-000
Tel: +55 73 3668 1137
Web: www.johansens.com/etnia

BRAZIL - MINAS GERAIS (TIRADENTES)

Pousada dos Inconfidentes
Rua João Rodrigues Sobrinho 91, 36325-000, Tiradentes, Minas Gerais
Tel: +55 32 3355 2135
Web: www.johansens.com/inconfidentes

BRAZIL - MINAS GERAIS (TIRADENTES)

Solar da Ponte
Praça das Mercês S/N, Tiradentes, Minas Gerais 36325-000
Tel: +55 32 33 55 12 55
Web: www.johansens.com/solardaponte

Hotels - The Americas

Properties listed below can be found in our Recommended Hotels, Inns, Resorts & Spas - The Americas, Atlantic, Caribbean & Pacific 2009 Guide. More information on our portfolio of guides can be found on page 13.

BRAZIL - PERNAMBUCO (FERNANDO DE NORONHA)
Pousada Maravilha LIDA
Rodovia BR-363, s/n, Sueste, Ilha de Fernando de Noronha, Pernambuco 53990-000
Tel: +55 81 3619 0028
Web: www.johansens.com/maravilha

BRAZIL - RIO DE JANEIRO (RIO DE JANEIRO)
Hotel Marina All Suites
Av. Delfim Moreira, 696, Praia do Leblon, Rio de Janeiro 22441-000
Tel: +55 21 2172 1001
Web: www.johansens.com/marinaallsuites

BRAZIL - PERNAMBUCO (PORTO DE GALINHAS)
Nannai Beach Resort
Rodovia PE-09, acesso à Muro Alto, Km 3, Ipojuca, Pernambuco 55590-000
Tel: +55 81 3552 0100
Web: www.johansens.com/nannaibeach

BRAZIL - RIO GRANDE DO NORTE (PRAIA DA PIPA)
Toca da Coruja
Av. Baia dos Golfinhos, 464, Praia da Pipa, Tibau do Sul, Rio Grande do Norte 59178-000
Tel: +55 84 3246 2226
Web: www.johansens.com/rocadacoruja

BRAZIL - RIO DE JANEIRO (ARMAÇÃO DOS BÚZIOS)
Villa Rasa Marina
Av. José Bento Ribeiro Dantas 299, Armação dos Búzios, Rio de Janeiro 28950-000
Tel: +55 21 2172 1000
Web: www.johansens.com/villarasamarina

BRAZIL - RIO GRANDE DO SUL (GRAMADO)
Estalagem St. Hubertus
Rua Carrieri, 974, Gramado, Rio Grande do Sul 95670-000
Tel: +55 54 3286 1273
Web: www.johansens.com/sthubertus

BRAZIL - RIO DE JANEIRO (BÚZIOS)
Casas Brancas Boutique-Hotel & Spa
Alto do Humaitá 10, Armação dos Búzios, Rio de Janeiro 28950-000
Tel: +55 22 2623 1458
Web: www.johansens.com/casasbrancas

BRAZIL - RIO GRANDE DO SUL (GRAMADO)
Kurotel
Rua Nações Unidas 533, P.O. Box 65, Gramado, Rio Grande do Sul 95670-000
Tel: +55 54 3295 9393
Web: www.johansens.com/kurotel

BRAZIL - RIO DE JANEIRO (BÚZIOS)
Insólito Boutique Hotel
Rua E1 - Lot 3 e 4 , Condomínio Atlático, Armação de Búzios, Rio de Janeiro 28,950-000
Tel: +55 22 2623 2172
Web: www.johansens.com/insolitos

BRAZIL - RIO GRANDE DO SUL (SÃO FRANCISCO DE PAULA)
Pousada do Engenho
Rua Odon Cavalcante, 330, São Francisco de Paula 95400-000, Rio Grande do Sul
Tel: +55 54 3244 1270
Web: www.johansens.com/pousadadoengenho

BRAZIL - RIO DE JANEIRO (PETRÓPOLIS)
Parador Santarém Marina
Estrada Correia da Veiga, 96, Petrópolis, Rio de Janeiro 25745-260
Tel: +55 24 2222 9933
Web: www.johansens.com/paradorsantarem

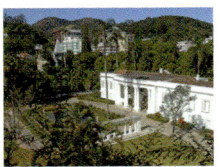

BRAZIL - SANTA CATARINA (GOVERNADOR CELSO RAMOS)
Ponta dos Ganchos
Rua Eupídio Alves do Nascimento, 104, Governador Celso Ramos, Santa Catarina 88190-000
Tel: +55 48 3262 5000
Web: www.johansens.com/pontadosganchos

BRAZIL - RIO DE JANEIRO (PETRÓPOLIS)
Solar do Império
Koeler Avenue, 376 - Centro, Petrópolis, Rio de Janeiro
Tel: +55 24 2103 3000
Web: www.johansens.com/solardoimperio

BRAZIL - SANTA CATARINA (PALHOÇA)
Ilha do Papagaio
Ilha do Papagaio, Palhoça, Santa Catarina 88131-970
Tel: +55 48 3286 1242
Web: www.johansens.com/ilhadopapagaio

BRAZIL - RIO DE JANEIRO (PETRÓPOLIS)
Tankamana EcoResort
Estrada Júlio Cápua, S/N Vale Do Cuiabá, Itaipava - Petrópolis, Rio de Janeiro 25745-050
Tel: +55 24 2103 3000
Web: www.johansens.com/tankamana

BRAZIL - SANTA CATARINA (PRAIA DO ROSA)
Pousada Solar Mirador
Estrada Geral do Rosa s/n, Praia do Rosa, Imbituba, Santa Catarina 88780-000
Tel: +55 48 3355 6144
Web: www.johansens.com/solarmirador

Hotels - The Americas

Properties listed below can be found in our Recommended Hotels, Inns, Resorts & Spas - The Americas, Atlantic, Caribbean & Pacific 2009 Guide. More information on our portfolio of guides can be found on page 13.

BRAZIL - SÃO PAULO (CAMPOS DO JORDÃO)
Hotel Frontenac
Av. Dr. Paulo Ribas, 295 Capivari,
Campos do Jordão 12460-000
Tel: +55 12 3669 1000
Web: www.johansens.com/frontenac

BRAZIL - SÃO PAULO (ILHABELA)
DPNY Beach Hotel
Av. José Pacheco do Nascimento, 7668, Praia do Curral,
Ilhabela, São Paulo 11630-000
Tel: +55 12 3894 2121
Web: www.johansens.com/dpnybeach

BRAZIL - SÃO PAULO (SÃO PAULO)
Hotel Emiliano
Rua Oscar Freire 384, São Paulo, SP 01426-000
Tel: +55 11 3068 4393
Web: www.johansens.com/emiliano

BRAZIL - SÃO PAULO (SÃO PAULO)
Hotel Unique
Av. Brigadeiro Luis Antonio, 4.700, São Paulo,
São Paulo 01402-002
Tel: +55 11 3055 4710
Web: www.johansens.com/hotelunique

BRAZIL - SÃO PAULO (SERRA DA CANTAREIRA)
Spa Unique Garden
Estrada Laramara, 3500, Serra da Cantareira,
São Paulo 07600-970
Tel: +55 11 4486 8700
Web: www.johansens.com/uniquegarden

CHILE - REGIÓN DE ARAUCANÍA (VILLARRICA)
Villarrica Park Lake Hotel
Camino a Villarrica km.13, Villarrica,
Región de Araucanía
Tel: +56 2 207 7070
Web: www.johansens.com/villarrica

CHILE - REGIÓN DE ATACAMA (SAN PEDRO DE ATACAMA)
Alto Atacama
Camino Pucarà S/N, Sector Suchor, Ayllú de Quitor,
San Pedro de Atacama, Región de Atacama
Tel: +562 436 0265
Web: www.johansens.com/altoatacama

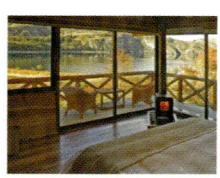

CHILE - REGION DE AYSEN (PATAGONIA - PUERTO GUADAL)
Hacienda Tres Lagos
Carretera Austral Sur Km 274, Localidad Lago Negro,
Puerto Guadal, Region de Aysen, Patagonia
Tel: +56 2 333 4122
Web: www.johansens.com/treslagos

CHILE - REGIÓN DE MAGALLANES (PATAGONIA - PUERTO NATALES)
Indigo Patagonia Hotel & Spa
Ladrilleros 105, Puerto Natales, Región de Magallanes
Tel: +566 141 3609
Web: www.johansens.com/indigopatagonia

CHILE - REGIÓN DE VALPARAÍSO (VALPARAÍSO)
Hotel Manoir Atkinson
Paseo Atkinson 165, Cerro Concepcion, Valparaíso,
Región de Valparaíso
Tel: +563 2235 1313
Web: www.johansens.com/hotelatkinson

CHILE - REGIÓN DE VALPARAÍSO (VIÑA DEL MAR)
Hotel Del Mar - Enjoy Hotels
Av. Perú Esquina Av. Los Héroes, Viña del Mar,
Región de Valparaíso
Tel: +56 32 284 6100
Web: www.johansens.com/hoteldelmarcl

CHILE - REGIÓN DO LOS LAGOS (PATAGONIA - PUERTO MONTT)
Nomads of the Seas
Puerto Montt, Región do los Lagos
Tel: +562 414 4600
Web: www.johansens.com/nomadsoftheseas

ECUADOR - AZUAY (CUENCA)
Mansión Alcázar Boutique Hotel
Calle Bolívar 12-55 Y Tarqui, Cuenca, Azuay
Tel: +593 72823 918
Web: www.johansens.com/mansionalcazar

ECUADOR - COTOPAXI (LASSO)
Hacienda San Agustin de Callo
77km south of Quito on the Panamerican Highway,
Lasso, Cotopaxi
Tel: +593 3 2719 160
Web: www.johansens.com/haciendasanagustin

ECUADOR - IMBABURA (ANGOCHAGUA)
Hacienda Zuleta
Angochagua, Imbabura
Tel: +593 6 266 2182
Web: www.johansens.com/zuleta

ECUADOR - IMBABURA (COTACACHI)
La Mirage Garden Hotel and Spa
Cotacachi, Imbabura
Tel: +593 6 291 5237
Web: www.johansens.com/mirage

Hotels - The Americas, Atlantic & Caribbean

Properties listed below can be found in our Recommended Hotels, Inns, Resorts & Spas - The Americas, Atlantic, Caribbean & Pacific 2009 Guide. More information on our portfolio of guides can be found on page 13.

PERU - LIMA PROVINCIAS (YAUYOS)
Refugios Del Peru - Viñak Reichraming
Santiago de Viñak, Yauyos, Lima
Tel: +511 421 7777
Web: www.johansens.com/refugiosdelperu

URUGUAY - MALDONADO (PUNTA DEL ESTE)
L'Auberge
Carnoustie y Av. del Agua, Barrio Parque de Golf,
Punta del Este CP20100
Tel: +598 42 48 2601
Web: www.johansens.com/laubergeuruguay

Recommendations in the Atlantic

ATLANTIC - BAHAMAS (GRAND BAHAMA ISLAND)
Old Bahama Bay by Ginn Sur Mer
West End, Grand Bahama Island
Tel: +1 242 350 6500
Web: www.johansens.com/oldbahamabay

ATLANTIC - BERMUDA (HAMILTON)
Rosedon Hotel
P.O. Box Hm 290, Hamilton Hmax
Tel: +1 441 295 1640
Web: www.johansens.com/rosedonhotel

ATLANTIC - BERMUDA (SOMERSET)
Cambridge Beaches Resort & Spa
Sandys, Somerset
Tel: +1 441 234 0331
Web: www.johansens.com/cambeaches

ATLANTIC - BERMUDA (SOUTHAMPTON)
The Reefs
56 South Shore Road, Southampton
Tel: +1 441 238 0222
Web: www.johansens.com/thereefs

Recommendations in the Caribbean

CARIBBEAN - ANGUILLA (RENDEZVOUS BAY)
CuisinArt Resort & Spa
P.O. Box 2000, Rendezvous Bay
Tel: +1 264 498 2000
Web: www.johansens.com/cuisinartresort

CARIBBEAN - ANGUILLA (WEST END)
Sheriva Villa Hotel
Maundays Bay Road, West End AI-2640
Tel: +1 264 498 9898
Web: www.johansens.com/sheriva

CARIBBEAN - ANTIGUA (ST. JOHN'S)
Galley Bay Resort & Spa
Five Islands, St. John's
Tel: +1 954 481 8787
Web: www.johansens.com/galleybay

CARIBBEAN - ANTIGUA (ST. JOHN'S)
Hermitage Bay Hotel
St. John's
Tel: +1 268 562 5500
Web: www.johansens.com/hermitagebay

CARIBBEAN - ANTIGUA (ST. JOHN'S)
The Verandah Resort & Spa
Indian Town Road, St. John's
Tel: +1 954 481 8787
Web: www.johansens.com/verandah

CARIBBEAN - ANTIGUA (ST. JOHN'S)
Blue Waters
P.O. Box 257, St. John's
Tel: +44 870 360 1245
Web: www.johansens.com/bluewaters

For further information, hotel search, gift certificates, online bookshop and special offers visit:

www.johansens.com

Annually Inspected for the Independent Traveller

Hotels - Caribbean

Properties listed below can be found in our Recommended Hotels, Inns, Resorts & Spas - The Americas, Atlantic, Caribbean & Pacific 2009 Guide. More information on our portfolio of guides can be found on page 13.

CARIBBEAN - ANTIGUA (ST. JOHN'S)
Curtain Bluff
P.O. Box 288, St. John's
Tel: +1 268 462 8400
Web: www.johansens.com/curtainbluff

CARIBBEAN - CURAÇAO (WILLEMSTAD)
Avila Hotel on the Beach
Penstraat 130, Willemstad
Tel: +599 9 461 4377
Web: www.johansens.com/avilabeach

CARIBBEAN - ANTIGUA (ST. MARY'S)
Carlisle Bay
Old Road, St. Mary's
Tel: +1 268 484 0000
Web: www.johansens.com/carlislebay

CARIBBEAN - DOMINICAN REPUBLIC (PUERTA PLATA)
Maxim Bungalows Resort and Spa
1 Paradise Drive, Cofresi Beach, Puerto Plata
Tel: +1 866 970 3364
Web: www.johansens.com/maximbungalows

CARIBBEAN - BARBADOS (CHRIST CHURCH)
Little Arches
Enterprise Beach Road, Christ Church
Tel: +1 246 420 4689
Web: www.johansens.com/littlearches

CARIBBEAN - DOMINICAN REPUBLIC (PUERTO PLATA)
Casa Colonial Beach & Spa
P.O. Box 22, Puerto Plata
Tel: +1 809 320 3232
Web: www.johansens.com/casacolonial

CARIBBEAN - BARBADOS (ST. JAMES)
Coral Reef Club
St. James
Tel: +1 246 422 2372
Web: www.johansens.com/coralreefclub

CARIBBEAN - DOMINICAN REPUBLIC (PUNTA CANA)
Agua Resort & Spa
Uvero Alto, Punta Cana
Tel: +1 809 468 0000
Web: www.johansens.com/aguaresort

CARIBBEAN - BARBADOS (ST. JAMES)
The Sandpiper
Holetown, St. James
Tel: +1 246 422 2251
Web: www.johansens.com/sandpiper

CARIBBEAN - DOMINICAN REPUBLIC (PUNTA CANA)
Sivory Punta Cana
Playa Sivory, Uvero Alto/Punta Cana
Tel: +1 809 333 0500
Web: www.johansens.com/sivory

CARIBBEAN - BRITISH VIRGIN ISLANDS (PETER ISLAND)
Peter Island Resort
Peter Island
Tel: +770 476 9988
Web: www.johansens.com/peterislandresort

CARIBBEAN - DOMINICAN REPUBLIC (PUNTA CANA)
Tortuga Bay, Puntacana Resort & Club
Dominican Republic
Tel: +1 809 959 2262
Web: www.johansens.com/puntacana

CARIBBEAN - BRITISH VIRGIN ISLANDS (PETER ISLAND)
The Villas at Peter Island
Peter Island
Tel: +770 476 9988
Web: www.johansens.com/villaspeterisland

CARIBBEAN - GRENADA (ST. GEORGE'S)
Spice Island Beach Resort
Grand Anse Beach, St. George's
Tel: +1 473 444 4423/4258
Web: www.johansens.com/spiceisland

CARIBBEAN - BRITISH VIRGIN ISLANDS (VIRGIN GORDA)
Biras Creek Resort
North Sound, Virgin Gorda
Tel: +1 248 364 2421
Web: www.johansens.com/birascreek

CARIBBEAN - JAMAICA (MONTEGO BAY)
Half Moon
Rose Hall
Tel: +1 876 953 2211
Web: www.johansens.com/halfmoon

Hotels - Caribbean

Properties listed below can be found in our Recommended Hotels, Inns, Resorts & Spas - The Americas, Atlantic, Caribbean & Pacific 2009 Guide. More information on our portfolio of guides can be found on page 13.

CARIBBEAN - JAMAICA (MONTEGO BAY)
Tryall Club
P.O. Box 1206, Montego Bay
Tel: +1 876 956 5660
Web: www.johansens.com/tryallclub

CARIBBEAN - ST. LUCIA (SOUFRIÈRE)
Anse Chastanet
Soufrière
Tel: +1 758 459 7000
Web: www.johansens.com/ansechastanet

CARIBBEAN - JAMAICA (OCHO RIOS)
Royal Plantation
Main Street, P.O. Box 2, Ocho Rios
Tel: +1 876 974 5601
Web: www.johansens.com/royalplantation

CARIBBEAN - ST. LUCIA (SOUFRIÈRE)
Jade Mountain at Anse Chastanet
Soufrière
Tel: +1 758 459 4000
Web: www.johansens.com/jademountain

CARIBBEAN - PUERTO RICO (OLD SAN JUAN)
Chateau Cervantes
Recinto Sur 329, Old San Juan
Tel: +787 724 7722
Web: www.johansens.com/cervantes

CARIBBEAN - ST. LUCIA (SOUFRIÈRE)
Ladera Resort
Soufrière
Tel: +1 758 459 7323
Web: www.johansens.com/ladera

CARIBBEAN - PUERTO RICO (RINCÓN)
Horned Dorset Primavera
Apartado 1132, Rincón 00677
Tel: +1 787 823 4030
Web: www.johansens.com/horneddorset

CARIBBEAN - ST. MARTIN (BAIE LONGUE)
La Samanna
P.O. Box 4077, 97064 CEDEX
Tel: +590 590 87 64 00
Web: www.johansens.com/lasamanna

CARIBBEAN - SAINT-BARTHÉLEMY (ANSE DE TOINY)
Hôtel Le Toiny
Anse de Toiny
Tel: +590 590 27 88 88
Web: www.johansens.com/letoiny

CARIBBEAN - THE GRENADINES (MUSTIQUE)
Firefly
Mustique Island
Tel: +1 784 488 8414
Web: www.johansens.com/firefly

CARIBBEAN - SAINT-BARTHÉLEMY (GRAND CUL DE SAC)
Hotel Guanahani & Spa
Grand Cul de Sac
Tel: +590 590 27 66 60
Web: www.johansens.com/guanahani

CARIBBEAN - THE GRENADINES (PALM ISLAND)
Palm Island
Palm Island
Tel: +1 954 481 8787
Web: www.johansens.com/palmisland

CARIBBEAN - ST. KITTS & NEVIS (NEVIS)
Montpelier Plantation
P.O. Box 474, Nevis
Tel: +1 869 469 3462
Web: www.johansens.com/montpelierplantation

CARIBBEAN - TURKS & CAICOS ISLANDS (GRACE BAY BEACH)
The Estate at Grace Bay Club
P.O. Box 128, Providenciales
Tel: +649 946 8323
Web: www.johansens.com/estateatgracebay

CARIBBEAN - ST. LUCIA (CASTRIES)
Windjammer Landing Villa Beach Resort & Spa
P.O. Box 1504, Castries, St. Lucia
Tel: 1 758 456 9000
Web: www.johansens.com/windjammerlanding

CARIBBEAN - TURKS & CAICOS ISLANDS (GRACE BAY BEACH)
Grace Bay Club
P.O. Box 128, Providenciales
Tel: +1 649 946 5050
Web: www.johansens.com/gracebayclub

Hotels - Caribbean & Pacific

Properties listed below can be found in our Recommended Hotels, Inns, Resorts & Spas - The Americas, Atlantic, Caribbean & Pacific 2009 Guide. More information on our portfolio of guides can be found on page 13

CARIBBEAN - TURKS & CAICOS ISLANDS (GRACE BAY BEACH)
The Regent Palms, Turks & Caicos
P.O. Box 681, Grace Bay, Providenciales
Tel: +649 946 8666
Web: www.johansens.com/regentpalms

CARIBBEAN - TURKS & CAICOS ISLANDS (GRACE BAY BEACH)
The Somerset on Grace Bay
Princess Drive, Providenciales
Tel: +1 649 946 5900
Web: www.johansens.com/somersetgracebay

CARIBBEAN - TURKS & CAICOS ISLANDS (PARROT CAY)
Parrot Cay & COMO Shambhala Retreat
P.O. Box 164, Providenciales
Tel: +1 649 946 7788
Web: www.johansens.com/parrotcay

CARIBBEAN - TURKS & CAICOS ISLANDS (POINT GRACE)
Point Grace
P.O. Box 700, Providenciales
Tel: +1 649 946 5096
Web: www.johansens.com/pointgrace

CARIBBEAN - TURKS & CAICOS ISLANDS (WEST GRACE BAY BEACH)
Turks & Caicos Club
West Grace Bay Beach, P.O. Box 687, Providenciales
Tel: +1 649 946 5800
Web: www.johansens.com/turksandcaicos

PACIFIC - FIJI ISLANDS (QAMEA ISLAND)
Qamea Resort & Spa
P.A. Matei, Taveuni
Tel: +649 360 0858
Web: www.johansens.com/qamea

PACIFIC - FIJI ISLANDS (SAVUSAVU)
Jean-Michel Cousteau Fiji Islands Resort
Lesiaceva Point, SavuSavu
Tel: +1 415 788 5794
Web: www.johansens.com/jean-michelcousteau

PACIFIC - FIJI ISLANDS (SAVUSAVU)
Namale - Fiji islands Resort & Spa
P.O. Box 244, Savusavu
Tel: +679 8850 435
Web: www.johansens.com/namale

PACIFIC - FIJI ISLANDS (SIGATOKA)
Myola Plantation
P.O. Box 638, Sigatoka
Tel: +679 652 1084
Web: www.johansens.com/myola

PACIFIC - FIJI ISLANDS (UGAGA ISLAND)
Royal Davui Island Resort - Fiji
P.O. Box 3171, Lami
Tel: +679 336 1624
Web: www.johansens.com/royaldavui

PACIFIC - FIJI ISLANDS (YAQETA ISLAND)
Navutu Stars Resort
P.O. Box 1838, Lautoka
Tel: +679 664 0553 and +679 664 0554
Web: www.johansens.com/navutustars

Recommendations in the Pacific

PACIFIC - FIJI ISLANDS (LABASA)
Nukubati Island, Great Sea Reef, Fiji
P.O. Box 1928, Labasa
Tel: +61 2 93888 196
Web: www.johansens.com/nukubati

PACIFIC - FIJI ISLANDS (LAUTOKA)
Blue Lagoon Cruises
183 Vitogo Parade, Lautoka
Tel: +679 6661 622
Web: www.johansens.com/bluelagooncruises

PACIFIC - FIJI ISLANDS (YASAWA ISLAND)
Turtle Island
P.O. Box 9317, Nadi, Yasawa Island
Tel: +1 360 256 4347
Web: www.johansens.com/turtleisland

PACIFIC - FIJI ISLANDS (YASAWA ISLAND)
Yasawa Island Resort & Spa
P.O. Box 10128, Nadi Airport, Nadi
Tel: +679 672 2266
Web: www.johansens.com/yasawaislan

Individuality Matters to our Partnership

We take pride in watching our clients' businesses grow and assisting them in that process wherever we can.

Goodman Derrick, founded over 50 years ago, have developed an acknowledged expertise in the areas of corporate and commercial law, litigation, property, employment and franchising law. We also have a leading reputation as legal advisors in the media, hotel and historic and collectors cars sectors. For personal matters, we also have a dedicated Private Client Group which provides a comprehensive and complementary range of services to the individual and their families.

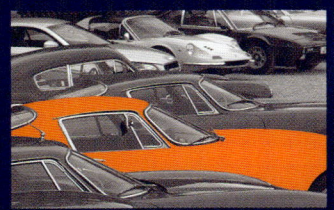

For more information about how we can help you or your business visit www.gdlaw.co.uk or contact Belinda Copland bcopland@gdlaw.co.uk tel: +44 (0)20 7404 0606

GOODMAN DERRICK LLP
CONDÉ NAST JOHANSENS PREFERRED LEGAL PARTNER

Index by Property

Index by Property

0-9

41	London	123
51 Buckingham Gate	London	140

A

Abbeyglen Castle	Clifden	214
Amberley Castle	Amberley	177
Ardanaiseig	Kilchrenan By Oban	235
Ardencote Manor Hotel	Warwick	185
Armathwaite Hall	Keswick	67
The Arundell Arms	Lifton	84
Ashdown Park Hotel	Forest Row	172
Ashford Castle	Cong	223
The Atlantic Hotel and Ocean Restaurant	Jersey	18
Auchen Castle	Moffat	237

B

Bailiffscourt Hotel & Spa	Arundel	178
Ballynahinch Castle Hotel	**Recess**	**216**
The Bath Priory Hotel, Restaurant & Spa	Bath	32
Beaufort House	London	130
Bedford Lodge Hotel	Newmarket	162
Bishopstrow House & Spa	Warminster	192
Black Swan Hotel	Helmsley	200
Bodysgallen Hall & Spa	Llandudno	255
The Brehon	Killarney	218
Brockencote Hall	Chaddesley Corbett	195
Buckland Manor	Buckland	194
Buckland-Tout-Saints	Salcombe Estuary	87
Budock Vean - The Hotel on the River	Falmouth	53
Bunchrew House Hotel	Inverness	243
Burleigh Court	Minchinhampton	103
Burythorpe House	Malton	202

C

Cahernane House Hotel	Killarney	219
Calcot Manor Hotel & Spa	Tetbury	105
Callow Hall	Ashbourne	74
The Capital Hotel & Restaurant	London	131
Cashel House	Connemara	215
The Castle at Taunton	Taunton	155
Castle House	Hereford	115
Cathedral Quarter Hotel	Derby	76
Celtic Manor Resort	Newport	259
Charingworth Manor	Chipping Campden	100
Charlton House Hotel	Shepton Mallet	154
Chewton Glen	New Milton	112
Chilworth Manor	Southampton	114
Cliveden & The Pavilion Spa	Maidenhead	40
The Club Hotel & Spa, Bohemia Restaurant	Jersey	19
Combe House	Exeter	81
Congham Hall	King's Lynn	142
Corse Lawn House Hotel	Tewkesbury	106
The Cottage in the Wood	Malvern Wells	197
Craigellachie Hotel of Speyside	Craigellachie	234
Cuillin Hills Hotel	Isle Of Skye	246

D

Dale Head Hall Lakeside Hotel	Keswick	69
Dale Hill	Ticehurst	176
Dalhousie Castle and Spa	Edinburgh	248
Danesfield House Hotel	Marlow-On-Thames	46
Deans Place Hotel	Alfriston	167
The Devonshire Arms Country House Hote	Bolton Abbey	198
Donnington Valley Hotel	Newbury	41
The Dower House Apartments	Bury St. Edmunds	158
Down Hall Country House	Near Stansted	118
Dukes Hotel	Bath	33
Dunbrody Country House & Cookery School	Arthurstown	228

E

Eastwell Manor	Ashford	119
The Egerton House Hotel	London	132
The Elms	Abberley	193
Esseborne Manor	Andover	108
The Europe Hotel & Resort	Killarney	220
The Evesham Hotel	Evesham	196

F

Falcondale Mansion Hotel	Lampeter	253
Fermain Valley Hotel	Guernsey	16
Fitzpatrick Castle Hotel	Killiney	213
Fowey Hall Hotel & Restaurant	Fowey	55
Fredrick's – Hotel Restaurant Spa	Maidenhead	39
The French Horn	Reading	43

G

The Garrack Hotel & Restaurant	St Ives	60
The George Of Stamford	Stamford	122
The Gibbon Bridge Hotel	Preston	120
Gidleigh Park	Chagford	80
Glenskirlie House & Castle	Banknock	249
The Goodwood Park Hotel	Chichester	179
The Grand Hotel	Eastbourne	171
The Grange Hotel	York	204
Great Fosters	Egham	164
Great Hallingbury Manor Hotel	Bishop's Stortford	116
Green Bough Hotel	Chester	49
The Greenway	Cheltenham	99

H

Hambleton Hall	Oakham	152
The Harlequin	Castlebar	224
Hart's Hotel	Nottingham	145
Harte & Garter Hotel & Spa	Windsor	44
Hartwell House Hotel, Restaurant & Spa	Aylesbury	45
Harvey's Point	Donegal Town	212
Hell Bay	Isles Of Scilly	56
Hintlesham Hall	Ipswich	160
Hoar Cross Hall Spa Resort	Lichfield	157
Holbeck Ghyll Country House Hotel	Ambleside	62
Holm House	Cardiff	266

Index by Property

Homewood Park	Bath	35
The Horse and Jockey Hotel	Thurles	227
Horsted Place Country House Hotel	Lewes	174
The Hoste Arms	Burnham Market	141
Hotel Dunloe Castle	Killarney	221
Hotel Riviera	Sidmouth	88
Howard's House	Salisbury	190
Hunstrete House	Bath	36

I

The Ickworth Hotel	Bury St Edmunds	159
Ilsington Country House Hotel	Ilsington	82
The Inn on the Lake	Lake Ullswater	71
Inverlochy Castle	Fort William	242
The Izaak Walton Hotel	Ashbourne	75

J

Judges Country House Hotel	Yarm	203
Jumeirah Carlton Tower	London	133
Jumeirah Lowndes Hotel	London	134

K

Kelly's Resort Hotel & Spa	Rosslare	230
Kensington House Hotel	London	127
Kesgrave Hall	Kesgrave	161
Kirroughtree House	Newton Stewart	238
Knockranny House Hotel & Spa	Westport	225

L

Lace Market Hotel	Nottingham	146
The Lake Country House	Llangammarch Wells	265
Lake Vyrnwy Hotel	Lake Vyrnwy	264
Lakeside Hotel on Lake Windermere	Windermere	73
Lamphey Court Hotel & Spa	Tenby	262
Langdon Court & Restaurant	Wembury	90
Lansdowne Place, Boutique Hotel & Spa	Brighton	169
Le Manoir Aux Quat' Saisons	Oxford	150
Lewtrenchard Manor	Lewdown	83
Linthwaite House Hotel	Windermere	72
Llangoed Hall	Brecon	263
The Lodore Falls Hotel	Keswick	68
Longueville House & Presidents' Restaurant	Mallow	211
Longueville Manor	Jersey	21
Lovelady Shield Country House Hotel	Alston	61
Lower Slaughter Manor	Lower Slaughter	101
Lucknam Park, Bath	Bath	187
The Lugger Hotel	Portloe	59
Luton Hoo Hotel, Golf & Spa	Luton	38
Lythe Hill Hotel & Spa	Haslemere	165

M

Maison Talbooth	Dedham	98
Mallory Court	Royal Leamington Spa	184
The Mandeville Hotel	London	136
Mar Hall Hotel & Spa	Glasgow	240
Marlfield House	Gorey	229
The Mayflower Hotel	London	125
Meudon Hotel	Falmouth	54
Middlethorpe Hall Hotel, Restaurant & Spa	York	205
Milestone Hotel	London	128
Miskin Manor Country House Hotel	Miskin	252
Moonfleet Manor	Weymouth	96
Mount Falcon Country House Hotel & Spa	Ballina	222
Mount Somerset Country House Hotel	Taunton	156
Mount Wolseley Hotel, Spa & Country Club	Tullow	210

N

Nailcote Hall	Coventry	183
The Nare Hotel	Carne Beach	51
Netherwood Hotel	Grange-Over-Sands	66
The New Linden Hotel	London	138
New Park Manor & Bath House Spa	Brockenhurst	110
Newick Park	Lewes	175
No.11 London	London	135
Northcote Manor Country House Hotel	Burrington	79
Nuremore Hotel and Country Club	Carrickmacross	226

O

Oakley Hall	Basingstoke	109
Ockenden Manor	Cuckfield	180
Old Bank Hotel	Oxford	148
Old Course Hotel Golf Resort & Spa	St Andrews	239
The Old Government House Hotel	Guernsey	17
The Old Parsonage Hotel	Oxford	149
Orestone Manor & The Restaurant at Orestone Manor	Torquay	89

P

Palé Hall	Bala	257
The Park	Bath	37
Park Hotel Kenmare & Sámas	Kenmare	217
The Parkcity Hotel	London	129
The Pear Tree At Purton	Swindon	191
Pelham House	Lewes	173
Penmaenuchaf Hall	Dolgellau	258
The Pheasant	Helmsley	201
The Polurrian Hotel	Mullion	58
The PowderMills	Battle	168
The Priory Hotel	Wareham	95

R

Riber Hall	Matlock	77
The Richmond Gate Hotel and Restaurant	Richmond-Upon-Thames	166
Risley Hall Hotel and Spa	Risley	78
The Ritz-Carlton Powerscourt	**Enniskerry**	**231**
Rocpool Reserve	Inverness	244
Rothay Manor	Ambleside	63
Rowton Hall Hotel, Health Club & Spa	Chester	50
The Royal Crescent Hotel & The Bath House Spa	Bath	34
Royal Highland Hotel	Inverness	245
The Royal Yacht Hotel	Jersey	20
Royal York Hotel	Brighton	170
Rushton Hall Hotel & Spa	Kettering	143

S

The Samling	Ambleside	64
Seaham Hall Hotel & Serenity Spa	Seaham	97

Index by Property/Location

Seckford Hall	Woodbridge	163
Sharrow Bay Country House Hotel	Lake Ullswater	70
Simonstone Hall	Hawes	199
Soar Mill Cove Hotel	Salcombe	85
Sofitel London St James	London	139
The Spread Eagle Hotel & Spa	Midhurst	181
The Springs Hotel & Golf Club	Wallingford	151
St Brides Spa Hotel	Saundersfoot	260
St Michael's Hotel & Spa	Falmouth	52
St Michael's Manor	St Albans	117
St Tudno Hotel & Restaurant	Llandudno	256
Stapleford Park Country House Hotel	Melton Mowbray	121
Stock Hill Country House Hotel & Restaurant	Gillingham	94
Stoke Park	Stoke Poges	48
Stoke Place	Slough	47
Ston Easton Park	Bath	153
Stonefield Castle	Tarbert	236
Stonehouse Court Hotel	Stonehouse	104
Summer Lodge Country House Hotel	Evershot	93

T

Talland Bay Hotel	Looe	57
Ten Square	Belfast	209
Thornbury Castle	Bristol	107
The Tides Reach Hotel	Salcombe	86
The Torridon	Torridon	247
Tufton Arms Hotel	Appleby-In-Westmorland	65
Tulloch Castle Hotel	Dingwall	241
Twenty Nevern Square	London	126
Tylney Hall	Rotherwick	113

V

The Vermont Hotel	Newcastle-Upon-Tyne	182
The Vineyard At Stockcross	Newbury	42

W

Warpool Court Hotel	St David's	261
Washbourne	Lower Slaughter	102
Watersmeet Hotel	Woolacombe	92
Westbury Hotel	London	137
Westover Hall	Lymington	111
Whatley Manor	Malmesbury	189
Whittlebury Hall	Northampton	144
The Woolacombe Bay Hotel	Woolacombe	91
Woolley Grange	Bradford-On-Avon	188
Wroxall Abbey Estate	Warwick	186
The Wyndham Grand London Chelsea Harbour	London	124

Y

Ye Olde Bell Hotel & Restaurant	Retford	147
Ynyshir Hall	Machynlleth	254

Index by Location

London

Buckingham Palace	41	123
Chelsea Harbour	The Wyndham Grand	124
Earls court	The Mayflower Hotel	125
Earls Court	Twenty Nevern Square	126
Kensington	Kensington House Hotel	127
Kensington	Milestone Hotel	128
Kensington	The Parkcity Hotel	129
Knightsbridge	Beaufort House	130
Knightsbridge	The Capital Hotel & Restaurant	131
Knightsbridge	The Egerton House Hotel	132
Knightsbridge	Jumeirah Carlton Tower	133
Knightsbridge	Jumeirah Lowndes Hotel	134
Knightsbridge	No.11 London	135
Mayfair	The Mandeville Hotel	136
Mayfair	Westbury Hotel	137
Notting Hill	The New Linden Hotel	138
Piccadilly	Sofitel London St James	139
Westminster	51 Buckingham Gate	140

England

A

Abberley	The Elms	193
Alfriston	Deans Place Hotel	167
Alston	Lovelady Shield Hotel	61
Amberley	Amberley Castle	177
Ambleside	Holbeck Ghyll Hotel	62
Ambleside	Rothay Manor	63
Ambleside	The Samling	64
Andover	Esseborne Manor	108
Appleby-In- Westmorland	Tufton Arms Hotel	65
Arundel	Bailiffscourt Hotel & Spa	178
Ashbourne	Callow Hall	74
Ashbourne	The Izaak Walton Hotel	75
Ashford	Eastwell Manor	119
Aylesbury	Hartwell House Hotel	45

B

Barnstaple	Northcote Manor Hotel	79
Basingstoke	Oakley Hall	109
Bassenthwaite Lake	Armathwaite Hall Hotel	67
Bath	The Bath Priory Hotel	32
Bath	Dukes Hotel	33
Bath	Homewood Park	35
Bath	Hunstrete House	36
Bath	Lucknam Park, Bath	187
Bath	The Park	37
Bath	The Royal Crescent Hotel	34
Bath	Ston Easton Park	153
Battle	The PowderMills	168
Berkswell	Nailcote Hall	183
Bishop's Stortford	Great Hallingbury Manor	116
Bolton Abbey	The Devonshire Arms	198
Borrowdale	The Lodore Falls Hotel	68
Boughton Lees	Eastwell Manor	119
Bowness	Linthwaite House Hotel	72
Bradford-On- Avon	Woolley Grange	188
Brighton	Lansdowne Place	169
Brighton	Royal York Hotel	170
Bristol	Thornbury Castle	107
Broadway	Buckland Manor	194

Index by Location

Location	Hotel	Page
Brockenhurst	New Park Manor	110
Bryher	Hell Bay	56
Buckland	Buckland Manor	194
Burnham Market	The Hoste Arms	141
Burrington	Northcote Manor	79
Bury St Edmunds	The Ickworth Hotel	159
Bury St. Edmunds	The Dower House Apartments	158

C

Location	Hotel	Page
Carne Beach	The Nare Hotel	51
Chaddesley Corbett	Brockencote Hall	195
Chagford	Gidleigh Park	80
Cheltenham	The Greenway	99
Chester	Green Bough Hotel	49
Chester	Rowton Hall Hotel	50
Chichester	The Goodwood Park Hotel	179
Chilworth	Chilworth Manor	114
Chipping	The Gibbon Bridge Hotel	120
Chipping Campden	Charingworth Manor	100
Claverdon	Ardencote Manor Hotel	185
Climping	Bailiffscourt Hotel & Spa	178
Colerne	Lucknam Park, Bath	187
Corse Lawn	Corse Lawn House Hotel	106
Coventry	Nailcote Hall	183
Cuckfield	Ockenden Manor	180

D

Location	Hotel	Page
Dartmoor	Ilsington Country House	82
Dedham	Maison Talbooth	98
Derby	Cathedral Quarter Hotel	76
Dorchester	Summer Lodge Hotel	93
Dovedale	The Izaak Walton Hotel	75

E

Location	Hotel	Page
Eastbourne	The Grand Hotel	171
Egham	Great Fosters	164
Evershot	Summer Lodge Hotel	93
Evesham	The Evesham Hotel	196
Exeter	Combe House	81

F

Location	Hotel	Page
Falmouth	Budock Vean - The Hotel on the River	53
Falmouth	Meudon Hotel	54
Falmouth	St Michael's Hotel & Spa	52
Fleet	Moonfleet Manor	96
Forest Row	Ashdown Park Hotel	172
Fowey	Fowey Hall Hotel	55

G

Location	Hotel	Page
Gatwick	Ockenden Manor	180
Gillingham	Stock Hill Country House	94
Glenridding	The Inn on the Lake	71
Goodwood	The Goodwood Park Hotel	179
Grange-Over-Sands	Netherwood Hotel	66
Great Milton	Le Manoir Aux Quat' Saisons	150
Grimston	Congham Hall	142
Gyllyngvase Beach	St Michael's Hotel & Spa	52

H

Location	Hotel	Page
Harome	The Pheasant	201
Haslemere	Lythe Hill Hotel & Spa	165
Hatfield Heath	Down Hall Country House	118
Hawes	Simonstone Hall	199
Heathrow	Stoke Park	48
Helmsley	Black Swan Hotel	200
Helmsley	The Pheasant	201
Helston	The Polurrian Hotel	58
Henlade	Mount Somerset Hotel	156
Hereford	Castle House	115
Hintlesham	Hintlesham Hall	160
Hinton Charterhouse	Homewood Park	35
Hoar Cross	Hoar Cross Hall Spa Resort	157
Honiton	Combe House	81
Horringer	The Dower House Apartments	158
Hunstrete	Hunstrete House	36
Hurstbourne Tarrant	Esseborne Manor	108

I

Location	Hotel	Page
Ickworth	The Ickworth Hotel	159
Ilsington	Ilsington Hotel	82
Ipswich	Hintlesham Hall	160
Ipswich	Kesgrave Hall	161

Isles Of Scilly	Hell Bay	56

K

Location	Hotel	Page
Kesgrave	Kesgrave Hall	161
Keswick	Armathwaite Hall and Spa	67
Keswick	Dale Head Hall Lakeside Hotel	69
Keswick	The Lodore Falls Hotel	68
Kettering	Rushton Hall Hotel & Spa	143
Kidderminster	Brockencote Hall	195
King's Lynn	Congham Hall	142
Kirklevington	Judges Country House	203

L

Location	Hotel	Page
Lake Thirlmere	Dale Head Hall Lakeside Hotel	69
Lake Ullswater	The Inn on the Lake	71
Lake Ullswater	Sharrow Bay Hotel	70
Launceston	The Arundell Arms	84
Lewdown	Lewtrenchard Manor	83
Lewes	Horsted Place Hotel	174
Lewes	Newick Park	175
Lewes	Pelham House	173
Lichfield	Hoar Cross Hall Spa Resort	157
Lifton	The Arundell Arms	84
Little Horsted	Horsted Place Hotel	174
Looe	Talland Bay Hotel	57
Lower Slaughter	Lower Slaughter Manor	101
Lower Slaughter	Washbourne Court	102
Luton	Luton Hoo Hotel, Golf & Spa	38
Lymington	Westover Hall	111

M

Location	Hotel	Page
Maidencombe	Orestone Manor	89
Maidenhead	Cliveden & The Pavilion Spa	40
Maidenhead	Fredrick's – Hotel Restaurant Spa	39

Index by Location

Location	Hotel	Page
Malmesbury	Whatley Manor	189
Malton	Burythorpe House	202
Malvern Wells	The Cottage in the Wood	197
Marlow-On-Thames	Danesfield House Hotel	46
Matlock	Riber Hall	77
Mawnan Smith	Budock Vean - The Hotel on the River	53
Mawnan Smith	Meudon Hotel	54
Melton Mowbray	**Stapleford Park Hotel**	**121**
Midhurst	The Spread Eagle Hotel	181
Milford on Sea	Westover Hall	111
Minchinhampton	Burleigh Court	103
Mortehoe	Watersmeet Hotel	92
Mullion	The Polurrian Hotel	58

N

Location	Hotel	Page
New Milton	Chewton Glen	112
Newbury	Donnington Valley Hotel	41
Newbury	The Vineyard At Stockcross	42
Newby Bridge	Lakeside Hotel on Lake Windermere	73
Newcastle-Upon-Tyne	The Vermont Hotel	182
Newick	Newick Park	175
Newmarket	Bedford Lodge Hotel	162
North Stoke	The Springs Hotel	151
Northampton	Whittlebury Hall	144
Nottingham	Hart's Hotel	145
Nottingham	Lace Market Hotel	146

O

Location	Hotel	Page
Oakham	Hambleton Hall	152
Okehampton	Lewtrenchard Manor	83
Oxford	Le Manoir Aux Quat' Saisons	150
Oxford	Old Bank Hotel	148
Oxford	The Old Parsonage Hotel	149

P

Location	Hotel	Page
Plymouth	Langdon Court & Restaurant	90
Portloe	The Lugger Hotel	59
Preston	The Gibbon Bridge Hotel	120
Purton	The Pear Tree At Purton	191

R

Location	Hotel	Page
Reading	The French Horn	43
Retford	Ye Olde Bell Hotel	147
Riber	Riber Hall	77
Richmond-Upon-Thames	The Richmond Gate Hotel	166
Risley	Risley Hall Hotel and Spa	78
Roseland Peninsula	The Lugger Hotel	59
Rotherwick	Tylney Hall	113
Rowton	Rowton Hall Hotel	50
Royal Leamington Spa	Mallory Court	184
Rushton	Rushton Hall Hotel & Spa	143

S

Location	Hotel	Page
St Albans	St Michael's Manor	117
St Ives	The Garrack Hotel	60
St Mawes	The Nare Hotel	51
Salcombe	Soar Mill Cove Hotel	85
Salcombe	The Tides Reach Hotel	86
Salcombe Estuary	Buckland-Tout-Saints	87
Salisbury	Howard's House	190
Seaham	Seaham Hall Hotel	97
Shepton Mallet	Charlton House Hotel	154
Shurdington	The Greenway	99
Sidmouth	Hotel Riviera	88
Silverstone	Whittlebury Hall	144
Skipton	The Devonshire Arms	198
Slough	Stoke Place	47
Soar Mill Cove	Soar Mill Cove Hotel	85
Sonning-On-Thames	The French Horn	43
South Sands	The Tides Reach Hotel	86
Southampton	Chilworth Manor	114
Stamford	The George Of Stamford	122
Stansted	Down Hall Country House	118
Stoke Poges	Stoke Park	48
Ston Easton	Ston Easton Park	153
Stonehouse	Stonehouse Court Hotel	104
Swindon	The Pear Tree At Purton	191

T

Location	Hotel	Page
Taplow	Cliveden & The Pavilion Spa	40
Taunton	The Castle at Taunton	155
Taunton	Mount Somerset Hotel	156
Teffont Evias	Howard's House	190
Tetbury	Calcot Manor Hotel & Spa	105
Tewkesbury	Corse Lawn House Hotel	106
Thornbury	Thornbury Castle	107
Ticehurst	Dale Hill	176
Torquay	Orestone Manor	89
Tunbridge Wells	Dale Hill	176

U

Location	Hotel	Page
Umberleigh	Northcote Manor Hotel	79
Upper Wensleydale	Simonstone Hall	199

W

Location	Hotel	Page
Wallingford	The Springs Hotel	151
Wareham	The Priory Hotel	95
Warminster	Bishopstrow House & Spa	192
Warwick	Ardencote Manor Hotel	185
Warwick	Wroxall Abbey Estate	186
Wembury	Langdon Court & Restaurant	90
Weymouth	Moonfleet Manor	96
Wick	The Park	37
Windermere	Lakeside Hotel on Lake Windermere	73
Windermere	Linthwaite House Hotel	72
Windsor	Harte & Garter Hotel & Spa	44
Woodbridge	Seckford Hall	163
Woolacombe	Watersmeet Hotel	92
Woolacombe	The Woolacombe Bay Hotel	91
Wroxall	Wroxall Abbey Estate	186

Y

Location	Hotel	Page
Yarm	Judges Country House	203
York	The Grange Hotel	204
York	Middlethorpe Hall Hotel	205

Index by Location/Consortium

Channel Islands

Guernsey	Fermain Valley Hotel	16
Guernsey	The Old Government House Hotel	17
Jersey	The Atlantic Hotel	18
Jersey	The Club Hotel & Spa	19
Jersey	Longueville Manor	21
Jersey	The Royal Yacht Hotel	20

N Ireland

Belfast	Ten Square	209

Ireland

Arthurstown	Dunbrody Country House	228
Ballina	Mount Falcon Hotel	222
Carrickmacross	Nuremore Hotel	226
Castlebar	The Harlequin	224
Clifden	Abbeyglen Castle	214
Cong	Ashford Castle	223
Connemara	Abbeyglen Castle	214
Connemara	Cashel House	215
Donegal Town	Harvey's Point	212
Enniskerry	The Ritz-Carlton Powerscourt	231
Gorey	Marlfield House	229
Kenmare	Park Hotel Kenmare & Sámas	217
Killarney	The Brehon	218
Killarney	Cahernane House Hotel	219
Killarney	The Europe Hotel & Resort	220
Killarney	Hotel Dunloe Castle	221
Killiney	Fitzpatrick Castle Hotel	213
Lough Eske	Harvey's Point	212
Mallow	Longueville House & Presidents' Restaurant	211
Recess	Ballynahinch Castle Hotel	216
Rosslare	Kelly's Resort Hotel & Spa	230
Thurles	The Horse and Jockey Hotel	227
Tullow	Mount Wolseley Hotel	210
Waterford	Dunbrody Country House	228
Westport	Knockranny House Hotel	225

Scotland

Banffshire	Craigellachie Hotel of Speyside	234
Banknock	Glenskirlie House & Castle	249
Bonnyrigg	Dalhousie Castle and Spa	248
Craigellachie	Craigellachie Hotel of Speyside	234
Dingwall	Tulloch Castle Hotel	241
Dumfries	Auchen Castle	237
Edinburgh	Dalhousie Castle and Spa	248
Fort William	Inverlochy Castle	242
Glasgow	Mar Hall Hotel & Spa	240
Inverness	Bunchrew House Hotel	243
Inverness	Rocpool Reserve	244
Inverness	Royal Highland Hotel	245
Isle Of Skye	Cuillin Hills Hotel	246
Kilchrenan By Oban	Ardanaiseig	235
Moffat	Auchen Castle	237
Newton Stewart	Kirroughtree House	238
Portree	Cuillin Hills Hotel	246
St Andrews	Old Course Hotel Golf Resort & Spa	239
Stirling	Glenskirlie House & Castle	249
Tarbert	Stonefield Castle	236
Torridon	The Torridon	247

Wales

Bala	Palé Hall	257
Brecon	Llangoed Hall	263
Cardiff	Holm House	266
Dolgellau	Penmaenuchaf Hall	258
Lake Vyrnwy	Lake Vyrnwy Hotel	264
Lampeter	**Falcondale Mansion Hotel**	**253**
Lamphey	Lamphey Court Hotel & Spa	262
Llandderfel	Palé Hall	257
Llandudno	Bodysgallen Hall & Spa	255
Llandudno	St Tudno Hotel	256
Llangammarch Wells	The Lake Country House	265
Llyswen	Llangoed Hall	263
Machynlleth	Ynyshir Hall	254
Miskin	Miskin Manor Hotel	252
Newport	Celtic Manor Resort	259
Penarth	Holm House	266
Penmaenpool	Penmaenuchaf Hall	258
St David's	Warpool Court Hotel	261
Saundersfoot	St Brides Spa Hotel	260
Tenby	Lamphey Court Hotel & Spa	262

Index by Consortium

Relais & Châteaux

England

The Royal Crescent Hotel & The Bath House Spa	B & NE Somerset	34
The Vineyard At Stockcross	Berkshire	42
Sharrow Bay Country House	Cumbria	70
Gidleigh Park	Devon	80
Summer Lodge Country House	Dorset	93
Lower Slaughter Manor	Gloucestershire	101
Chewton Glen	Hampshire	112
Le Manoir Aux Quat' Saisons	Oxfordshire	150
Hambleton Hall	Rutland	152
Amberley Castle	West Sussex	177
Mallory Court	Warwickshire	184
Lucknam Park, Bath	Wiltshire	187
Whatley Manor	Wiltshire	189
Buckland Manor	Worcestershire	194

Channel Islands

Longueville Manor	Channel Islands	21

Ireland

Marlfield House	Wexford	229

Scotland

Inverlochy Castle	Highland	242

Wales

Ynyshir Hall	Ceredigion	254

Index by Consortium

von Essen

England

Homewood Park	B & NE Somerset	35
Hunstrete House	B & NE Somerset	36
The Royal Crescent Hotel	B & NE Somerset	34
Cliveden & The Pavilion Spa	Berkshire	40
Fowey Hall Hotel & Restaurant	Cornwall	55
The Samling	Cumbria	64
Sharrow Bay Country House	Cumbria	70
Lewtrenchard Manor	Devon	83
Moonfleet Manor	Dorset	96
Seaham Hall Hotel	Durham	97
The Greenway	Gloucestershire	99
Lower Slaughter Manor	Gloucestershire	101
Washbourne Court	Gloucestershire	102
Thornbury Castle	S Gloucestershire	107
New Park Manor	Hampshire	110
Congham Hall	Norfolk	142
Mount Somerset Country House	Somerset	156
Ston Easton Park	Somerset	153
The Dower House Apartments	Suffolk	158
The Ickworth Hotel	Suffolk	159
Amberley Castle	West Sussex	177
Bishopstrow House & Spa	Wiltshire	192
Woolley Grange	Wiltshire	188
Buckland Manor	Worcestershire	194
The Elms	Worcestershire	193

Scotland

Dalhousie Castle and Spa	Midlothian	248

Wales

Ynyshir Hall	Ceredigion	254

Ireland's Blue Book

Ireland

Longueville House & Presidents' Restaurant	Cork	211
Cashel House	Galway	215
Park Hotel Kenmare & Sámas	Kerry	217
Dunbrody Country House	Wexford	228
Marlfield House	Wexford	229

Pride of Britain members

England

The French Horn	Berkshire	43
Hartwell House Hotel	Buckinghamshire	45
The Nare Hotel	Cornwall	51
Holbeck Ghyll Country House	Cumbria	62
Buckland-Tout-Saints	Devon	87
Northcote Manor Hotel	Devon	79
The Priory Hotel	Dorset	95
Maison Talbooth	Essex	98
Calcot Manor Hotel & Spa	Gloucestershire	105
Eastwell Manor	Kent	119

Charlton House Hotel	Somerset	154
Bailiffscourt Hotel & Spa	West Sussex	178
Ockenden Manor	West Sussex	180
The Pear Tree At Purton	Wiltshire	191
The Devonshire Arms	North Yorkshire	198
Judges Country House Hotel	North Yorkshire	203
Middlethorpe Hall Hotel	North Yorkshire	205

Scotland

The Torridon	Highland	247

Wales

Bodysgallen Hall & Spa	Conwy	255
The Lake Country House	Powys	265

Leading Hotels of the World

England

Milestone Hotel	London	128

Ireland

Ashford Castle	Mayo	223

Scotland

Old Course Hotel Golf Resort	Fife	239

Small Luxury Hotels of the World

England

The Bath Priory Hotel	B & NE Somerset	32
Luton Hoo Hotel, Golf & Spa	Bedfordshire	38
Danesfield House Hotel	Buckinghamshire	46
Hartwell House Hotel, Restaurant & Spa	Buckinghamshire	45
Stoke Park	Buckinghamshire	48
Holbeck Ghyll Country House	Cumbria	62
Tylney Hall	Hampshire	113
Stapleford Park Country House	Leicestershire	121
The Capital Hotel & Restaurant	London	131
Hintlesham Hall	Suffolk	160
Great Fosters	Surrey	164
Ashdown Park Hotel	East Sussex	172
The Grand Hotel	East Sussex	171
The Devonshire Arms	North Yorkshire	198

Channel Islands

The Atlantic Hotel	Jersey	18

Ireland

Park Hotel Kenmare & Sámas	Kerry	217
Dunbrody Country House	Wexford	228

Scotland

Mar Hall Hotel & Spa	Glasgow	240
The Torridon	Highland	247

The Perfect Gift...
Condé Nast Johansens Gift Vouchers

Condé Nast Johansens Gift Vouchers make a unique and much valued present for birthdays, weddings, anniversaries, special occasions or as a corporate incentive.

Vouchers are available in denominations of £100, £50, €140, €70, $150, $75 and may be used as payment or part payment for your stay or a meal at any Condé Nast Johansens 2009 Recommended property.

To order, call +44 (0)207 152 3558
or purchase direct at www.johansens.com

Tell us about your stay

Following your stay in a Condé Nast Johansens Recommendation, please spare a moment to complete this Guest Survey Report. This is an important source of information for Condé Nast Johansens, in order to maintain the highest standards for our Recommendations and to support our team of Inspectors. It is also the prime source of nominations for Condé Nast Johansens Awards for Excellence, which are held annually and include properties from all over the world that represent the finest standards and best value for money in luxury, independent travel.

1. Your details

Your name:

Your address:

Postcode:

Country:

Please leave your email address if you would like to receive our monthly e-newsletter, with details of special offers and competitions

E-mail:

Please tick if you would like to receive information or offers from The Condé Nast Publications Ltd by SMS ☐ or E-mail ☐. Please tick if you would like to receive information or offers from other selected companies by SMS ☐ or E-mail ☐. Please tick this box if you prefer not to receive direct mail from The Condé Nast Publications Ltd ☐ and other reputable companies ☐

2. Hotel details

Name of hotel:

Country:

Date of visit: .... Room No:

3. How did you book?

○ Telephone   ○ E-Mail   ○ Hotel Website
○ Internet   ○ Travel Agent

Are you: ○ Guide User   ○ Web User   ○ or both

4. Any other comments

If you wish to make additional comments, please write separately to the Publisher, Condé Nast Johansens Ltd, 6-8 Old Bond Street, London W1S 4PH, Great Britain

5. Your rating of the hotel

Please tick one box in each category below (as applicable)

	EXCELLENT	GOOD	DISAPPOINTING	POOR
Bedrooms				
Comfort	○	○	○	○
Amenities	○	○	○	○
Bathroom	○	○	○	○
Public Areas				
Inside	○	○	○	○
Outdoor	○	○	○	○
Housekeeping				
Cleanliness	○	○	○	○
Maintenance	○	○	○	○
Service				
Check in/out	○	○	○	○
Professionalism	○	○	○	○
Friendliness	○	○	○	○
Dining	○	○	○	○
Internet Facilities				
Bedrooms	○	○	○	○
Public Areas	○	○	○	○
Ambience	○	○	○	○
Value for Money	○	○	○	○
Food and drink				
Breakfast	○	○	○	○
Lunch	○	○	○	○
Dinner	○	○	○	○
Choice of dishes	○	○	○	○
Wine List	○	○	○	○
Did The Hotel Meet Your Expectations?	○	○	○	○

I most liked:

I least liked:

My favourite member of staff:

Please fax your completed survey to +44 (0)207 152 3566